PUBLIC CHOICE, PUBLIC FINANCE AND PUBLIC POLICY

Photo: Mrs Trevor S. Wilkinson

PUBLIC CHOICE, PUBLIC FINANCE AND PUBLIC POLICY

Essays in Honour of Alan Peacock

Edited by

David Greenaway
Reader in Economics
University of Buckingham

and

G. K. Shaw
Rank Foundation Professor of Economics
University of Buckingham

Basil Blackwell

First published 1985

Basil Blackwell Ltd
108 Cowley Road, Oxford OX4 1JF, UK

Basil Blackwell Inc.
432 Park Avenue South, Suite 1505,
New York, NY 10016, USA

British Library Cataloguing in Publication Data
Public choice public finance and public policy:
  essays in honour of Alan Peacock.
  1. Finance, Public
  I. Peacock, Alan, 1922–   II. Greenaway, David
  III. Shaw, G. K.
  336   HJ141
  ISBN 0-631-14313-0

Library of Congress Cataloging in Publication Data
Main entry under title:
  Peacock, Alan
Public choice, public finance, and public policy.
  Papers from a conference held at the University
  of Buckingham, Sept. 5–7, 1984.
  Bibliography: p.
  Includes index.
  Contents: Public finance and distributive justice/
  Richard A. Musgrave – Marginal cost pricing/
  Mark Blaug – Toward a Theory of bureaucratic behaviour/
  Charles Rowley and Robert Elgin – [etc.]
  1. Finance, Public – Congresses.
  2. Economic policy – Congresses.
  3. Peacock, Alan, 1922–   –Congresses.
  I. Peacock, Alan, 1922–.   II. Greenaway, David.
  III. Shaw, G.K. (Graham Keith), 1938– .
  HJ113.P85 1985   338.9   85-1441
  ISBN 0–631–14313–0

Typeset by Keytec, Bridport, Dorset
Printed in Great Britain by The Camelot Press Ltd, Southampton

Contents

Foreword

When we first seriously discussed the possibility of a Festschrift conference for Professor Alan Peacock in July 1983 we were motivated by several considerations. First, there was a deep-rooted respect and affection for a valued colleague. Second, there was a feeling that the enormous contribution that Alan Peacock had made to the development of the University of Buckingham at a particularly crucial period in its growth merited some recognition. Both of these, however, were only necessary, rather than sufficient, considerations for a Festschrift. After all, friendship *per se* is hardly a criterion; and, significant as his contribution to the Economics Department at Buckingham University undoubtedly was, his legacy to the university transcended particular disciplines. Thus, any university 'gesture' would be (and subsequently proved to be) university-wide. The third and most important consideration and, as it were, the sufficient condition, was the feeling that the economics profession owed Alan a Festschrift. For some thirty-five years he has been a practising economist in all senses of the adjective: as a contributor to professional journals, as a communicator to students, as a consultant to many public organisations, and as an advisor to many governments. Over the years, this prodigious activity has served as an example to his younger colleagues, and the product of his labours has been a source of credit to the profession.

In working closely with someone, there is of course always a danger that the individual's attributes are perhaps exaggerated, even if only a little. It was therefore gratifying to find that our judgement with respect to Alan's case for a Festschrift was truly vindicated when we issued invitations to contributors. Each and every 'first choice' contributor accepted without hesitation and agreed to come to Buckingham on 5–7 September 1984 to participate in what turned out to be a very happy event. We would like publically to express our gratitude to this very distinguished group of contributors, not only for participating in the conference but for providing us with such a straightforward editorial function. We would also like to thank those who acted as discussants, namely Peggy Musgrave (University of California), Jack Wiseman (University of York), Nic Tideman (Virginia Polytechnic Institute), Ilde Rizzo (University of Catania) Chris Milner (University of Lough-borough), John Burton (Institute of Economic Affairs) and Martin Ricketts, Mike McCrostie and Norman Barry (University of Bucking-ham). All of the discussants provided worthwhile and perceptive commentaries on the papers; our only regret with respect to the entire event is that the detailed discussion of papers could not be included in this volume.

Finally, we would like to express our gratitude to the following, without whose generous financial support the conference would not have been possible: Anglo-German Foundation for the Study of Industrial Society; Atlantic Economic Society; Cambridge Design; Economist Intelligence Unit; Fairchild Martindale Centre; Mr and Mrs D. Franklin; Friends of Buckingham; Dr V. Kanapathy; Shell International; Spicer and Pegler; Wincott Foundation; and the late Mr Ralph Yablon.

David Greenaway
G. K. Shaw
Buckingham, 1984

Preface

JACK WISEMAN

The papers in this volume are presented as a Festschrift in honour of Alan Peacock. There is a good deal of difference of opinion as to what a Festschrift should be, when it should properly occur and, indeed, whether the enterprise can be justified at all. I personally have no strong feelings in the matter: I am content to judge by results. By this criterion, I consider the present venture to have been outstandingly successful, and in important ways a model for others. Its success owed much to Alan Peacock's qualities, and to the excellence of the editorial and administrative organization. But while these may not easily be reproducible, the general nature of the occasion can and should be. The papers were presented at a conference in which Alan Peacock himself participated, symbolic of the fact that the occasion being celebrated was a new departure in his academic life – namely, his retirement from the Vice-Chancellorship of the University of Buckingham – and in no way the end of it. The conference itself was a congress of friends, which was important not only socially but also, I believe, to the quality of the papers. The members, heterogeneous in age, sex, nationality, academic interests and political opinions, shared Alan Peacock's own faith in liberal intellectual enquiry and a mutual desire to make the final product of their efforts worthy of its progenitor. This kind of scrutiny is not usually encountered by the contributors to Festschriften; and a common characteristic of Alan Peacock's catholic academic circle is a quality of intellectual independence (indeed, forthrightness) which left its mark on the discussion.

I feel the more free to write in this vein because I am not myself a contributor. The editors suggested that, given my long and close association with Alan Peacock, I might prefer to write a general Preface. (The unworthy thought did cross my mind that they wanted to avoid the possibility that Alan would wish to be co-author of any paper I was invited to submit!) In the spirit of the invitation, I shall devote my remaining space to the *raison d'être* of the volume. Further comment on the papers themselves would be neither necessary nor useful. The distinction of the authors is itself a tribute to Alan Peacock, and the quality of their contributions can be left to speak for itself. Not one of the papers received the amount of discussion it deserved: that would have required as many days as we in fact had hours. Nothing here is 'off the shelf', and the breadth of the subject matter covered reflects the embracing interests of their celebrant.

My own academic and personal association with Alan Peacock goes back – like the realization that one is teaching one's old students' children – longer than either of us particularly cares to remember. But I hope I may be forgiven for using it to exemplify a more general evaluation.

Our early collaboration was marked by a king of Schumpeterian 'intellectual creative destruction'. We developed a thesis by argument, or, more accurately if less politely by a process of conflict resolution. A brief anecdote may give the flavour of our early relationship. I once visited Alan at the University of Edinburgh, after he had left the LSE to become Head of Department there, in order to discuss his first draft of a chapter of the joint book on which we were engaged. We met over coffee in his room, which also served as the economist's staff common room. After greeting friends, I responded to his request for my thoughts on his draft. I told him, in my usual style, that I liked it: if we reversed the order of argument, rewrote it to tighten the logic, ... Alan Peacock exploded, also as usual: he did not take readily to the mutilation of his brainchildren. Discussion began. Five minutes later, I observed that his room was empty save for the two of us. Inevitably, time has changed all this: as we learned each other's minds, the combat became more muted, though I hope not, therefore, less sophisticated. Yet I sometimes wonder if we were not at our most innovative when also at our most combative.

I tell this story not because I enjoy the reminiscence – though I do – but because of what it tells about Alan Peacock. First, nothing in the academic relationship touched our personal regard, save I believe to strengthen it. Second, I never felt that our collaboration used me: only that I had to match my collaborator's contribution, that I was enlarged by it, and that I dared – and achieved – more, both within our collaboration and elsewhere, because of it. It is these qualities – of intellectual integrity, of stimulation and of personal loyalty untouched by intellectual differences – that make it a pleasure and a privilege for me to write this Preface.

I believe – indeed, I know – that this view of Alan Peacock is shared by others, the participants in the Festschrift among them. The profile of those participants has some interesting features. They are the entire 'first line' who were invited to contribute: all accepted, and all participated in the Conference; they include compatriots, a few generations of ex-students and a broad mix of nationalities, reflecting, together with the subject matter of the papers, the breadth of both Alan Peacock's own intellectual interests and his scholarly network; almost all the participants have written in collaboration with him. What better evidence could there be of the qualities I have cited?

It is usual for a Festschrift to concentrate on the recipient's contribution to scholarship. I have so far said nothing of that, though I shall. But for me, Alan Peacock's most outstanding quality lies in his inspiration of others. He is a democrat in principle, a leader by instinct, and the kind of leader who does not like to lead from behind. It is this, tempered by the qualities I have described, that gives him the firm hold that he has on our respect and our affection.

Yet this could not be so were he not himself a respected economist. Had he not had the qualities I have chosen to elaborate, I could have written this Preface simply around his deserved international reputation as a scholar. His writings, alone and in collaboration, are both creative and remarkably extensive. His reputation in his primary field of specialization, public finance, needs no advertisement from me. But the breadth of his scholarship and writings goes far beyond this; he has, for example, been at the forefront of the developments broadening his specialization into the study of the public sector in all its manifestations; he is a reputable historian of thought and an authority on the German literature; and he has turned his hand productively to many other matters attracting his interest, such as the economics of the performing arts.

I began by asking what a Festschrift was. One reason for doubt is that it is sometimes a kind of farewell, but sometimes not. There is no doubt about this in the present case. Observation, at the conference and elsewhere, suggests that our subject is in prime intellectual and physical condition: a likely candidate, if the thought be not too frivolous, for many future Festschriften!

Perhaps, for the present, we should simply be grateful that he failed in at least one career ambition to which he admits: to be a musician who treated economics as a hobby. I have nothing but respect for Alan Peacock's musical abilities, but can imagine no cost–benefit appraisal that would persuade me that such a translation would not have left us the poorer.

List of Contributors

HILDA BAUMOL   Professor of Economics, New York University

WILLIAM BAUMOL   Professor of Economics, Princeton University

MARK BLAUG   Professor of Economics, University of London and University of Buckingham

ANIBAL CAVACO-SILVA   Professor of Economics, Portuguese Catholic University, Lisbon

ROBERT ELGIN   Research Fellow, George Mason University

FRANCESCO FORTE   Professor of Economics, University of Rome

HERBERT GIERSCH   Professor of Economics, University of Kiel

KEITH LUMSDEN   Professor of Economics, Heriot Watt University

RICHARD MUSGRAVE   Professor of Economics, University of California

MAURICE PESTON   Professor of Economics, Queen Mary College, University of London

CHARLES ROWLEY   Professor of Economics, George Mason University

ALEX SCOTT   Senior Research Fellow, Heriot Watt University

ALAN WILLIAMS   Professor of Economics, University of York

JOHN WILLIAMSON   Professor of Economics, Institute for International Economics, Washington

THOMAS WILSON   Professor of Economics, University of Glasgow

JACK WISEMAN   Professor of Economics, University of York

1

Public Finance and Distributive Justice

RICHARD A. MUSGRAVE

1.1 INTRODUCTION

My purpose in this essay is to trace the relationship between philosophies of social justice and the redistributive function in the development of fiscal theory. I do so, even though I am aware that distribution interacts with other aspects of that theory, and that our conference is meant to address the positive rather than normative issues of public finance. However, I suspect that the normative–positive dichotomy is easily overdone. For one thing, positive findings are of interest as viewed against the background of normative standards – this being what distinguishes social science from botany. For another, ideas matter, even in the course of events; and events sooner or later penetrate the philosopher's den. I thus suspect my theme to be of interest to our laureate, my co-editor of the *Classics*, (Musgrave and Peacock, 1967), to which this paper might be added as a footnote.

Theories of distributive justice that had a major impact on the development of fiscal doctrine include (1) Locke's principle of entitlement by natural law, (2) the utilitarian case for maximum happiness as based on reason, and (3) derivation of distributive rules from justice as fairness. The still earlier Hobbesian framework of conflict resolution is omitted here, as it points towards game theory rather than normative analysis. Moreover, in Hobbes' own formulation it is rendered barren as a matter of distributive justice by the assumption that bargaining, in the state of nature, occurs among individuals of equal strength.

1.2 ENTITLEMENT AND THE NATIONAL ORDER

We here consider the basic framework as laid down by John Locke and then proceed to its amendment by Adam Smith.

John Locke

Man, so Locke argued, has a right in his person, and what his hands create are properly his. 'Whatever then he removes out of the state that nature have provided – he has mixed his labor with, and joined to it something that is his own, and thereby makes it his Property'. (Locke, 1960, p.328) Locke offers no defence for this proposition; rather, it is taken as a self-evident truth, based on the teaching of natural and divine law. He then adds two provisos. According to the first, permissible accumulation is limited by spoilage. According to the second, man may freely mix his labour with land and retain the produce 'at least where there is enough and as good left in common for others'. But land is given to mankind to be held in common, and this entitlement ceases when land becomes scarce. Locke noted that the first proviso became inoperative with the development of storage and trade, but he was less successful in resolving the second. Indeed, it became the foundation for a long succession of authors who viewed land as the prime, if not the single, source of taxation.

Though a fascinating aspect of the Lockean doctrine, we will here bypass the dichotomy of land and labour and deal with the latter only.[1] Given the entitlement to earnings, political or civic society must then be established to protect property. But man, being created free and equal, cannot be subordinated thereto without his consent or that of majority rule. To finance the provision of protection, each member of society should pay out of his estate in proportion for its maintenance. But this is all: the construction of highways and canals, later noted by Smith, is not pressed, and a redistributive use of taxation – as distinct from voluntary giving – falls outside the Lockean system. The Lockean model, with its explicit anchor in the entitlement doctrine, thus points to a minimal state.

The central presumption of desert, from which the rest follows, may, in the modern eye, seem to lack analytical foundation, and modern Lockeans such as Nozick have been criticized for not proving their premise (Nagel, 1975). But though I would not choose the Lockean premise myself, theories of distributive justice must in the end be derived from an ethical base rather than being deduced from reason alone.

It is necessary, however, to be specific and to define clearly what the doctrine implies, a requirement that was met by neither Locke himself nor by Nozick's modern restatement (Nozick, 1974). Thus it need be considered whether earnings from capital have the same claim to desert as do earnings from labour. St Thomas and the Scholastics did not think this obvious. Also, there is a question of whether exchange as the legitimate means of transferring title *must* be conducted in competitive markets, or whether the simple requirement of voluntarism suffices.

The answer to this question is important, because only in the former case will Lockean justice – as J.B. Clark (1914) argued – also meet the requirement of economic efficiency. Moreover, the question must be faced of how externalities are to be dealt with. If A's action generates externalities which interfere with B's property rights, Lockean justice calls for compensation, along with other measures to protect property rights. Then there is the problem of how to deal with transfers at death, leading to acquisitions not legitimized by being the fruit of one's own labour. Rowley and Peacock (1975) proceed from a Lockean base but recognize that these qualifications need to be addressed.

Adam Smith

We now turn to Adam Smith, the customary point of departure for travels in the history of fiscal thought.[2] Adam Smith, in Book V of the *Wealth of Nations*, spends considerable time groping for the reasons why certain services need to be provided publicly. Defence, the administration of justice and education are examined. So are certain public works, 'which it can never be for the interest of any individual, or small number of individuals, to erect and maintain; because the profit could never repay the expense to any individual or small number of individuals, though it may frequently do much more than repay it to a great society.'

The puzzle of social goods, and why the market cannot provide them, is not resolved although it is at least confronted. But very little is said about the distributive aspects of the fiscal system. To be sure, government should show some concern for the education of the common people, lest the division of labour destroy their intellectual, social and marital values. Also, Smith criticizes the settlement laws as unfair to the poor, but these are minor exceptions to a vision of the social order that takes drastic inequality for granted.

To understand this vision, one has to turn to Smith's *Theory of Moral Sentiments*. In that earlier treatise – which is essential to an understanding of Adam Smith – we are given a fascinating panorama of the human condition and of the complex system that comprises the order of natural liberty. We find a social engine driven by the passions and aspirations of its individual actors, producing an interaction designed (be it by natural or divine law) to secure a beneficent outcome. Self-interest, to be sure, is the strongest of individual motivations, and self-preservation is a worthy goal. But self-interest is not the entire story. Smith's view of society is not that of a Hobbesian jungle, tamed by utilitarian agreement to provide protection. Protection of property is part of the order; and prudence (the pursuit of self-interest) is one of the three major virtues, but it is the 'least admirable' of them. Prudence is outranked by justice, with benevolence regarded as the highest of virtues. The individual views his conduct in relation to these virtues. He watches the image that he presents from the outside to an 'impartial observer', seeking to be approved by him and to draw the approbation of others. But the 'man inside' not only seeks praise: he also seeks to be praiseworthy. Thus, self-interest is constrained by regard for the higher virtues. Drawing upon this structure of human psychology – with its manifold virtues, vices and follies – the invisible hand then translates this micro-universe into a harmonious whole. In the process, the hand is not beyond tricking its pawns into appropriate behaviour. But natural (or divine) law offers this order, and man would be foolish not to avail himself of its majestic and benevolent design.

Obviously, then, Smith's view of the world is not one-dimensional, with self-interest 'the only game in town' (as some modern Smithians would have us believe).[3] Nor does Smith share Mandeville's conclusion that prosperity is a product of the vices (read 'self-interest') and hence incompatible with the pursuit of virtue. Taking a middle road, Smith was concerned with resolving the tension between (1) self-interest, as the key to efficient operation of the economic engine, and (2) the role of benevolence and sympathy as the highest of virtues. This is done by granting self-interest, the duty of self-preservation, the status of a minor virtue but justifying its major role as needed for the functioning of the market and thus for securing the common good. Man after the Fall, so Smith might have said, cannot function by his highest virtues alone. The author of *The Theory of Moral Sentiments* must accommodate the author of *The Wealth of Nations* to produce a workable system.

The same concern with constructing an order, both moral and workable, enters into Smith's treatment of distribution. Justice, the second-ranked virtue, is defined as putative justice only, i.e. as the protection of the individual against interference with his personal and property rights. On this point, Smith is a radical egalitarian, believing that all are entitled to an equal and impartial administration of justice. But not so with regard to the distribution of holdings: while Smith does not advance an explicit endorsement of the Lockean view of entitlement, the claim to earnings would be justified by the role of self-interest as necessary to the workability of the system.

But Smith evidently felt uneasy about the problem of distribution. On the one hand, a highly unequal distribution was considered a necessary part of the natural order. On the other, the resulting contrast of wealth and poverty evidently bothered the moral philosopher, or his impartial observer. This may be concluded from the fact that Smith found it necessary to demonstrate why inequality is in the general interest. In *The Wealth of Nations*, he argues that economic progress created by the market system greatly advances the welfare not only of the rich but also of the poor. Their position, while below the extravagance of the rich, 'exceeds that of many an African king'. Moreover, as argued in *The*

Theory of Moral Sentiments, the gain from riches is largely a fiction. The wealthy landlord, in imagination, may consume his whole harvest, but 'the capacity of his stomach bears no proportion to the immensity of his desires, and will receive no more than that of the meanest peasant.' The rich consume little more than the poor, to whom the rest is passed. There follows a remarkable passage, the first in which the 'invisible hand' makes its appearance: 'Thus they [landlords] are led by an invisible hand to make nearly the same distribution of the necessities of life which would have been made had the earth been divided into equal portions among all its inhabitants.' Moreover, the rich have burdens to bear that are not placed upon the poor. 'In what constitutes the real happiness of human life,' Smith states, 'they are in no respect inferior to those who would seem so much above them. In ease of being and peace of mind, all the different ranks of life are nearly upon a level, and the beggar, who suns himself by the side of the highway, possesses a security which kings are fighting for.'

Even a fervent admirer of Smith must admit that this somewhat overstates matters, and Smith himself appears uneasy with his model of distributive justice. But, alas, providence once more turns man's fallibility to the best purpose. Charmed with the beauty of palaces, he is willing to strive, 'and it is well that nature imposes on us in this matter. It is this deception which arouses and keeps in continual motion the industry of mankind'. It is the motion that matters, as much as the outcome; and the system of natural liberty, involving its use of deception as a central device, is what keeps the engine of human advancement going.

In conclusion, Smith saw the need for public services, for the canals and highways which it does not pay private interest to supply, but he assigned little weight to distributive objectives of expenditure policy. The natural order, while recognizing externalities (to use the modern term), did not call for such measures. This is also the background against which his views on the distribution of the tax burden should be seen. His approach, not surprisingly, begins with a preference for fee finance; and where fees are inapplicable, taxation can be rendered distributionally neutral by using a benefit proxy. Thus, 'the subjects of every state ought to contribute towards the support of the government, as nearly as possible in proportion to their respective abilities; that is, in proportion to the revenue which they respectively enjoy under the protection of the state.' Although in another passage Smith suggests that some degree of progression might be desirable, and notes that subsistence wages cannot be taxed anyhow, his essential position was one of proportional taxation. He took this view, we gather, as an approach to benefit taxation (assuming the cost of protection per dollar to be constant) rather than as a reflection of ability to pay.

Individuals interacting through the market are the key, but

government also has its function in the social order. The public welfare matters, and 'constitutions of government are valued as they tend to promote the happiness of those who live under them.' The prince is counselled to keep this in mind, and Smith appears confident that he will do so. But government must not be extended beyond its natural role. The 'man of system' who would reconstruct this order by his own devices is doomed to failure.

1.3 FROM BENTHAM TO PIGOU

We now come to the utilitarian setting. Gone is Smith's mysterious world of human motivations and divine design. Man is placed on his own and, capable of reason, is challenged to make the best of his condition. But once more, a harmonious outcome is within reach. As each individual following reason endeavours to maximize happiness, it is the business of society as a whole to secure maximum happiness for the group as a whole. Each individual maximizes utility within the constraints set for him by the market, and society as a whole should aim to maximize welfare for the sum of its members. But total happiness also depends on distribution, so that the utilitarian rule points to distribution as a prime issue. This is most evident if the size of the pie is taken as given, but it remains so (though in more complex form) once distribution is seen to affect the size of the pie or, in modern terms, once the efficiency cost of redistribution is accounted for.

Jeremy Bentham

A surprisingly clear statement of the utilitarian position on distribution was presented at the very outset. As early as 1803, Jeremy Bentham argued that (1) a person's happiness increases with his wealth; that (2) the gain in happiness decreases with successive additions to wealth; so that (3) total happiness increases with equality of wealth. However, satisfaction derived from wealth is only one part of happiness: security is no less important, and indeed is a prerequisite to the creation of property. 'If all property were equally divided, at fixed periods, the sure and sudden consequence would be that presently there would be no property to divide.' In other words, inequality can be reduced but not removed; and when in conflict it must yield to security. Given this theme, which is stated at the beginning of the debate, the follow-up over the next two centuries would be one of refinement only.

John Stuart Mill

John Stuart Mill, in his *Principles of Political Economy* (written in

1849), first questioned whether society would be served best by a system based on private property or by socialist models, such as those proposed by Owen, St Simon or Fourier. But he then proceeded to a private property setting and the guiding rule that 'laissez-faire should be the general practice: every departure from it, unless required by some great good, is a certain evil'. Nevertheless, this stricture leaves certain functions to be performed by government. They include the protection of person and property, the establishment of certain legal institutions in which business can function, and 'a variety of cases in which important public services are to be performed, while yet there is no individual specially interested in performing them, nor would any adequate remuneration naturally or spontaneously attend their performance'. The lighthouse enters as prime illustration; but no major progress is made in understanding the nature of social goods.

Turning to the distribution of the tax burden incurred in providing these services, Mill rejects the benefit principle. Benefits are too general to be assigned, and application of the rule might in fact call for regression, as the poor have greater need for protection. The basic principle is not to be *quid pro quo*, but equality should apply in all affairs of government. In the context of taxation, equality calls for imposition of equal sacrifice, and equal sacrifice is taken to call for proportional taxation. To this he mistakenly adds that this 'is the mode by which least sacrifice is occasioned on the whole'. Mill evidently did not accept or grasp Bentham's earlier doctrine of decreasing marginal utility, a premise that should have led him to call for maximum progression.

But the principle of equality is applied to the financing of public services only; it is not extended to redistribution as a budgetry function. To be sure, Mill recognizes a claim to help, created by destitution and the need for a public system of charity. Indigents should not be left to starve, but public support is to be kept to a minimum to avoid abuse. With this limited exception, inequality in the distribution of earnings is accepted as part of the system of liberty; but two further qualifications are made. One pertains to the ownership of land, which, as had been argued by Locke, is to be held in common. The other pertains to the right to leave bequests; this right, previously accepted by Locke, is now to be limited severely.

Mill resumed his discussion of distributive justice in his later essay on 'Utilitarianism' (written in 1861). Here, the issues of equality and equal treatment are viewed in a broader context. Like Bentham, Mill postulates that 'each person count for one, and as only so', and that 'maximum total happiness' be the goal. Unlike Bentham, he does not move from the one to the other by postulating declining marginal utility. Rather, 'an equal claim to all the means of happiness' appears to be derived directly from a proposition of equal worth and recognition of the golden rule. But, like Bentham, Mill's case for equality is highly tentative. The maxim is limited by the 'unavoidable conditions of human life and the general interest', and 'it bends to every person's ideas of social expediency'.

Sidgwick and Edgeworth

Subsequent utilitarians adhered more closely to Bentham's route. Thus Sidgwick (1883), arguing from Bentham's premise, arrived at the 'obvious conclusion' that aggregate sacrifice is minimized by equal distribution of wealth. But, like Bentham, he qualifies his conclusion by allowing for effects on total output and social conditions, including factors other than wealth.

Edgeworth's 'Pure Theory of Taxation' (written in 1897) viewed Bentham's derivation of maximum total happiness with scepticism. In its place, Edgeworth saw the principle as the outcome of a bargain among self-interested parties. In the absence of a competitive mechanism, neither party to the bargain can in the longer run expect to obtain the larger share of total welfare. Evidently, the Hobbesian assumption of equal strengths is resumed. Given this bargaining prospect, maximum collective utility will also afford each party the greatest individual utility. From this it follows that 'minimum sacrifice, the direct emanation of pure utilitarianism, is the sovereign principle of taxation.' Taxation therefore should level down incomes from the top until the necessary revenue is obtained. Moreover, the solution 'in the abstract is that the richer should be taxed for the benefit of the poor up to the point at which complete equality of fortunes is allowed. The acme of socialism is thus for a moment sighted, but it is immediately clouded over by doubts and reservations'. These doubts, as for Bentham and Sidgwick, include detrimental effects on output and growth, and beyond this the spectre of 'dull equality'; and differences in the capacity for happiness are cited. Thus, the 'high tableau of equality' cannot be reached, and the extent to which progressive taxation and income equalization should in fact be carried is left wide open.

A. C. Pigou

Decades later, the discussion was resumed by Pigou (1928), but the basic framework remained the same. The assumption of similar declining and comparable marginal utility of income schedules is retained, and equal marginal sacrifice is ranked ahead of the alternative rules of equal absolute proportional sacrifice. In the utilitarian spirit, the former is preferred as a matter of efficiency (in order to secure least total sacrifice) rather than as a matter of equity (in granting equal treatment). And, as before, the desirable degree of progression and redistribution is qualified by allowing for resulting effects. Pigou's major innovation was in how these effects are viewed.

Following the Marshallian analysis of tax burden in terms of consumer surplus, the 'announcement effects' of raising the same revenue from alternative taxes is compared and the excess loss of welfare (loss, that is, over and above revenue gains) is explored. Thus, the basis for the modern theory of optimal taxation was laid. The least total sacrifice rule would call for deriving a given revenue from a particular taxpayer so as to burden him least, as well as for distributing these minimized burdens among individual taxpayers so as to secure a minimum total sacrifice. This now might call for a rate structure substantially less progressive than that suggested by moving to the point of zero marginal revenue.

1.4 THE NEW WELFARE ECONOMICS

Whereas the Pigouvian sacrifice doctrine had stayed within the framework of the traditional welfare economics, its very foundation was soon questioned. Following Robbins (1938), the hypothesis of cardinal, comparable and similar utility functions came to be rejected as scientifically unacceptable and not open to empirical verification. This left economic analysis with two choices. One was to withdraw from the issue of optimal distribution and to seek refuge in the safer waters of Pareto efficiency. The economist, according to this view, was to deal with efficiency only, and had no business addressing the issue of distribution. The other was to formulate the problem of distribution in a more tenable fashion.

The theory of public finance, more than any other branch of economics, had a major stake in this choice. To be sure, a limited treatment of the distribution issue would be possible within the Paretian context. Based on interpersonal utility interdependence, individuals would give so as to maximise their welfare (Hochman and Rogers, 1964). If such satisfaction was limited to one's own giving, it would be a truly private affair. But if the satisfaction was derived from seeing the position of the poor improve, independent of who gave, a free-rider problem would again arise, calling for a budgetary (tax-transfer) solution. Even in this case, however, the resulting state of distribution would still be a function of the initial (pre-giving) distribution, thus leaving unresolved the basic issue of primary distribution (Musgrave, 1970). Provided that jealousy is disallowed, it may be readily agreed that, beginning from a position within the frontier, a north-east movement is desirable. But points on the frontier cannot be chosen without ethical judgement. Nor can it be argued without such judgement (i.e. without a social welfare function) that welfare might not be improved by moving off the frontier (Samuelson, 1948).

With such judgement involved in many fiscal issues, it is not surprising that fiscal analysis came to rely on the use of a social welfare function. Thus it has become common practice in recent years to apply distributional weights to alternative outcomes, be it in the context of cost–benefit analysis or, more recently, in optimal taxation. Typically, these weights assign declining social utilities to dollars of income when moving up the income scale. The argument that once slayed the old welfare economics by ruling out interpersonal comparison no longer applies: social utility weights reflect a socio-political judgement (individuals are treated 'as if' they were comparable), and the argument proceeds on that basis. But not all such judgements are equally valid, and new issues arise. These include the process by which the judgement is obtained and the feasibility of arriving at an unambiguous outcome without cycling. It is also important for the economist who wishes to apply the criteria to understand the ethical judgement that society wishes to impose. He will thus do well, whether as a visiting scholar or *ex officio*, to explore the internal structure and consistency of such judgements.

1.5 JUSTICE AS FAIRNESS

Since the appearance of John Rawls's *Theory of Justice* (1971), attention has been directed at the concept of fairness as an alternative point of departure; alternative, that is, to Lockean entitlement or utilitarian summation. Fairness, in line with the Golden Rule of the Scriptures or the Kantian principle of universality, calls for each person to do to others as he would have others do to him. Applied to the division of a given cake, A, though stronger, will not take all, since he would not want B to do so if the roles were reversed. Thus, A will be satisfied with one-half, since to demand more (or leave less) would not meet the spirit of the Golden Rule. An equal division will result. The outcome is the same as for Hobbes, but the reason differs. According to Hobbes, equal division results from a bargain, based on equal 'strength'. Without that assumption, the bargain (or battle) would sustain inequality. Whatever happens, the outcome is not a justice-based solution. Under the fairness rule, on the other hand, relative strength does not matter since fairness requires it to be disregarded. The same applies where we deal with the distribution of income among two earners who have different but *fixed* earnings. A earns 10 and B earns 5, so that the size of the pie equals 15. Absent the Lockean premise, earning ability does not give entitlement, and division is to be by the Golden Rule. Once more, A reasons that if he were B (and B were A), he would want A to transfer 2.5 to him; and, being A, this is what he will offer to B. B, in turn, will ask for the same since, if he were A, he would not be willing to give more.

Economists, uncomfortable with reasoning from ethical premises, have translated behaviour under the Golden Rule into two steps. Step 1, still ethical in nature, calls for impartiality, i.e. willingness to disregard one's own strength or capacity to earn. Step 2, however, moves to the more congenial ground of utility maximization under uncertainty. Returning to the disposition of a given cake or fixed earnings, let A and B both be confronted with equal odds to obtain shares ranging from zero to 100 per cent. Given risk aversion (slight or extreme), both will choose a 50–50 solution as this maximizes utility under uncertainty. Thus, the same conclusion is arrived at as by direct application of the Golden Rule. The similarity of outcome is not surprising, since the very willingness of both players to accept the gamble at equal odds already implies a willingness to adopt the Golden Rule solution.

Notwithstanding the distinguished line of economists, from Lerner (1944) and Vickrey (1945) to Harsanyi (1953), who have viewed the problem in gambling terms, the introduction of risk aversion seems to me of questionable value. It suggests that the solution stems from Paretian calculus (utility maximization) rather than from the acceptance of disinterestedness, here in the form of willingness to accept the premise of equal odds. But is it not inconsistent to accept equal odds (i.e. to act in line with the Golden Rule) and then to maximize utility (i.e. to pursue self-interest)? Some authors propose to overcome this difficulty by drawing a sharp distinction between the 'constitutional state', in which disinterestedness reigns, and the subsequent condition, in which constitutional rules are needed to regulate conduct of a selfish society. I find this difficult to accept. Constitutional rules are needed, to be sure, to avoid a continuing reconsideration of the social order and to permit the conduct of mundane affairs. Yet constitution-setting (or the setting of basic rules) is not a once-and-for-all historical occasion, but something that needs to be reconsidered by each generation (Musgrave, 1974).

Now, it might be argued that all this matters little, since the Golden Rule and utility maximization under uncertainty both point to equal distribution. But this no longer holds for the more complex and realistic situation in which labour supply is permitted to vary. Let A command a higher wage than B; but, acting under the veil, let each maximize utility as if they did not know their identity. Their choice must now allow for a further consideration: namely, that taxation reduces labour supply, so that the size of the pie varies inversely with the degree of redistribution. Now, the outcome will depend on the degree of risk aversion. Given extreme risk aversion, redistribution will be carried to the point of maximin, while it will fall short thereof if risk aversion is less severe, i.e. if the marginal utility of income schedule falls less sharply.

This is no longer the result that follows if the Golden Rule is applied directly. Suppose that, in the absence of equalization, A's earnings will be 100 while B's earnings will be only 50. According to the rule, A will offer 25 to B just as A would want B to offer that amount if the roles were reversed. Disincentive effects on labour supply, which are allowed for in the utility maximization model – and which, combined with extreme risk aversion, are crucial to Rawls's maximin solution – do not enter under the Golden Rule. Once more, it is puzzling why individuals who first accept the ethical axiom to act under the veil should then proceed to avoid its implications by restricting labour supply in response to taxation. The problem of inconsistency again arises, and now has a major bearing on the outcome.

It is intriguing to consider how the analysis of distributive justice should have come to be converted into risk aversion. The answer, it appears, lies in the double role of declining marginal income utility. This decline is significant (1) because it bears on the relative welfare position of various individuals with different incomes, i.e. on the philosopher's problem of distributive justice; but also (2) as a basis for developing economic propositions about gambling behaviour and risk aversion. This technical linkage has permitted the analysis to slip from (2) to (1), even though they deal with entirely different problems. Following the economist's lead, the philosopher's attention is thus diverted from the essential fairness proposition.

There is, of course, a distinction between the pure theory of justice and its application. It need hardly be noted that application of the Golden Rule is not feasible in practice. People who are unwilling to follow the Rule will respond so as to generate announcement effects, and there is no impartial referee to whom potential earning capacities are known, so that tax liabilities could be related to potential rather than actual earnings. But this hardly justifies the formulation of the theory of distributive justice in inconsistent terms. Moreover, our concerns may not be without practical implication. Thus, it may be questioned whether the social welfare function, by which redistributive policies are assumed, should be constructed so as to allow for all deadweight losses. To be sure, such taxes as are imposed on A and such subsidies as are granted to B should be designed so as to minimize their deadweight loss. B's gain should be arrived at the least cost to A. This is the range over which the strictures of optimal taxation fully apply. But it is not obvious that the then remaining deadweight loss should be allowed for in the social welfare function and in judging the desired degree of redistribution. These losses result from responses that run counter to society's intent to apply a certain rule of fairness. It is questionable whether individuals who fight the implementation of the rule should be rewarded for the consequences of their non-cooperation.[4]

The preceding argument has provided a plea for defining fairness in more consistent terms. But this is not to say that 'fairness' should be the only controlling criterion. Society may well choose to view distributive justice as involving combinations of both Lockean entitlement and 'fairness'. By combining the two principles with certain weights attached to each, various forms of social welfare function may be constructed. Thus, the rule of fairness may be limited to provide for a cetain level of minimum income, be it in absolute terms or as a percentage of the median, while permitting the remainder of the income flow to be in line with the Lockean rule.

1.6 CONCLUSION

In conclusion, I briefly return to how the theory of distributive justice bears on that of public finance. My premise has been that the issue of distribution (and redistribution) is an inherent part of both fiscal theory and practice. While I have argued over the years (and still hold) that the allocation and distribution issues are separable in theory, and, in most respects, are better separated in practice, they are nevertheless intertwined. In the Wicksellian system, a just distribution of income must prevail to begin with if the prices of public goods generated by a voting system are to approximate a just solution (Wicksell, 1896). This prior of just distribution is made very clear by Wicksell but tends to be overlooked by modern 'Wicksellians' whose concern is only with efficient resource use, based on a given distribution. In Samuelson's model, the Paretian part of the argument comes first and leads to a utility frontier, but the choice of the optimum then draws upon a social welfare function with its implicit view of welfare distribution. In either model, a theory of distributive justice is an inherent part of a complete theory of public finance. But a theory of distibutive justice cannot be derived from the tools of economic analysis alone, although these tools have much to say about the consequences of alternative distributive arrangements. The theory of public finance, therefore, has to transcend what is usually defined as economics. I do not feel this a disadvantage, and once more suspect that our laureate will agree.

Nor do I think philosophical reasoning can prove the unique validity of a particular theory of distributive justice. Such a theory, in the last resolve, has to rest on one or another prior. This is the case for the fairness model, as well as for the utilitarian and Lockean solutions. The first step, then, is to define each model clearly and to see what its internal logic requires. The next step, not to be examined here, is to explore the consequences of implementation, allowing for the constraints of a real-world setting. This may lead two observers who favour models X and Y respectively to agree on model Z as the best available outcome. The luxury of first-choice solutions is rarely available in social affairs. However, available outcomes cannot be ranked without reference to a normative framework, so that fiscal theory has to comprise both dimensions.

NOTES

1 For a discussion of the land issue, see Musgrave (1983).
2 Among a large literature on this fascinating theme see Viner (1927), Stigler (1975b), Peacock (1975), Mizuta (1975), Cropsey (1975), Wilson (1976), Cairnes (1976), Buchanan (1976) and Musgrave (1976).
3 As an example, see Stigler (1975b), who chides Smith for failing to consider all problems as solvable via a self-interest mechanism.
4 Perhaps some of these difficulties might be avoided if the focus of distributive justice were shifted to relative wage rates rather than income (or welfare) positions. However, this formulation is complicated by non-pecuniary job differentiation.

2
Marginal Cost Pricing: No Empty Box

MARK BLAUG

2.1 INTRODUCTION

The belief that 'efficiency' and 'equity' can somehow be separated represents one of the oldest dreams of economics. A half-century before Pareto, J.S. Mill distinguished between the immutable 'laws of production' and the pliant 'law of distribution' in an attempt to persuade his readers that questions about the size of the cake can be divorced from questions about its slices. Virtually every economist before Pareto analysed particular economic policies as if it were possible, first, to discuss the effects on allocative efficiency given the distribution of income and, second, to round off the analysis by adding a value judgement about the associated changes in income distribution. The two stages of the argument were never clearly distinguished, however, so it was often difficult to see just where interpersonal comparisons of utility entered in.

The value of Pareto's definition of social welfare was to make the distinction between efficiency and equity crystal clear. But Pareto continued to believe that significant pronouncements about economic policy could be laid down solely on the basis of efficiency considerations, and the same ideal inspired the advocates of the 'new' welfare economics that flourished in the 1930s. In particular, the 'new' welfare economics featured the doctrine that the Pareto optimality conditions for maximum economic welfare required all prices to equal marginal costs, even in cases where marginal costs were less than average costs for the entire range of operations of an enterprise, so that total costs are never recovered by receipts from sales. This, in a nutshell, is the concept of marginal cost pricing (MCP).

What I want to do in this paper is to take you through the tortured history of MCP, moving quickly through the prewar phases of the debate, which have been so brilliantly reviewed by Nancy Ruggles

(1947, 1949), and somewhat more slowly through the postwar phases and particularly the recent years. This will not be history of economic thought for its own sake: the story has a point. In the course of telling it, it will quickly become apparent that MCP is one of those orthodox doctrines that has been continually criticized and rejected by experts in the field of public utility pricing but nevertheless remains part and parcel of the corpus of received economic ideas. Even now, the precise status of the concept is a matter of frequent misunderstanding.

2.2 THE PREWAR PERIOD

The doctrine that the whole of the overhead costs of decreasing-cost industries or 'natural monopolies' must be financed out of general tax revenues, and that the price of their output must depend only on marginal operating costs, makes its first explicit appearance in the railway literature of the late nineteenth century, in particular in the writings of such railway economists as Wilhelm Launhardt and Arthur Hadley, although hints of it are found in the much earlier work of Jules Dupuit and his disciples at the Ecole des Ponts et Chaussees in Paris.[1] When Harold Hotelling resurrected the concept of MCP for public enterprises in a famous paper (Hotelling, 1938), he advanced the general principle that the resulting deficits of decreasing-cost industries must be financed out of 'lump-sum taxes', that is out of taxes that do not affect the behaviour of economic agents at the margin because they leave the *pattern* of post-tax income the same as that of pre-tax income. His claim for the superiority of MCP and the exclusive reliance on neutral, lump-sum taxes was based on the 'new' welfare economics in the sense of Pareto. Hotelling's advocacy of MCP ran almost immediately into a barrage of furious criticism.

Ruggles's classic review of the debate surrounding the Hotelling thesis included many of the great names of modern economics, such as Frisch, Lerner, Samuelson, Lewis, Meade, Coase and many others. It was a confusing discussion, which, we can now see, involved almost as many fallacies as valid objections. Some argued, incorrectly, that prices need only be proportional, not equal, to marginal costs, in which case it might be possible to meet all the marginal conditions of Pareto optimality and at the same time cover total costs out of sales receipts. Some thought that MCP required identical tariffs for public utilities during peak and off-peak periods, whereas the exact opposite is true. Some said that perfect price discrimination would satisfy the marginal conditions, which is true, and that perfect price discrimination is preferable to MCP, which is not true, since discriminatory charges are only one of many ways of pricing intra-marginal units. In particular, a special form of price discrimination, namely multipart pricing, with a fixed, uniform 'admission' fee to all users or consumers to finance overhead costs plus a variable charge equal to marginal costs to recover operating costs, was held to be superior to MCP because it satisfied the benefit principle of taxation at the same time that it solved the deficit problem of decreasing-cost industries. Finally, it was argued that MCP failed to provide a profit–loss test of misconceived investment, and that any change from average cost pricing to MCP without compensation payments by gainers (consumers of the public service) to losers (all taxpayers) necessarily leads to a change in income distribution, which is to say that the results of MCP are simply not comparable with those of average cost pricing.

After sorting out the sense from the nonsense in these criticisms, Ruggles nevertheless rejected the Hotelling thesis. At best, Hotelling had shown that a shift to MCP would entail a *potential* Pareto improvement (PPI), not an actual one. He believed that, if deficits were financed by lump-sum taxes, the case for MCP rested on *actual* Pareto improvements because lump-sum taxes fall only on the intra-marginal consumers' and producers' surpluses. Ruggles argued that Hotelling was simply wrong, because even lump-sum taxes are borne in part by those who make little or no use of a public service and hence involve a redistribution of income between users and non-users. Either we must decide to ignore this effect by assuming that the utility of income is the same for all individuals, which takes us right back to the 'old' welfare economics of Marshall and Pigou, or we must deny that the associated redistribution is uniquely related to the incomes of users and non-users, which may or may not be true, depending on the public service in question.

Ruggles's criticism of Hotelling has withstood the test of time, and it is now a commonplace of writers on welfare economics to declare that the 'new' welfare economics can only approve a potential Pareto improvement: an actual Pareto improvement requires the addition of a specific distributional judgement. This admission is sometimes regarded as marking the effective failure of the 'new' welfare economics, which had, after all, promised to provide important and significant statements on policy issues without invoking interpersonal comparisons of utility, thus separating questions of allocative efficiency from those of distributive equity. If the conclusions of welfare economics have to be confined to potential Pareto improvements rather than actual ones, the sceptics argue, the promised separation of efficiency and equity is achieved only at the cost of practical irrelevance. Hotelling himself believed that taxes on land rents, inherited income and current income all qualified as neutral, lump-sum taxes, from which it followed that a PPI could always be realized in practice. The notion that taxes on land rents and inherited incomes are lump-sum taxes that do not affect the marginal conditions for maximizing welfare must be put down as a piece of old-fashioned, nineteenth-century economics. Stranger still was Hotelling's notion that an income tax is a lump-sum tax when an income tax obviously alters the marginal rates of substitution between work and leisure.[2] That leaves us with a poll tax or head tax as the only candidate for a lump-sum tax. Unfortunately, such taxes appear to be politically impracticable. If so, there would seem to be no way in which we could ever realise a PPI in practice without committing ourselves to some interpersonal comparison of utility.

2.3 THE POSTWAR PERIOD: PHASE I

The late 1950s saw a number of major contributions to the debate, all of which endorsed Ruggles's central conclusion that the impracticability of lump-sum redistributions of income or wealth represented the Achilles Heel of the theory of MCP.

A careful reading of Ian Little's knock-down assault on the doctrine of marginal cost pricing in his *Critique of Welfare Economics* (1957) shows that it rests essentially on second-best reasoning, that is, the impossibility in a mixed economy of achieving first-best conditions, coupled with a denial of the view that the redistributive effects of a switch from average cost pricing to MCP in public services is random. On the other hand, here and there he made a number of concessions to MCP. In general, Little concluded that cases of zero or near-zero short-run marginal costs (e,g, museums, parks, bridges, passenger trains, buses, broadcasting, water supply and uncongested roads) justified zero or near-zero prices so as to equate demand to supply. Nevertheless, in the final analysis he insisted that 'nationalized industries should *at least* aim to cover total costs' (p. 201), and it is precisely this conclusion that typifies the standpoint of all those who oppose MCP.

Similarly, Jan de Graaff's devastating survey of the 'new' welfare economics in 1957 returns again and again to the impossibility of separating efficiency from equity because of the impracticability of lump-sum redistributions of income or wealth (de Graaff, 1957, pp.77–80). The assertion that lump-sum transfers are not practicable, or even that they are not feasible – a much stronger assertion – is so common in the literature (see for example Samuelson, 1948, pp.147–9) that we ought to spend a moment examining it.

Lump-sum transfers are frequently but incorrectly defined as taxes and subsidies that do not influence any economic decision, which of course guarantees the conclusion that the set of lump-sum transfers is empty. Instead, they should be defined as transfers that do not directly change the terms of any economic choice, or, more precisely, as transfers that do not produce substitution effects. In principle, we can think of at least four types of taxes that will meet this requirement: (1) a poll tax or an undifferentiated, uniform levy on everyone; (2) a differential head tax, which is a function of the personal characteristics of individuals, provided these characteristics are not subject to choice, such as age, measured IQ in the preschool years or the number of letters in one's last name; (3) an excise tax on goods, the demand for which is completely price-inelastic; and (4) an equiproportionate tax on all economic alternatives, including not only leisure but all of the non-pecuniary advantages of different occupations. It is sometimes said that differential lump-sum taxes and subsidies are not feasible because the information on which we would like to base such transfers is not observable and, moreover, economic agents have incentives not to reveal it (Atkinson and Stiglitz, 1980). It is evident that this objection applies with full force to the last two of the four types, but it is not easy to see why it should apply to the first two. A poll tax or a differential head tax is perfectly feasible from an economic point of view. Of course, such taxes are politically impossible because no elected government would swallow the notion of arbitrary levies unrelated to the economic circumstances of taxpayers. At any rate, let us stop saying that lump-sum transfers are not feasible when what we really mean is that they are politically inconceivable.[3]

To return to de Graaff. Like Little, he too rejects MCP on second-best grounds:

> It seems fairly clear that the conditions which have to be met before it is correct (from a welfare viewpoint) to set prices equal to marginal costs in a particular industry are so restrictive that they are unlikely to be satisfied in practice. The survival of the marginal cost pricing principle is probably no more than an indication of the extent to which the majority of professional economists are ignorant of the assumptions required for its validity. How else can we account for the glib advocacy of the principle in a society where the marginal rate of income-tax is certainly not zero, where optimum taxes are certainly not imposed on both imports and exports, where external effects in consumption are of the first importance, where uncertainty and expectation play a major role in making life worth living, where ...? (de Graaff, 1957, p. 154)

In the following year, Coenraad Oort published a book-length study of *Decreasing Costs as a Problem of Welfare Economics* (Oort, 1958), which once again rejected MCP, particularly as a guide to pricing the products of decreasing-cost industries. To stop at the demonstration that MCP creates the conditions for a PPI, while handing over to politicians the job of converting a potential into an actual Pareto improvement, he concluded, is to abandon policy-making at the point where all the interesting economic issues first arise (Oort, 1958, pp. 149–50).

Since all these writers agree, there would seem to be little left to say about MCP. Nevertheless, we have not yet taken account of Jack Wiseman's 'empty box' paper (Wiseman, 1957), the most frequently cited and most uncompromising of all the attacks published on MCP in the 1950s. Wiseman did not mince words: 'No general pricing rule or rules can be held unambiguously to bring about an "optimum" use of resources by public utilities even in theory. Indeed, failing some universally acceptable theory of public economy, the economist can offer no *general* guidance at all to a government how to decide a price policy for such utilities.'

Wiseman's argument is based essentially on the fact that there exists no method of implementing the MCP rule for decreasing-cost industries – which for him comprise the typical case – that does not entail a system of financing the resulting deficit, thus altering the distribution of income, which alteration however cannot be evaluated according to the 'new' welfare economics. In short, decreasing-cost industries provide the outstanding example of how pricing rules based on principles of allocative efficiency necessarily imply a simultaneous decision about income distribution.

Wiseman made two further points, both of which have proved to be productive of further developments. He rejected miltipart pricing as a solution to the problem of deficits in decreasing-cost industries because it failed to avoid interpersonal comparisons of utility. Multipart pricing, we recall, consists of a lump-sum licence fee to cover deficits and a variable charge per unit of utilization equal to the marginal cost of provision (such two-part tariffs are now common in many countries, for example telephone charges in the United Kingdom). The uniform licence fee, Wiseman noted, may be interpreted as an admission charge to a voluntary 'club' of users, whose members decide unanimously on quantity and price. It is true that multipart pricing changes the distribution of income among users of the service, but this does not matter because it is the product of a voluntary and unanimous choice. If the fixed admission charge did not discourage potential customers, the two-part tariff would be Pareto-efficient. However, since the admission charge is essentially a regressive head tax, the two-part tariff is not distributionally neutral, and its adoption therefore implies an interpersonal comparison of utility. A later paper by James Buchanan took up this idea of economic 'clubs', applying it to the study of efficiency rules for allocating impure 'public goods' characterized by excludable benefits, resulting in what is now a vast if inconclusive literature on the economic theory of clubs (see Sandler and Tschirhart, 1980).

Wiseman also made much of the fact that the MCP principle gives no guidance in selecting the appropriate time period for deciding on public utility prices, and hence no guidance in selecting the length of the relevant planning period. He argued that the only practical planning period is one as long as the lowest common multiple of the life-periods of the assets involved, implying that MCP would always have to be supplemented by or associated with an exercise in investment planning.

Martin Farrell (1958) wrote what is generally considered to be the definitive reply to Wiseman. It is noteworthy that he concedes all the standard, second-best arguments against MCP, avoids discussion of the special difficulties created by decreasing-cost industries, and ultimately rests his case for MCP on the still greater deficiencies of average cost pricing.[4] But William Vickrey (1955), writing two years before the Wiseman attack, had used exactly the same sort of argument as Farrell. 'One may for various and sufficient reasons', wrote Vickrey, 'hesitate to embrace marginal cost pricing in all its ramifications as an absolute standard. But no approach to utility pricing can be considered truly rational which does not give an important and even a major weight to marginal cost considerations.' He conceded that popular notions of equity, the need to provide internal efficiency checks on the operation of public enterprises and the high cost of raising the revenues required to implement MCP in the case of 'natural monopolies', such as railroad freight services, made it desirable to depart from the strict MCP rule in a number of cases. Nevertheless, in most cases, and he singled out railroad passenger services as a good example, pricing based on incremental costs yields better results than the type of pricing based on 'fully distributed costs' which is commonly practised by public enterprises in most countries. 'In general,' he concluded

> marginal cost pricing must be regarded not as a mere proposal to lower rates generally below the average cost level but rather as an approach which implies a drastic rearrangement of the patterns and structure of rates. Indeed, it is this restructuring of rates that is likely to be the greatest contribution of marginal cost pricing to the improvement of the overall efficiency of our economy. (Vickrey, 1955, p. 114)

Similar sentiments with particular reference to railroad pricing were voiced by a team of economists led by William Baumol a few years later (Baumol *et al.*, 1962).

In all of these defences of MCP that were penned in the late 1950s, we have clearly travelled a long way from the dogmatic pronouncements of the early advocates of MCP in the golden halo created by the 1938 Hotelling paper. The new argument for MCP is not that it is a perfect policy rule for public enterprises, but that it is a policy rule superior to average cost pricing.

2.4 THE POSTWAR PERIOD: PHASE II

The early 1960s witnessed a new twist to the MCP debate, which seemed at last to answer Wiseman's earlier criticism that MCP requires a decision on the length of the run over which marginal costs are defined, and yet provides no basis for such a decision. The answer takes its cue from the well-known theorem that short-run and long-run marginal costs coincide when capacity is optimally adjusted to demand – from which it follows that any difference between the short-run and the long-run implications of MCP is a sure sign that capacity is not adjusted to its optimal level. If there is excess demand at a price determined by short-run marginal costs, MCP tells us that prices must be raised until demand equals capacity. At the same time, however, capacity should be raised to meet the demand that would be forthcoming at the price that is optimal on the basis of long-run marginal costs. In other words, if there is an optimal investment policy, there is no contradiction between short-run and long-run MCP, and if there is such a contradiction, it constitutes a criticism not of the MCP principle, but of the investment policy that is being pursued.

This argument is the gist of the contributions of a number of French economists, particularly Marcel Boiteux and Pierre Massé, who were connected with Electricité de France in the late 1940s and 1950s.[5] They noted that, in electricity pricing at any rate, there was little alternative to pricing based on long-run marginal costs. 'Short-run marginal costs' could mean the cost either of increasing output quickly or of increasing it temporarily; but, whatever the operational meaning of the term, administrative constraints on frequent tariff charges forced managers of electricity generating boards to focus on permanent output changes and hence on long-run marginal costs (Turvey, 1969a).

The theory of optimal capacity of the French engineers-cum-economists has been vigorously taken up by Ralph Turvey in his writings on the pricing problems of the British electricity industry. In his major study, *Optimal Pricing and Investment in Electricity Supply* (1968), Turvey defines long-run marginal costs in present-value terms as 'the greatest worth of all system costs as they will be with the increment in load which is to be costed, less what they would be without that increment', and shows that information about the structure of marginal costs is provided as a byproduct of the calculations required for rational investment planning. Elsewhere, too, Turvey has come down firmly on the side of MCP as a second-best pricing rule, arguing that the prices of public enterprise products sold within the public sector should equal their long-run marginal costs, while those sold outside the public sector should be proportional to long-run marginal costs, the markup over marginal costs being determined by the prices of their private sector substitutes (Turvey, 1969b).[6]

The striking feature of the French contributions to the MCP literature is their total failure to deal with the problem of deficits in decreasing-cost industries – which, indeed, is hardly ever mentioned.[7] If there really are 'natural monopolies', that is public enterprises in which costs continue to decline monotonically for all foreseeable levels of output, it is of little help to be told that short-run marginal costs will be equal to long-run marginal costs when capacity is optimally adjusted, because the optimum level of capacity of 'natural monopolies' is infinitely large. It is true, of course, that the evidence that there are increasing returns to scale in most public services is actually very thin, and it has been argued that even decreasing costs in railways are really due to excess capacity and do not represent a true long-run equilibrium phenomenon.[8] But even if we reject the notion of genuine decreasing-cost industries, the problem of deficits forms an integral part of the MCP principle.

Most UK and US writers on MCP illustrate the problem of deficits with examples of nationalized industries, such as railway transport, the demand for which has been shrinking for such long periods that financial deficits are really due to excess capacity. In that case, even prices equal to short-run marginal costs will not cover long-run marginal costs and will generate financial losses. We can, of course, raise prices to cover average costs in order to remove the deficit, but that only redistributes the social costs of carrying excess capacity, from all taxpayers to users of the service. The French writers on MCP avoid discussing such issues of equity connected with pricing rules of public enterprise because they appear to be thinking of the electricity industry, for which demand is growing and for which costs are almost certainly non-decreasing in the long run.

2.5 THE POSTWAR PERIOD: PHASE III

We are now very close to the heart of the matter, which, in popular parlance, is the question, Should public enterprises be expected to pay their own way? Those who advocate MCP, even with many ifs and buts, deny any presumption that public enterprises ought always to make a profit or even to break even; they focus on current costs, and treat historic costs as bygones that are forever bygones. Furthermore, they insist on keeping questions of allocation and pricing analytically separate from questions of finance and equity. On the other hand, those who reject marginal cost pricing in any and all of its varieties, maintaining that only average cost pricing provides an accounting check on management and denying that efficiency and equity can ever be separated, end up insisting that every public enterprise must be expected to pay its own way, which paradoxically undermines the very case for public ownership that gave rise to the debate on public utility pricing in the first place. In other words, the opponents of MCP would appear to solve the pricing problem of public enterprises by dissolving it.[9]

We come now to the last and most recent phase of the long controversy over the Hotelling thesis. The views of the early advocates of MCP, such as Hotelling and Lerner, that Pareto optimality requires MCP in the public sector on the assumption that prices are equated to marginal costs in the private sector is nowadays dismissed as extraordinarily naive. Given imperfect competition, uncorrected externalities and non-lump-sum taxes, MCP in public enterprises can be only a second-best solution. But apart from all these considerations, there is the old problem of financing the deficit of decreasing-cost industries. Since the deficit must be financed by taxation, and since any tax other than a poll tax or an arbitrary head tax induces price distortion, MCP must involve the problem of maximizing output in the presence of an added constraint: the revenues of government must equal the algebraic sum of the deficits (or surpluses) of the individual firms in the economy – which is precisely the definition of a second-best problem. Even if there is no such thing as a 'natural monopoly', public enterprises or privately regulated enterprises may be required by law to meet historic as well as current costs, in consequence of which MCP would once again involve the problem of maximizing output subject to an added revenue constraint. In either case, MCP is inherently a second-best problem, at least so long as lump-sum taxes are ruled out as being impossible in practice. It can be shown, however, that the second-best case for MCP requires not that prices equal marginal costs, but that prices deviate systematically from marginal costs. It is this theorem that Baumol and Bradford have labelled the 'Mislaid Maxim', in the sense that it goes back to the public finance literature of the 1920s, for example to Pigou (1928), and even further back to the public utility pricing literature of the nineteenth century.[10]

Far from setting prices equal to or even proportionate to marginal costs, second-best, quasi-optimal prices should deviate unequally from marginal costs throughout the economy, the deviation in any particular case being greater, the more price-inelastic is the demand for the product in question. In the simple case where all cross-elasticities of demand are zero, the rule is that the deviation from marginal costs for any one product should be inversely proportional to its price elasticity of demand (Baumol and Bradford, 1970). This idea of an optimal set of deviations from MCP in a second-best world is now a recognized feature of modern discussions of applied welfare economics, being the other side of the coin of the currently fashionable topic of 'optimal taxation' (see Atkinson and Stiglitz, 1980, pp. 461-74).

These developments are clearly a far cry from the original Hotelling article. Neverthless, they remain in the Hotelling tradition, not simply because long-run marginal costs remain the reference point to pronouncements on optimal resource allocation, but because the century-old separation of efficiency from equity characterizes second-best as it did first-best welfare economics. Even in this literature, the First Commandment of the 'new welfare economics' – 'Thou Shalt Not Make Interpersonal Comparisons of Utility' – is scrupulously obeyed. But for this First Commandment, we could meet the revenue constraint that inhibits us from achieving a first-best solution by average cost pricing rather than marginal cost pricing. The case for MCP, or, as we should now say, the case for making MCP a point of departure for a set of optimal prices, stems basically from the fundamental conditions for Pareto-optimal efficiency; and, of course, Pareto optimality is defined only with reference to a particular distribution of income or, rather, resource endowments. If we are unwilling to divorce efficiency from equity, at least for the sake of argument, neither the concept of MCP nor that of optimal deviations from MCP makes any sense.

2.6 COST–BENEFIT ANALYSIS

In the final analysis, therefore, it is the willingness to analyse efficiency arguments apart from problems of income distribution that divides the advocates from the critics of MCP. The fundamental distinction between efficiency and equity is rarely defended in so many words by modern writers on MCP, but it is frequently and explicitly discussed in the literature on cost–benefit analysis.

Cost–benefit analysis appraises economic projects in terms of their net total benefits over total costs on the assumption that it is desirable to maximize the sum of producers' and consumers' surpluses. But producers' surplus is simply the absolute value of the money amount by which the total costs of production of a particular output exceed the revenue which that output yields under strict MCP, while the consumers' surplus is the money amount by which the consumers' total valuation of that output exceeds the revenue they have paid out, again under strict MCP. Hence, cost–benefit analysis subsumes the MCP principle and is unthinkable without it.[11]

Virtually all modern exponents of cost–benefit analysis are careful to point out that it can only show that a particular project is capable of generating a PPI in which gainers could compensate losers and still themselves remain better off. It offers no opinion on whether such compensation payment *should* be made; that is, it stops at the point at which it has enumerated the gains and losses to various individuals and ventures no judgement on how these gains and losses should be distributed. Since the actual adoption or rejection of a project by a public authority implies both a cost–benefit calculation and a distributional judgement, a number of writers have in recent years suggested that such distributional judgements should be integrated into cost–benefit analysis by means of weights attached to the benefits that accrue to various income groups.

This proposal to use distributional weights has been vigorously opposed by Arnold Harberger (1971, 1978) on a number of different grounds. He argues, first, that economists are unlikely to agree on any particular set of weights. The view that distributional weights ought to decline with income, because of some notion of diminishing marginal utility of income, would no doubt command universal assent among economists. Nevertheless, the distributional weighting functions reflecting this viewpoint can be shown to involve vastly different weights. Even the suggestion of a single premium magnifying the net benefits of beneficiaries below the poverty line is problematic. In general, the use of distributional weights would in most cases make project evaluation depend critically on how the project is actually financed. Hence, if we are concerned to reach a professional consensus in the area of applied welfare economics, we are well advised to ignore distributional effects in cost–benefit analysis.

Besides, even conventional valuations of social income, in which an increase in the size of the national income is regarded as 'good' and a decrease as 'bad', in effect assume that the size of the cake can be treated independently of the sharing out of its slices. In evaluating a change in national income, we typically accept base-year or final-year prices as if the choice involved no value judgement, and we ignore concomitant changes in the distribution of income, thereby attaching equal weights to the gainers and losers of the change. To do anything else would mean that we could not welcome an increase in measured national income without prior agreement on the social welfare function.

Harberger is not denying that the evaluation of the distributional effects of an economic project forms part of the decision to accept or reject the project. The argument is simply that, instead of incorporating distributional weights into cost–benefit analysis, we should sum the monetary value of costs and benefits algebraically across relevant individuals or groups of individuals, leaving the addition of alternative distributional weights to a later stage. In this way we can show that society may have to pay a price in terms of efficiency for each incremental distibutional 'benefit' obtained. In one of the most perceptive appraisals of cost–benefit analysis that I know of, Alan Williams (1972) comes to identical conclusions: he rejects the concept of amalgamating efficiency and equity effects but recommends attaching incidence calculations to each cost–benefit appraisal, so that the principles underlying distributional weights can be gradually improved.

2.7 EQUITY VERSUS EFFICIENCY AGAIN

We end this long and complex story, therefore, by reasserting the old distinction between efficiency and equity which runs right through the entire literature on welfare economics, as far back as Pareto, Pigou, Marshall and even Ricardo, and without which its elaborately constructed apparatus collapses like a house of cards. This is not to say that efficiency questions are 'positive', 'objective' economics, involving no value judgements. Even first-best Pareto optimality rests on definite value judgements, as Alan Peacock has recently reminded us (Rowley and Peacock, 1975). Efficiency is necessarily a value-laden concept, and cannot be freed from the notion that it is somehow more desirable than inefficiency.[12] Nevertheless, there is little advantage, and much disadvantage, in cluttering up the conclusions of welfare economics by indiscriminately combining the value judgements underlying the concept of Pareto optimality with those relating to the economic justice of different distributions of income.

Consider, for example, what is implied by the opposite attitude. If we refuse, even in principle, to distinguish allocative efficiency from distributive equity, we must perforce reject the whole of welfare economics and with it any conventional presumption in favour of competitive markets – and, indeed, in favour of the price mechanism as a method of allocating scarce resources. Arguments for coordinating economic activity by markets would then have to be expressed in terms of political philosophy – for example, that markets diffuse economic power – and economics would in consequence have to become a totally different subject.[13] Moreover, it is perfectly clear that economists do judge such practical questions as, Should parking meters be used to control road congestion? Should public transport be free? Should governments subsidize petrol, medical care and public housing? and so on by means of sequential reasoning, in which the efficiency of various alternatives is judged before considering any possible adverse distributional effects that may or may not be capable of being offset by taxes and transfers (for evidence see Brittan, 1973). It is true that most decisions of public policy proceed exactly the other way round: they are expressly designed to aid a favoured group at the expense of every other, the more so as the benefits of economic policies are often extremely visible, whereas the costs are so widely diffused that most people are hardly aware of paying any part of it. Jacob Viner once defended the economist as 'the special custodian for society of the long view in economic matters' (Viner, 1958, pp.112-13). Similarly, we must insist on the role of the economist as a special custodian for society of the efficiency view of economic problems, because all the evidence suggests that, if economists do not draw attention to the trade-off between efficiency and equity, no one else will.

2.8 THE SUBJECTIVITY OF COSTS

Even so, we are not yet home and dry. Recent years have seen an entirely new objection to MCP, new in the sense that it makes explicit an objection that one can now see has been at the back of much of the criticism of MCP. It is an argument that has been vigorously advocated by James Buchanan, who goes so far as to claim that it represents the outlook of an entire 'school' of LSE economists (Buchanan, 1970; Buchanan and Thirlby, 1973). Buchanan argues that opportunity costs in the real world are personal, subjective valuations of the utility of forgone alternatives, and not the objective market prices of resources that figure in the diagrams of textbooks in price theory. In a world of fully competitive equilibrium, he readily admits, objective *ex post* cost data would indeed coincide with subjective *ex ante* estimates of forgone alternatives; but in actual situations of disequilibrium, imperfect knowledge and pervasive uncertainty, there is no reason to think that the two are systematically related. Buchanan mentions some practical implications of his argument and is particularly scathing about cost–benefit analysis; he is silent, however, on the question of the pricing of public utilities.

However, in a critical assessment of Buchanan's argument, Karen Vaughn (1980) specifically considers the problem of pricing rules for regulated monopolies. It is, of course, precisely when governmental decisions pre-empt market decisions that models of markets in full equilibrium are likely to be particularly misleading. In other words, the Buchanan critique cuts most deeply at the very point under considera-tion: if in practice the regulatory agency has no method for ascertaining the costs perceived by the regulated enterprise, MCP falls to the ground.

But this is merely to say that MCP suffers all the shortcomings of applied welfare economics cast in the traditional Paretian mould: it is a proposition about the nature of end-point equilibrium states and has nothing whatever to say about the process by which an actual economy converges on equilibrium. Economists have usually been confident that, provided one is certain about one's destination, the journey to that destination is of little consequence; in other words, they have shrugged off the political and administrative problems of imposing MCP on an enterprise pursuing a pricing rule based on average costs. Much doubt has recently been cast on that approach by Demsetz (1968), Stigler (1975a) and Alan Peacock (1979) himself. Faced with a genuine natural monopoly situation, it is no longer as obvious to the present generation of economists as it was to previous generations that only outright nationalization or regulation of some kind can achieve the MCP solution required by Paretian principles. Nevertheless, this is no objection to MCP in cases where the industry has long been in public ownership or subject to public regulation. And, besides, the natural monopoly case is only half the story of MCP.

2.9 CONCLUSIONS

So, Ruggles, Little, Graaff, Oort and Wiseman notwithstanding, the theory of MCP is no empty box. Of course, MCP is a method, not a dogma. It is grounded in Pareto optimality and the maximization of consumers' and producers' surpluses, but, then, so are all the policy views of economists. In addition, MCP requires empirical judgements on a product-by-product basis about market structure, indivisibilities, externalities and elasticities of demand and supply; in short, it is a systematic check-list of what to look for in pricing a public service. It does not, therefore, furnish any simple pronouncements about public pricing, except perhaps that public enterprises should not necessarily be expected to break even and that almost any pricing rule is better than average cost pricing. Moreover, standing by itself, it furnishes no case for nationalizing or regulating all industries with natural monopoly characteristics.

These may be simple truths, but nevertheless they directly contradict popular doctrine about public sector pricing. Here as elsewhere, economists find themselves solidly ranked against some of the great myths of our times.

NOTES

1 See Ekelund and Herbert (1983) and the literature cited there, not least their own researches.
2 Most of the early participants in the controversy over the Hotelling thesis agreed with Hotelling that an income tax is superior to an excise tax as a method of raising revenue to finance the MCP system. This thesis, soon to be known as the 'excess burden of indirect taxation', attracted almost as much debate in the 1940s and 1950s as the concept of MCP. It took almost two decades to arrive at the correct view, namely that there is no simple way of ranking taxes according to their 'excess burden' (see Walker, 1955, and Musgrave, 1959, ch. 7).
3 This conclusion is essentially due to Oort (1958, pp. 40–4, 122–5).
4 Farrell (1958) is reprinted with considerable amendment, taking account of Wiseman (1959), in Turvey (1968a).
5 See Dreze (1964), Turvey (1964) and Nelson (1968).
6 See also Turvey and Anderson's popular exposition of MCP in the electricity industry (Turvey and Anderson, 1975). This concludes: 'If we ignore complications relating to income distribution, externalities and pricing distortions elsewhere, and if we ignore stochastic variations in demand and in the availability of productive capacity, the rules for optimal resource allocation are simple. There is the pricing rule that price should equal whichever is the higher of marginal operating costs, or the price necessary to restrict demand capacity. There is also the investment rule that the present worth of the dual (shadow) value of capacity should be equated with its marginal capacity costs' (p. 355).
7 I owe this insight to Millward (1971, pp. 244–5).
8 The typical long-run average cost curve of a firm appears to be L-shaped, falling at first then becoming horizontal, which is to say that there is no

evidence for continually falling costs even in the case of railways. In other words, while there is clear evidence of unexploited economies of scale in many industries, there are few unambiguous cases of 'natural monopolies'; see Johnston (1960); Walters (1963, 1968); Smith (1955); Silbertson (1972).

9   For an admittedly confusing example of this style of anti-MCP reasoning see Melody (1974) and the reply by Kahn (1974). The tension between these two points of view is at the back of the complex argument of Nove (1973). He rejects the belief of 'many economists [who] insist on identical criteria in the nationalized and private sectors' and yet recommends Wiseman's 'proper scepticism about marginal cost pricing' in the apparent belief that MCP suggests that every part of an integrated public enterprise should be run at a profit and that there should never be cross-subsidization between them. But the MCP philosophy suggests the very opposite, so Nove's criticisms are properly directed not at MCP, but at average cost pricing.

10 Pigou (1928) contains an extensive summary of optimal pricing solutions for an industry in which MCP fails to recover total costs, including a statement of the 'Mislaid Maxim'. Thus, a decade before Hotelling's paper Pigou had already conceived MCP as a second-best problem.

11 As Millward (1971) has said, 'It is amazing how the topic of marginal cost pricing has been bombarded with criticisms, many of which are equally applicable to cost–benefit analysis which often escapes Scot-free' (p. 282). Actually, this is less amazing when it is realized that the intimate connection between MCP and cost–benefit analysis is little appreciated even by those who malign MCP.

12 Only a minority of economists would disagree with this view, principally Archibald and Hennipman. For details see Blaug (1980, pp. 142–8).

13 As Mishan (1971) has said, 'If economists reject welfare economics, they may well have to reject also the economists' conventional presumption in favour of a competitive market. The economist could of course approve of the market for other than allocative reasons: for instance, on the grounds that it is a cheap and relatively non-political administrative institution for coordinating economic activity' (p. 308).

3

Towards a Theory of Bureaucratic Behaviour

CHARLES ROWLEY AND ROBERT ELGIN

3.1 INTRODUCTION

The early theories of bureaucracy tended to be dominated by Weberian notions of impartial, efficient service by government officials concerned to serve the public interest as interpreted by their elected government (Weber, 1947). Economists for the most part took little account, in analysing market failure and recommending efficiency-enhancing bureaucratic interventions, of the undercurrent of popular criticism of bureaucrats on grounds of laziness, insensitivity to citizen preferences, and/or self-seeking. (The 'busy loafers', as Peacock, 1983, reminds us, was Kruschev's contemptuous label for them.)

Early challenges to this nirvana model stemmed from Tullock (1965) and Downs (1967), both analysing the internal organization of bureaucracy, subjecting bureaucratic agents to critical scrutiny and noting the inevitable loss of control associated with this form of economic organization.[1] However, it was only in 1971, with the publication of Niskanen's seminal text (Niskanen, 1971), that bureaucracy was subjected to a comprehensive economic critique with respect to both its internal organization and its external environment. This contribution stimulated a rich literature, in which bureaucracy is analysed on the basis of universal self-seeking assumptions and the public interest model is discarded.

Bureaucracy is a concept that can be defined broadly or narrowly, with some, like Breton and Wintrobe (1982), extending its domain even to include private corporate organizations that raise their revenues by selling commodities at a per-unit price. It is the essence of this paper, however, that the concept should be narrowly drawn in the sense of Niskanen – indeed, more tightly even than his definition, since we wish to exclude from consideration private non-profit organizations which otherwise satisfy his criteria. Thus 'bureaus' here are defined as public sector organizations in which the 'owners' and employees cannot appropriate any part of the difference between revenues and costs as direct personal income, and in which a significant part of the recurring revenues derive from other than the sale of output at a per-unit price.

This paper surveys recent contributions to the theory of bureaucracy within the monopoly/bilateral monopoly framework established by Niskanen. This approach is contrasted with the competitive, exchange-orientated theory of bureaucracy developed notably by Breton and Wintrobe. The issue of input preference also is analysed.[2] Finally, recent contributions which employ notions of property rights and rent-seeking are synthesized in a principal–agent approach which appears to us to offer important insights into the organization and behaviour of central (or federal) government bureaucracies, and which generalizes many of the results previously analysed.

3.2 THE MONOPOLY/BILATERAL MONOPOLY THEORY OF BUREAUCRACY

Niskanen's theory of bureauracy and representative government (he stresses the importance of the dual relationship)[3] is predicated on the self-seeking generative assumption associated with all senior bureaucrats who exercise responsibility over bureau budgets. Of the several variables that enter the bureaucrat's utility function – salary, perquisites of office, public reputation, power, patronage, output of the bureau, ease of making changes and ease of managing the bureau – Niskanen suggested that all except the last two were a monotonic increasing function of the total budget of the bureau. Thus he employed budget maximization as a relevant proxy for utility maximization by senior bureaucrats, predicting that bureaucrats produce the output level that yields the highest possible budget rather than, for example, the output level that maximizes the difference between revenues and costs.

Niskanen further assumes that government bureaus possess supply monopolies and, for the most part, bargain against governments or their appropriations committees over their budgets from positions of information advantage.[4] Given that they trade a total output for total budget, this enables them to exercise monopoly power in a manner comparable to perfect price discrimination, extracting the total consumers' surplus from their commodity provisions.

Niskanen's model posits a senior bureaucrat acting under a budget constraint given by

$$B = aQ - bQ^2 \tag{1}$$

where B is the budget that the government is willing to grant the bureau for a given expected level of output, Q. He further assumes an increasing marginal cost function, of the form

$$TC = cQ + dQ^2 \tag{2}$$

If the total cost is less than or equal to the total budget at the budget-maximizing output (the case of the demand-constrained bureau), the choice of output by the bureau head will be $Q = a/2b$ where the budget is maximized. If the total cost exceeds the budget at that output (the case of the budget-constrained bureau), the bureau will settle for a constrained maximum which assures equality of total cost with budget, namely

$$Q = \frac{(a - c)}{(b + d)}$$

These solutions suggest to Niskanen that a primary problem with bureaucracy is over-supply, in the sense that output exceeds that which would maximize net value to the government sponsor. Note that this concept is remote from that of Pareto optimality, since the government and not individual citizens have articulated demand. A secondary problem, save only in the limiting case of budget-constrained output, is that output will be supplied at above minimum possible cost. A third problem, sensed rather than fully articulated by Niskanen, is that bureaus will tend to over-employ capital in order to boost the present value of the budget. In general, therefore, Niskanen-type bureaus diverge sharply from the Weberian ideal.

Although a number of commentators, for example Orzechowski (1977) and Miller (1977), criticize Niskanen for his emphasis upon bureau monopolies in the context of sponsor passivity, this criticism is justified only in connection with the 'basic model'. For, in the relatively neglected Part V of his text, Niskanen models the review process in representative government, utilizing the median voter theorem in this connection, albeit concluding that, 'although the interests of the review committee and the bureau are not identical, they are often (maybe generally) consistent' (p. 153). He also relaxes the assumption of bureau monopoly to explore bureaucratic behaviour in a competitive environment, emphasizing the beneficial effects of such competition upon the cost effectiveness of supply in the demand-constrained environment and upon the provision of supply information to government sponsors.

In an important paper which retained the monopoly assumption of Niskanen's basic model, Migué and Bélanger (1974) challenged Niskanen's budget maximization hypothesis as internally inconsistent, in that it fails to differentiate between the bureau output and all other perquisites of office attainable via budget discretion. The Niskanen bureaucrat is seen to derive zero utility from fiscal residuum. Instead, he pursues the productive efficiency of the competitive firm without any regard for taking rents from the bureau for himself.

Migué and Bélanger suggest that bureau heads may value rewards of office independently from bureau output and may expend less than the total budget on output in order to retain a discretionary budget, given by

$$D = aQ - bQ^2 - cQ - dQ^2 \tag{3}$$

where the symbols are as defined above.

Thus, the output level that maximizes the discretionary budget in this example is

$$Q = \frac{(a - c)}{2(b + d)} \tag{4}$$

The level of ouput here achieved is that preferred by the sponsor, but it is supplied inefficiently with the total surplus appropriated by the bureau. As Migué and Bélanger recognize, this is the alternative polar case to that posited by Niskanen, and intermediate cases are anticipated in which bureau heads maximize a utility function of the form

$$U = f(Q, D) \tag{5}$$

The comparative statics of the Niskanen and the Migué–Bélanger models also differ, since the Niskanen model predicts that bureaus respond to a demand increase by expanding both output and budget in pro rata terms, whereas the Migué–Bélanger model predicts a relatively large budget increase associated with an increase in unit cost. Since Migué and Bélanger do not specify the particular input preference of the bureaucrat, their model is silent on the issue of bureaucratic bias in resource utilization.

Both models leave little role for the legislature or its representatives concerning the final output of the bureau, other than in the budget negotiations, which are seen in any event to be determined by the bureaus. Thus, over-production and/or successful rent-seeking by bureau heads is not viewed as provoking legislative response. Both models ignore property rights and their delineation as a basis for analysing bureaucracy and, in consequence, take no account of the principal–agent relationship which is central to an understanding of bureau behaviour.

3.3 BUREAU BEHAVIOUR IN A COMPETITIVE ENVIRONMENT

Although Niskanen is best known for his monopoly theory of bureau behaviour, in fact he devoted a chapter of his book to an analysis of bureaucratic behaviour in a competitive environment. At local government level, he noted the importance of exit as a mechanism for imposing competitive discipline on bureaus offering alternative service–tax packages, with the inference that even 'monopoly' bureaus would supply near-optimal levels of output at near-minimum production cost. At national government level, however, he suggested that the effect of competition among bureaus must depend on the nature of the review process and the political structure of the government.

Bureau competition is encouraged in certain areas of public good provision, notably in the armed forces in the United States. Niskanen analyses the case in which two bureaus supply the same service to national government under somewhat different cost conditions. The budget–output proposals are jointly reviewed by a committee that is dominated by representatives of a group with a relatively high demand for the service, which forwards a total budget and output for approval by a majority of the entire body of representatives.

Niskanen establishes that such a review committee would select the same total output and budget from the competing bureaus as would a monopoly bureau, in the budget-constrained situation. Under such conditions, bureau competition does not increase efficiency in supply, nor does it reduce service over-supply. However, in the demand-constrained situation, the difference between the budget and the minimum production cost of a monopolistic bureau may be considerable. Competition then will induce efficiency in two ways: (1) by increasing demand elasticity for the services of each bureau, and (2) by providing the review committee with a contemporary basis for comparison. However, bureau competition does not reduce the general problem of bureau over-supply, but rather reduces total expenditure without changing output.

Breton and Wintrobe (1982), while explicitly recognizing the importance of demand forces via the legislature or its review committees for the overall determination of bureaucratic outputs, nevertheless concentrated upon the development of an exchange-based theory of supply with significant internal trading and competitive characteristics. Although their theory is utilized to determine bureaucratic behaviour in both government and corporate organizations here it is reviewed only from the former perspective. Their theory, which continues to provide a role for authority, emphasizes the importance of trade, and thus breaks both with Weberian traditions of bureaucracy as rational and efficient and with the early public choice perspective that bureaus are inherently inefficient in their output provisions.

Relationships between superiors and subordinates are viewed in general as being governed by exchange and trade, with superiors purchasing obedience from their subordinates, and with subordinates competing and trading among themselves. To assist their task, the authors introduce three notions essentially ignored by the early public choice approach, drawn from the conventional literature in bureaucracy.

The first such notion is that of trust. Trade essentially requires the existence of property rights, which for the most part, it is argued (unjustifiably in our view), cannot be supported by legal instruments in the case of bureaucratic relationships but instead are supported by trust. The existence of trust – confidence in some degree by one bureaucrat that another will effect his promise – enables trade to take place where otherwise it would be impossible. Trust networks are therefore the analogues of markets, just as trust is the analogue of law and law enforcement. The structure of networks in the organization is referred to as the informal structure and is treated as a variable, the extent, complexity and influence of which are all under bureaucratic control. In particular, trusts and networks are accumulated by rational individuals who wish to trade with one another over time.

The formal structure, in contracts, is seen to be important essentially as a significant determinant of the cost of accumulating or maintaining networks rather than for its authority role; for Breton and Wintrobe, in our view incorrectly, reject the relevance for bureaucracy of principal–agent analysis , arguing first that monitoring the behaviour of agents in the context of contractual, enforceable law is of necessity different from monitoring in the context of relationships based on trust, and second that, since monitoring typically is conducted by bureaucrats, the problem remains as to who should monitor the monitors. Monitoring, for Breton and Wintrobe is ancillary to trust.

The second concept employed by Breton and Wintrobe is that of selective behaviour, the essence of which is that bureaucrats choose whether to be efficient or inefficient within the limits of their capacity. Essentially, selective behaviour is viewed as the outcome of a trading process – a set of explicit or implicit negotiations conducted via bureaucratic networks between superiors and subordinates on the one hand and among subordinates on the other. The outcome is determined by forces of demand and supply, with the price offered by superiors for efficient service compared with the rewards available to subordinates from inefficiency. These forces are determined themselves by the cost of monitoring and by the distribution of trust in the network.

The third concept introduced is that of bureaucratic competition (in the modern Austrian sense),[5] which Breton and Wintrobe claim to be a dominant feature of bureaucracy, both within and between specific bureaus. Within bureaus, there is competition for jobs, together with a less well recognized form of competition for network ties. Between bureaus, there is competition for territory. For Breton and Wintrobe these various forms of competition are viewed as substitutes, with imperfections in one form compensated for by competition in others. Somewhat unconvincingly, they claim that the world of bureaucracy is essentially a world of competition.

On the basis of these concepts, a theory of bureaucracy is developed which is logically self-contained and, with careful attention to the definition of observable proxies for 'trust', is capable of generating testable predictions.[6] They claim to have developed a model in which both competition and bureaucratic behaviour play important roles, and they claim that this is an accurate reflection of the world. Competition, in their theory, does not eliminate selective behaviour, whether efficient or inefficient – hence the authors' recognition of a role for direct monitoring, reorganization and regulation by sponsors to combat inefficient behaviour. Yet these latter concepts play only a shadowy role in their text and operate essentially outside any notion of property rights as usually defined. In our view, these are very serious deficiencies which are likely to relegate the theory to a peripheral position in the literature on bureaucracy and representative government.

3.4 ISSUES OF BUREAUCRATIC INPUT PREFERENCES

Even the competition-orientated theories of bureaucracy do not deny the possibility of residual discretionary power which may give rise to inefficiency in supply, while analyses based on the superior monopoly advantages of bureaus suggest that a relatively large fiscal residuum arises, from which senior bureaucrats indirectly may extract wealth. The manner in which such wealth is extracted, however, is not clarified, either by Niskanen or by Migué and Bélanger – or, indeed, by Breton and Wintrobe.

Orzechowski (1977) attempted to remedy this deficiency by employing the notion of Migué and Bélanger (that bureaucrats indeed divert the fiscal residuum generated by their agencies for their own purposes) in a model of bureau behaviour that incorporates explicitly the resource preferences of bureaucrats. He noted the emphasis placed by C. N. Parkinson (1970), in early studies of bureau behaviour, upon the strong internal preference for staff (the so-called Parkinson's Law, that the growth rate of staff in public bureaus approximates a positive constant over time). He noted also the confirmation of this preference by O. E. Williamson (1964) for utility-maximizing managers of firms imbued with non-trivial discretionary power. He further noted the contribution of Borcherding, Bush and Spann (1977), which emphasized the vote motive for bureaucrats to extend their bureaus and thereby to enlarge the political base for their activities, and which indeed demonstrated statistically for the United States that voter participation rates were highest among bureaucrats. In contrast, he noted the view of De Alessi (1969) that bureaus may tend to favour relatively capital-intensive production methods since these draw in a larger proportion of supply costs over a shorter time horizon. Orzechowski then derived a model of bureaucracy capable of incorporating elements of both approaches, but one that, in his application, assumes that labour is the dominant preference variable.

Thus, the Orzechowski model defines a utility function for senior bureaucrats containing two variables: output (following Niskanen) and the size of labour input. Bureaus are assumed to maximize this function:

$$\max U = U(Q, L) \tag{6}$$

subject to a total budget constraint $B = R(Q)$:

$$R\{f(K, L)\} = wL + rK \tag{7}$$

Using the Lagrangean method, and substituting $f(K, L)$ for Q to convert the choice problem into one involving two variables, Orzechowski manipulates the first-order conditions to yield an expression that indicates the pattern of resource usage by bureaus:

$$\frac{f_K}{f_L} = \frac{r}{w - U_2/\lambda} \tag{8}$$

With λ and U_2 (the marginal utility of labour) both positive, the implication derived is that

$$\frac{f_K}{f_L} \neq \frac{r}{w} \tag{9}$$

On this basis, Orzechowski establishes that the bureau will employ factor inputs inefficiently, with the ratio of marginal products not equalling their price ratio and, on his assumptions, with labour the over-employed factor input, for any linear-homogeneous or homothetic production function.

The comparative static implications of this model also differ from those of standard profit maximization. For example, the bureaucrat's response to a decrease in the price of capital will have an ambiguous effect on the labour–capital ratio, possibly inducing the use of more labour relative to capital. Moreover, the response of the bureau to demand shocks is also ambiguous, with the Migué and Bélanger thrust suggesting greater inefficiency as the bureau budget expands, but the Parkinson thrust suggesting that staff size expands as budgets experience significant cuts.

Peacock (1983), while judging Orzechowski's model to be a distinct improvement on those based upon the budget maximization generative assumption, suggested that it fails to encapsulate two 'widely recognized' features of bureaucratic leadership: caution and laziness.

Peacock denied that the taste for leisure by senior bureaucrats was appropriately captured by employing labour input as a preference variable, since staff enlargement, in his view, tends to be associated with an increase in managerial and administrative responsibilities.

Emphasizing European bureaucracies (where senior bureaucrats tend to be tenured) in contrast with US bureaucracies (where they are not), Peacock specified a utility function for senior bureaucrats with no expectation of further promotion as follows:

$$\max U = U(N, L, S) \qquad (U_n, U_l, U_s > 0) \tag{10}$$

where N represents the number of administrative grade officials under his command, L represents 'on-the-job leisure' and S represents the surplus (fiscal residuum) over and above the wages and other emoluments payable to administrative-grade staff.

Peacock retained the bureau monopoly assumption of Niskanen, but introduced as an objective constraint the inability of the senior bureaucrat to fix salary rates within the bureau. Assuming (for simplicity) that all administrators are of the same grade and receive identical salaries, the budget constraint is

$$B = \overline{w}N + S \tag{11}$$

The leisure constraint upon senior bureaucrats is

$$L = L(N) \quad \text{with } L_n < 0 \text{ and } L_{nn} < 0 \tag{12}$$

implying a Lagrangean of the form

$$W = U(N, L, S) + \lambda_1\{L - L(N)\} + \lambda_2(B - wN - S) \tag{13}$$

The first-order conditions for utility maximization simplify to

$$U_n + U_l \cdot L_n = U_s \overline{w} \tag{14}$$

Thus the bureaucrat maximizes utility where the marginal utility derived from increasing administrative manpower is equated with the marginal utility derived from using the wages of the marginal administrator for surplus activities. Once N is determined, so is L on Peacock's assumptions. Given the exogenous determination of the cost of labour input, the limitation on the demand for labour is determined by the maximum size of the budget. The upper limit on output expansion is provided by the loss of utility from leisure marginally induced by an expansion in administrative staff. In Peacock's model, output may lie below the level of the perfectly competitive industry, in contrast to both the Niskanen and the Orzechowski models. Technical inefficiency via excessive leisure and fiscal residuum objectives clearly is a predictable outcome of this monopoly model.[7]

3.5 THE ROLE OF THE LEGISLATURE

At best, the legislature, or its representatives, are seen to exercise only a shadowy role in bureau surveillance in the important analyses of bureaucracy so far reviewed. At worst, they are seen to exercise no role at all. Since we shall argue that this is an important weakness, a brief survey of the relevant perspectives is provided in this section.

Niskanen (1972), in his basic model, noted that most bureaus are financed by a single or dominant collective organization, which in turn is financed by tax revenues or by compulsory contributions. The officers, or representatives of the collective (which in the United States may be some amalgam of the executive and the legislature) are usually elected by the wider constituency but are often effectively self-perpetuating (at least within a specific election period). These officers review (in single or in multi-stages) the bureau's proposed activities and budget; approve the budget; monitor the performance of the bureau; and, usually, approve the appointment of the bureau head. Given the monopoly nature of Niskanen's bureau, the relationship between bureau head and review officers is viewed as one of bilateral monopoly characterized 'by both threats and deference, by both gaining and appeals to a common objective' (p. 24).

However, because the officers typically are more concerned with re-election issues than with bureau-monitoring, and are aware that their constituents are ill-informed of their committee contributions – and in any event typically vote for a 'package' of policies – Niskanen argues that they tend to be diverted from their bureau-monitoring responsibilities. Given the differential access to relevant information by bureau heads, the bureau is provided with 'overwhelmingly dominant monopoly power' (p. 30). Niskanen suggests that this monopoly model is probably most applicable to national and state governments and less applicable to local governments, where committee responsibilities are presumably more central to the re-election issue, and where constituent exit costs are significantly lower in response to bureau alienation.

Even in subsequent analysis of the review process in representative government, where Niskanen departs from the passive sponsor assumption, he remains very sceptical about significant sponsor control, especially at national government level, whether in the United States or in Western Europe, as the following passage indicates:

> Under such conditions, the committee review process is a farce. The bureaus estimate the largest budget that will be approved by the larger body of representatives and add a few per cent based on the historical record of reductions made by the committee. The review committees oblige by making the expected reductions. The larger body of representatives dutifully approve the budget recommended by the committee. Most

of the participants in this process, I suppose, believe that they are acting in the public interest. (Niskanen, 1972, p. 153)

Niskanen claims as his most important conclusion the notion that, although the interests of the review committee and the bureau are not identical, they are often (indeed, perhaps generally) consistent, not least because the committees tend to be backed by 'special interest' legislators. Even when they are inconsistent, the low incremental benefits to the review committee and the high cost of an effective review will often induce the committee to accept the bureau's solution.

For the most part, Migué and Bélanger swallow without question Niskanen's notion of the passive sponsor, which is central to their own model. They relax the assumption only at the conclusion of the paper, when they adjust the bureau financing mechanism from block grant budgets to per-unit subsidies for local bureaus otherwise enjoying complete autonomy. In such circumstances, the central government must exercise initiative in defining the level of subsidy to be granted, since the local bureaus simply respond competitively, albeit without new entry threats, to the subsidy on offer. However, the notion of per-unit subsidies extends the concept of bureaucracy beyond the definitional scope of this paper.[8]

Breton and Wintrobe downplay the importance of sponsors in their book, not because they accept the notion of the passive review committee, but because they are concerned more centrally with the competitive exchange paradigm of bureau behaviour. They note in passing, however, that politicians are aware that bureau information is indeed distorted and incorrect as a means of financing inefficient production. In consequence, the sponsors are seen to allow fewer resources to bureaus than would be the case if such known distortions could be policed without cost. In this view, the budget of the bureau will be smaller than would be the case if bureaucrats did not attempt to maximize it by information distortions. If true, this creates a real dilemma for the Niskanen bureaucrat!

In any event, in an earlier note Breton and Wintrobe (1975) specifically addressed the problem of the legislature, arguing that the assumption of passive sponsors was 'the basic flaw' in Niskanen's theory. Politicians, concerned about their prospects for re-election, obviously would attempt to exploit their monopsony power as purchasers of the bureau's output. At some cost, information concerning bureau production and cost functions can be obtained from bureau heads. In such circumstances, the legislature may well gain access to some of the surplus created by bureau outputs. The actual budget will then fall between the total cost curve and the total evaluation curve, with part of the surplus retained by the agency head, part retained by the legislature and part dissipated in monitoring cost.

Niskanen (1975) has conceded that this model provides a starting point for analysing the review process, but he has noted, correctly, that it incorporates neither the specific institutions of the review process nor the incentives of the legislators. He has re-emphasized the importance (especially in the United States) of the review committee rather than the legislature in bureau-monitoring and has reaffirmed his view that most such committees are dominated by legislators with higher demands for the services under review than the median demand in the legislature. In support of this view, he has cited studies of the committee assignment process – by Rohde and Shepsle (1973), by Shepsle (1975) and by Cohen (1974) – which establish as facts that most legislators receive the committee assignments they request and that requests are correlated with services that are most important to their regional constituencies. He has confirmed that, in the United States, committee decisions very seldom are amended or reversed by the whole legislature. In such circumstances, his claim is that bureau and review committee objectives typically are consistent and cannot be rejected out of hand, with the implication that more consumers' surplus will be siphoned off by bureau heads in the form of over-supply than Breton and Wintrobe would allow.

Of course, a high-demand committee has the same incentives to control inefficiency in supply as a randomly selected committee. Indeed, given the cost of control instruments to reduce over-supply and to control inefficiency in supply, the high-demand committee will utilize more control instruments over the latter than would the randomly selected committee, unless supply inefficiency manifests itself in purchasing high-cost factor inputs from those constituencies represented in the review committee.

Furthermore, Niskanen argued that the monitoring function is a public good within the legislature, in that the benefits accrue to the whole population as a function of their tax costs. In consequence, a substantial free-rider problem exists, with the implication that monitoring activities will be under-supplied. Modelling this situation, Niskanen suggested that a legislature will spend time on activities specific to his constituents and contributors as a negative function of the vote effect of taxes paid, of the time cost of reducing bureau costs, and of the share of taxes paid by his constituents.

Niskanen emphasized the role of the party leadership in monitoring individual legislators to limit the size of efficiency losses. However, in political systems such as that of the United States, the party leadership cannot deny membership in the legislature as a sanction. In consequence, a substantial free-rider problem exists in the monitoring function, even for the party leadership, but in much more pronounced form for individual voters.

Orzechowski (1977), for the most part, restricted discussion to internal bureau maximands, implicitly accepting in this respect the Niskanen bureau monopoly solution. However, in explaining the Parkinson bureau output expansion path, he relied on the notion of incremental budgeting, suggesting that bureaus typically experience only small changes in their budgets. An explanation of this is the high relative cost of attempts by appropriations committees to review an entire budget, save perhaps only in the case of the largest bureaus, where the review benefits may be substantial.

Miller (1977), in his review of some of the literature surveyed in this paper, was critical of Niskanen, of Migué and Bélanger and of Breton and Wintrobe for their respective emphases upon one-sided equilibria, whether as a consequence of passive sponsors or of passive bureaus. Indeed, he argued that both the agency head and the party in power determine the output of the agency, the latter by its appropriations decision and the former by its output response. This approach leads to an analysis based on games with an infinite but countable number of pure strategies – games that are not easy to handle. Moreover, such games may well not offer unique solutions but instead may result in multiple equilibria, unstable equilibria, divergent games, mixed strategy solutions or even prisoners' dilemmas. Miller then proceeded to explore likely game solutions under specified hypothetical conditions.

The governing party, following Niskanen, is designated an evaluation function:

$$Mg = aQ - bQ^2 - B \tag{15}$$

and the agency head, following Migué and Bélanger, is designated a maximand made up of output and managerial discretionary profit:

$$Mh = Mh(Q, MDP) \tag{16}$$

If, as is the case with Niskanen, Mg is concave in G and Mh is concave in H, then at least one pair of equilibrium strategies exists. If Mg should be convex in H and if Mh should be convex in G, then equilibrium would be unique. However, this condition will not hold in the likely event that the governing party maximizes net benefit and has a decreasing marginal evaluation of Q. The resulting concavity of Mg in H then precludes a unique equilibrium in the bureaucratic game.

Peacock (1983), although essentially endorsing the monopoly bureau hypothesis, clearly was aware of the reward cost structure as a monitor of bureaucratic behaviour. For example, the relevance of job security for senior European bureaucrats in encouraging their pursuit of leisure preferences is outlined, as is the likely pressure for monitoring constraints in response to negative externalities from 'busy loafing'.

Peacock suggested that the problem of bureau monitoring is more appropriately studied via a framework that displays the interdependencies between bargaining groups within the economy rather than via the legislator–bureaucrat confrontation model central to the post-Niskanen literature. Legislators are seen to offer 'facilitation services' to consumers and firms, particularly those in their respective constituencies. The prospect of collaboration between legislators and bureaucrats also cannot be denied. Of course, recognition of such interplays takes the theory of bureaucracy well away from the partial equilibrium analysis of Niskanen. Whether the loss of precision is justified by the increase in generality is a complex methodological issue.

3.6 THE RELEVANCE OF PROPERTY RIGHTS

Notable for its absence in the literature here reviewed is the notion of property rights and their influence upon sponsor–bureau relationships. Those analysts who rely on the bureau monopoly or the sponsor monopoly models clearly obviate all discussion of contractual relationships. Even those like Miller (and to a lesser extent Peacock), who allow sponsor–bureau interactions do so essentially within a strict bargaining rather than within a property rights framework (Peacock's discussion of job tenure excepted). Most extreme of all is the view advanced by Breton and Wintrobe (1982) that property rights cannot be supported by legal instruments in the case of bureaucratic relationships, and therefore do not exist, and that trust networks replace rights as the basis for exchange relationships.

It is a central thrust of this paper that neglect of property right considerations, with a few recent exceptions in the economic analysis of bureaucracy, simply has mirrored much earlier work in the theory of the firm, potentially with very similar disadvantages.

Specifically, the vast literature on the theory of the firm under discretionary conditions, initiated by the contributions of W. J. Baumol (1958) and J. Williamson (1966) and O. E. Williamson (1964), eventually deteriorated into a sequence of special cases, each with testable implications which, for the most part, were not tested, and with no apparent integrative theory. Only with the important contributions by Demsetz (1967) and Alchian and Demsetz (1972), which reintroduced property rights into the theory of the firm, was this vicious cycle curtailed and a more general theory re-established. A direct consequence of this latter contribution is the recent literature on principal–agent analysis which is our chosen route of analysis for a reconstituted theory of bureaucracy. First, however, it is important to confront the view of Breton and Wintrobe that there are no property rights in bureaucracy.

The departure point for Alchian and Demsetz was their categorical rejection as a 'delusion' of the notion that firms are characterized by the power to settle issues by fiat, by authority or by disciplinary action superior to that available in the conventional market. Instead they presented a theory of the firm as a set of contracts, longer- or shorter-term, between all factor inputs. Recognizing the free-rider problem in team production, incentives exist for the selection of a centralized contractual agent who will monitor productive efficiency on behalf of all factor inputs. In the view of Alchian and Demsetz (later challenged by the principal–agent literature), the specialist who receives the residual rewards will be the monitor managing the use of cooperative inputs, with the right to alter individual membership and performance of the team.

Thus, the bundle of rights defining 'ownership' in the classical capitalist firm comprises: (1) the right to be a residual claimant; (2) the right to observe input behaviour; (3) the right to be the central party common to all contracts with inputs; (4) the right to alter the membership of the team; and (5) the right to sell these central contractual rights. This category of firm, it was argued, emerged because it resolves the shirking-information problem of team production better than would the non-centralized contractual arrangement.

Of course, the classical capitalist firm no longer dominates as an organization form in the advanced Western democracies. Its position has been eroded by the relative advance of corporate enterprise, with its separation of ownership and control; by the growth of public enterprise; and by the major advance of government bureaucracy. Inevitably, these changes in organization form have served to truncate property rights in central residual status, and thus to alter the nature of the monitoring relationship, creating the so-called principal–agent problem now viewed as a central issue in the organization of production.

3.7 PRINCIPAL–AGENT ANALYSIS

Fama (1980) extended the contribution of Alchian and Demsetz by arguing that the separation of security, ownership and control that is typical of large corporations (notwithstanding the diminution in monitoring incentives from equity stockholders) nevertheless might be an efficient form of economic organization. Utilizing a nexus of contracts approach,[9] which defines the firm as a set of contracts, ownership of the firm is viewed by Fama to be an irrelevant concept. Indeed, with management and risk-bearing now treated as separate factors of production, it is by no means clear that the capital market exercises the dominant monitoring function ascribed to it by conventional economic theory. Risk-bearers in the modern corporation have markets for their services which allow then to shift among teams with relatively low transaction costs and to hedge against failure by diversifying their holdings across teams. In contrast, the managers of a firm rent a substantial part of their wealth – their human capital – to the firm, with rental rates signalled by the managerial labour market, depending on the relative success or failure of the firm. The transaction costs of management shifts across teams are typically much higher than for capital shifts. Thus, it is argued, management may have a greater incentive to monitor.

The notion of the outside managerial market monitoring organizational performance becomes quite important in bureaucracy where capital market pressures do not exist, although, as we shall suggest, the legislature as principal may well exert a significant monitoring influence. The managerial market monitors both via entry and via quits, since able management is identified with successful organizations. There is also much internal monitoring by managers, both in the upward and downward direction, given the jointness of marginal products inherent in team production.

The monitoring problem, both in corporations and in bureaucracy, becomes acute at the highest level – the issue of who will monitor the monitor. For, having reached the top, management may decide that expropriation of security holder wealth (in the case of corporations) or of consumers' surplus (in the case of bureaus) is more congenial than competing among themselves. In corporate enterprise, the stock market is viewed as the monitoring principal (despite Fama's doubts). In bureaucracy, the legislature (and behind it the voters) is viewed as exercising 'property right' controls, albeit of a different, much truncated, nature.

3.8 THE PRINCIPAL–AGENT THEORY OF BUREAUCRACY

The problems of monitoring bureaus are widely believed to be much more serious than those of monitoring corporate enterprises – hence presumably the bureau monopoly model originally advanced by Niskanen.[10] There are a number of important principal–agent features that give rise to this judgement. First, there is no capital market mechanism in bureaucracy and thus no means such as stock option schemes of enabling bureau management to share in the present value of generated fiscal residua. Second, many bureaus are more protected from competition (though by no means all) than are their private counterparts.

Third, the concept of output is more nebulous in the case of bureaus, with obvious difficulties for signalling management success to the outside labour market. Even where output itself is discernible, legislative objectives may be less distinct than the profit signal from corporate production. Fourth, it is much more difficult to assess the underlying production function of a monopolistic bureau than that of a competitive corporation, once again blunting the monitoring process.

Nevertheless, an effective monitoring system does appear to exist.[11]

In this section, the legislator–bureau relationship is analysed with reference to the US environment, reflecting the main emphasis of the extant literature on the economics of bureaucracy. Although details differ, in certain respects non-trivially, in Europe, many of the general issues raised apply also to the various European models of bureaucracy.

Legislators here are assumed to behave as if motivated by vote maximization – a close approximation to reality in the United States, where failure to select electorally popular policies renders a politician extremely vulnerable, and where voter party allegiance is less well developed than in much of Europe. As Weingast (1984) has argued, the assumption that bureaus depend on Congress, like the assumption that firms depend on customers, is the key to understanding the principal–agent relationship (see also Faith, Leavens and Tollison, 1982; Grier, 1984).

Legislators, tied to specific constituencies whence they receive electoral support, provide a flow of policy benefits to the interest groups with whom they are identified. Congressional institutions are tailored to facilitate this process, with committees forging the essential link between interest groups and bureau benefit provisions. Committees indeed dominate policy–making, with each committee's subcommittee accorded a truncated property right over a designated range of bureaucratic activities. This 'right' typically includes a near monopoly over proposals to alter budgets and a complete veto (through agenda manipulation) over proposals made from outside the committee. As Weingast emphasizes, this agenda power provides committee majorities (even the committee chairman) with very significant monitoring powers; however, it rarely may be overturned by determined congressmen taking the issue to the floor through a discharge petition.

Committee membership is determined by a self-selection process influenced by seniority, with members typically selecting committee seats, as far as possible, reflecting their highest attainable re-election potentials, and with changes in the composition of constituency support inducing policy changes and member movements within the subcommittee system. Thus, although voters are the ultimate principals, legislators are the surrogates in dealings with senior bureaucratic agents.

There is a sense, therefore, in which the typical government bureau faces an institutional constraint not dissimilar from that imposed by the capital market upon corporate enterprise, but in this case via the legislative oversight committee(s) responsible for appropriations to the bureau. However, important distinctions exist between the risk-takers of Fama's corporate enterprise and the risk-bearing re-election-seeking politicians of the bureau oversight committees. The Fama risk-taker is viewed as being indifferent as to the precise composition of his stock portfolio as long as the mean–variance values of the portfolio satisfy his attitude towards risk. Typically, the risk-averse stockholder diversifies his portfolio instead of concentrating his holdings and thereby increasing his vulnerability to risk. In contrast, oversight committee members, including the more senior ones who face a loss of seniority and the more junior ones who face relatively high switching costs, are induced to develop and retain a personal interest in their subcommittee's activities. In this respect, the transferability of rights is much truncated, although senior legislators would not hesitate to switch between subcommittees if the expected re-election net benefits of alternative bureaus are seen to shift in relative terms.[12]

Although congressmen typically will not expend a great deal of time in detailed monitoring of their respective bureaus, this does not imply that they are ill-informed to the degree suggested by Niskanen. In practice, their own constituencies and special interest groups, where they perceive net benefits, effect the monitoring, identify strengths and weaknesses and advise their legislators on acceptable interventions. Information flows are not as effective as in capital markets, which are highly specialized in this exercise; but they are not entirely deficient in a self-seeking society.

Niskanen models bureaus, for the most part, as though the budget preference functions of their sponsors are stable, even exogenously determined. This is far from the truth. Budgets do change over time, both positively and negatively, and not always at the instigation of the specific bureau heads. Legislators may well fund budget increases explicitly for bureau activities that they perceive to be vote-winners, or they may implicitly encourage bureau heads to experiment on their behalf by shifting discretionary funds. If experiments fail, or if existing activities become unpopular, bureau allocations are shifted – in some cases without overall budget implications, but in others with non-trivial budget cuts or increases.[13]

Moreover, in areas where bureau monitoring is especially costly, or where bureau discretionary power might prove to be particularly embarrassing to specific oversight committees, Congress does not hesitate to legislate to place agency employees in excepted service, thereby eliminating bureau vertical network discretion and in some cases offering additional hire and fire incentives for bureau monitoring, in the sense of Fama. Some extremely important agencies and bureaus, including the Board of Governors of the Federal Reserve, the Nuclear Regulatory Commission and the US Postal Service, currently have all their employees in excepted service.[14] Notably, however, the last mentioned exception is to be seen as isolating aggressive union behaviour rather than as improving bureau monitoring, in that the Office of Personnel Management's authority is subverted through legislative action. This indicates the caution with which the excepted services monitoring mechanism must be treated in empirical analysis.

3.9 CONCLUSION

The contrasting approaches of monopoly theories of bureaucracy and of principal–agent theories of bureaucracy and representative government provide a rich agenda for empirical research – an agenda that as yet has scarcely been attacked. Early results from work by Weingast, Shepsle and Grier are not at all unfavourable to the principal–agent approach – though much more research is required before confidence can be placed in its fundamental precepts. Just as the property rights initiative of Alchian and Demsetz resuscitated the general theory of the firm, replacing *ad hoc* modelling, so the principal–agent model may rescue the theory of bureaucracy from the not-dissimilar *ad hoc* modelling to which it had become dangerously prone.

NOTES

Constructive comments from the Festschrift conference are gratefully acknowledged. The helpful comments by participants at the Center for Study of Public Choice seminar also are acknowledged.

1 Tullock employed a model of a maximizing bureaucrat to examine the personal relations and advancement procedures within bureaus. Downs developed a comprehensive theory of management processes within bureaus but made no attempt to relate this theory to budget and output performance.
2 Niskanen offered no theory concerning the input preferences of senior bureaucrats. It is relatively easy, however, to assimilate such preferences into his theory.
3 However, a number of commentators collapse his analysis into the bureaucracy dimension alone.
4 He assumes this in the development of his basic model; he relaxes this assumption subsequently to incorporate notions of bureau competition.
5 This notion is sharply in contrast to the otherwise neoclassical thrust of their text.
6 They claim that trust, both vertical and horizontal, is endogenous, dependent on such facts as the amount of turnover, the amount of perquisites, such as bonuses for subordinates, and the frequency of promotions. These latter variables are measurable; thus, productivity per employee can be evaluated against variables that affect the amount and distribution of trust.
7 Peacock does not incorporate the budget-constrained bureau as a polar case in his own analysis.
8 It extends the concept, indeed, well beyond any of the recent literature concerning the economics of bureaucracy.
9 The nexus of contracts approach is an extension of earlier work by Alchian and Demsetz, which first appeared in Jewson and Meckling (1976).
10 Alchian and Demsetz (1972) recognized this acute problem for the non-market sector.

11 Bureau monitoring takes the form of constituents (policy recipients) signalling to their representatives the success or failure of policy outcomes. Oversight committee members (risk-takers in the sense of Fama) weigh the returns and shift to the highest valued accessible assignments.

12 Seniority, together with leadership vote screening, plays a key role in the ease with which legislators may shift to preferred assignments among subcommittees, thus better serving their constituent interests.

13 *Congressional Quarterly (Weekly Report)* reveals that funds frequently are shifted across items in an agency's budget. Hence, the final appropriation may look quite different from the initial agency budget request, reflecting the preferences of oversight committee members over those of bureau heads (1984, p. 928).

14 US Government Printing Office (1984, p. 6).

4

Forced Loans: Tax Element, Equity and Effects on Consumption

ANIBAL A. CAVACO-SILVA

4.1 INTRODUCTION

Forced loans have received scant attention in the economic literature. Since the scheme proposed by Keynes in 1940 in 'How to pay for the war' perhaps less than a dozen articles on the subject have appeared in the economic journals.

However in a realistic world, forced loans cannot be excluded from the list of revenue sources that may be chosen by governments and they are not an exclusive device of war finance. After World War II several countries (not only developing countries)[1] have made use of forced loans and in other countries governments have considered that possibility. For example, they have been used by Denmark, South Africa and Israel. The Portuguese Government tried to issue a forced loan in 1976 and France has introduced one in the summer of 1983. We may be sure that in the future some governments will, at least, think about compelling the private sector to lend them money. On the other hand, the knowledge of economists about this technique can hardly be considered complete.

Thus, the apparent indifference of economic research to forced loans is not justifiable. This paper deals, at a theoretical level, with the measurement of the tax element in a forced loan, the equity in its distribution and its effects on private consumption.

4.2 THE IMPLICIT TAX ELEMENT

The economic literature on the forced or compulsory loan emphasizes the possibility that it contains an implicit tax element for the individual who is required to lend to the state.[2] In this section we shall consider the question of the size of that tax element.

If the forced loan gives the lender a negotiable debt certificate, that question does not raise any difficulty. The implicit tax on the forced lender is simply measured by the excess of the amount that he has to pay for the public bond that he is required to purchase over its market price (it is assumed that the debt certificate can be sold at any time after the issue date and that the transaction costs are zero). The tax element equals the reduction in the value of the individual's net wealth at the market rate of interest. If an individual is forced to purchase for price d a one-period bond paying interest at a rate r^d, while the market rate of interest is r for assets with the same maturity and risk, this implies a tax in the amount

$$t = d(r - r^d)(1 + r)^{-1}$$

The forced loan d may be viewed as a mixture of a tax t and a loan to the state in the amount $(d - t)$ paying interest at the market rate.

If the forced loan certificates are negotiable, their rate of interest r^d would presumably be lower than the market rate of interest r. If $r^d = r$, the loan is in fact voluntary. As Shoup (1944, pp. 129–30) points out, 'Those of the forced contributors who are involuntary buyers will quickly sell their holdings to those who are not forced to buy as much as they would have purchased voluntarily. The net result is no decrease in the net worth of any of the contributors, hence no tax element in the forced loan.'

In general, the forced loan certificates are not negotiable, or else they acquire such status only after a certain time period has elapsed,[3] and they are redeemable only at a stipulated date. The question of the measurement of the implicit tax element in the non-negotiable case does not have a simple answer and will be discussed in the remainder of this section.

In such a case, the tax element in the forced loan cannot in principle be directly measured. Shoup (1969, p. 425; 1944, p. 128–9) suggests the following method to isolate the amount of the implicit tax element: 'In general the forced lender will be indifferent between (1) the forced loan and (2) a tax, smaller than the forced loan, of an amount such that, were this tax imposed on him, he would then freely subscribe to the redemption amount of the loan with the balance of the money that the government wants from him.' This amount of tax, according to Shoup, measures the element of taxation on the lender that is implicit in the forced loan.

The question of the measurement of the implicit tax may be clarified by making use of a model of intertemporal consumer behaviour with two periods to facilitate the graphic explanation. The individual is assumed to have a utility function $U(c_1, c_2)$, defined over his consumption in two periods.

Liquidity-constrained Lenders

Consider first the case of a genuinely liquidity- or borrowing-constrained individual, that is an individual who is quite unable to borrow owing to lack of collateral or credit rationing and who holds no non-human assets. (The analysis would remain unchanged if the individual holds assets that are non-marketable or illiquid.)

Denoting by y_1 and y_2 the individual's net labour incomes in the current and future periods and by r the market rate of interest and the rate that he can earn on his savings, the line AB, with slope $-(1 + r)$, in figure 4.1 depicts the individual's opportunity budget line. Levels of consumption in the current period that are larger than the current disposable income y_1 are not available to the consumer as he cannot borrow against future labour income. Besides the wealth constraint,

$$y_1 + y_2(1 + r)^{-1} = c_1 + c_2(1 + r)^{-1}, \tag{1}$$

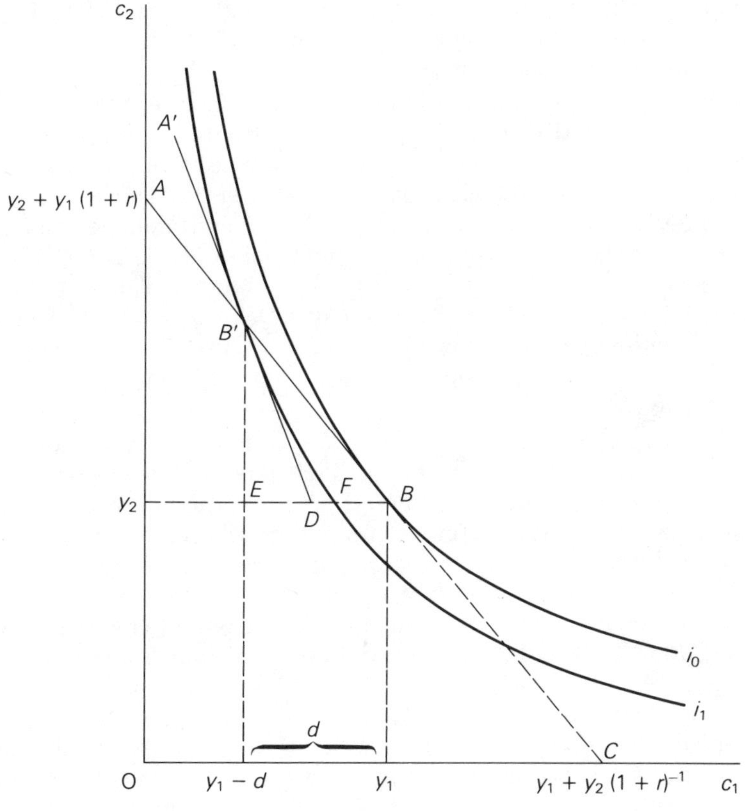

Figure 4.1

the individual is subject to the liquidity constraint, $c_1' < y_1$, so that the effective consumption possibility frontier in figure 4.1 is ABy_1.

Suppose that, in the absence of the forced loan, the individual is at the point of tangency B, where the utility is maximized so that current consumption equals current disposable income: $c_1 = y_1$. Consider now the case in which the government issues a one-period non-negotiable forced loan paying interest at the market rate r and the individual is required to lend an amount d. The loan is unexpected, perceived as non-recurrent, and the individual does not expect to pay any additional future taxes to service it.

Such a forced loan does not change the individual's net worth at the market rate of interest, but the section of the opportunity budget line at the right of B' is no longer available to him. The individual has to reduce his current consumption by the amount that he is forced to lend because the liquidity constraint is binding. Utility is now maximized at corner B', which is on the indifference curve i_1, lower than the curve i_0 that the individual would have attained in the absence of the forced loan. Thus the loan implies a reduction in the individual's welfare which is given by the movement from indifference curve i_0 to i_1.

The reduction in the individual's welfare would have been the same if, instead of the forced loan d, the government would have imposed on him a tax smaller than d and offered free subscription public bonds carrying a rate of interest higher than r such that the individual's budget line would move to $A'D$, which is tangent to the indifference curve i_1 at point B'. Then the tax imposed on the individual would be $\overline{DB}$ in figure 4.1, and the rate of interest on the public bond would be $r' = \overline{EB'}/\overline{ED} - 1$. The individual would freely pay $\overline{ED}$ for a bond that would repay $\overline{EB'}$ in one period's time. This price $\overline{ED}$ plus the tax $\overline{DB}$ equals the amount d that the government wants from the individual through the forced loan.

$\overline{DB}$ is the tax element in the forced loan according to Shoup's method. Its size depends on the amount that the individual is forced to lend and on the slope of the indifference curves, which indicate the individual's marginal preference for current consumption relative to future consumption. If the individual has a strong preference for maintaining his current level of consumption, the tangent to the indifference curve i_1 at the point B' intersects the horizontal line y_2B at a point to the right of E but close to it, so that the forced d, from the individual's viewpoint, is not much different from a tax of the same amount. In the case of liquidity-constrained lenders, the tax implicit in the forced loan cannot be directly measured precisely because of its dependency on the marginal rates of substitution of current for future consumption, which are unknown.

If the successive indifference curves have the same slope along a horizontal line, Shoup's method to isolate the tax element in the forced loan is equivalent to Holzman's suggestion (1957, p. 393) that the amount of tax is measured by the difference between the price d that the individual is forced to pay for the debt certificate and the price at which he would be willing to purchase it, should it have been sold on a voluntary basis.

If we assume that both current and future consumption are subject to declining marginal utility of income, so that the slope of the successive indifference curves rises when moving to the left along a horizontal line, Holzman's method determines an amount of tax that is smaller than that suggested by Shoup. It is easy to see that, had the government imposed on the individual a tax determined by Holzman's method, he would not freely pay for the debt certificate the difference between that and the

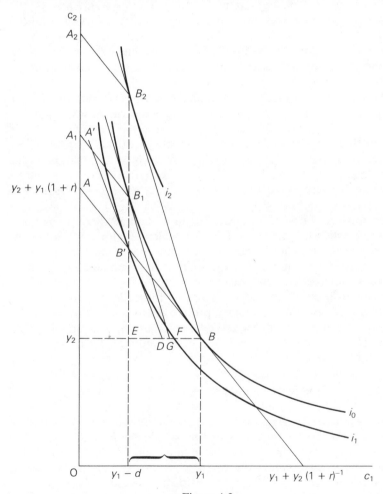

Figure 4.2

amount *d* that the government wants from him. Thus, Holzman's method is clearly inferior to that of Shoup since it makes a comparison between a forced loan and a mixture of tax and voluntary loan which does not leave the individual at the same utility level.

Shoup's method for isolating the tax element in the forced loan, although superior to Holzman's, has a great inconvenience inasmuch as a forced loan, paying an interest rate that enables the individual to achieve a higher level of welfare, may still embody a positive tax element.

Figure 4.2 duplicates the initial situation depicted in figure 4.1. In the case in which the rate of interest on the forced loan r^d equals the market rate r, the budget line is AB'. If the forced loan carries a rate of interest $r_1^d > r$ such that the budget line moves to A_1B_1 ($r_1^d = \overline{EB_1}/\overline{EB} - 1$), the best that can be done is a corner maximum at point B_1, which is on the same indifference curve i_0 that the individual would have attained in the absence of the loan. Thus a forced loan *d* carrying a rate r_1^d leaves the individual's welfare unchanged, but it still contains a tax element in the amount $\overline{GB}$ according to Shoup's method.

If the rate of interest on the forced loan is $r_2^d > r_1^d$ such that the budget line moves up to A_2B_2($r_2^d = \overline{EB_2}/\overline{EB} - 1$), the individual will achieve a higher utility level than without the loan. r_2^d is the rate of interest at which the individual would freely buy the debt certificate for price *d* and is therefore the rate of interest at which the element of taxation in the forced loan is zero, according to Shoup's method. For a liquidity-constrained individual, r_2^d may be substantially higher than the market rate of interest.

Therefore, at rates of interest beteen r_1^d and r_2^d, Shoup's method implies a positive tax element for the forced lender although his welfare improves. This does not seem correct: the individual would not be willing to pay any tax not to be required to lend an amount *d* to the state at a rate of interest r^d such that $r_1^d \leqslant r^d < r_2^d$.

It is better to define the tax element in a forced loan more simply as the amount of tax that would have produced an equal reduction in the individual's welfare. Thus, a forced loan that, though affecting the individual's mix of current and future consumption by changing the opportunity budget line, leaves his utility level unchanged has no implicit tax element.

In the case of the forced loan *d* at the market rate of interest depicted in figure 4.1, the tax would be measured by $\overline{FB}$ instead of $\overline{DB}$, as for Shoup's method. If the government had imposed a tax $\overline{FB}$ on the individual, the best attainable position would be F, which is on the indifference curve i_1, like the equilibrium position B' in the case of the forced loan. It is true that, were the tax $\overline{FB}$ imposed on the individual, he would not freely buy the debt certificate for the price $\overline{EF}$, which, added to the amount of tax, equals the money that the government wants to obtain from him; but his utility level would remain the same had the government forced him to pay that price: B' would still be the best attainable position.

In what follows I shall interpret the tax element in the forced loan as the equivalent tax in terms of reduction in welfare. Its size continues to depend on the amount that the individual is forced to lend and on the marginal rate of substitution of current for future consumption. The correction made in the measurement of the tax element is important because of its impications for the solution of the problem of equity in the distribution of the forced loan.

Consider now the case in which the forced loan pays interest at a rate r^d lower than the market rate of interest r. The individual's budget line shifts parallel to the left by the vertical distance $d(r - r^d)$. In figure 4.3, which reproduces the initial situation depicted in figure 4.1, the opportunity budget line of the liquidity-constrained individual shifts from AB to A_1B_1 if $r^d = 0$ ($\overline{EB} = \overline{EB_1}$) and the best position that he can attain is B_1. The forced loan implies a reduction in the individual's

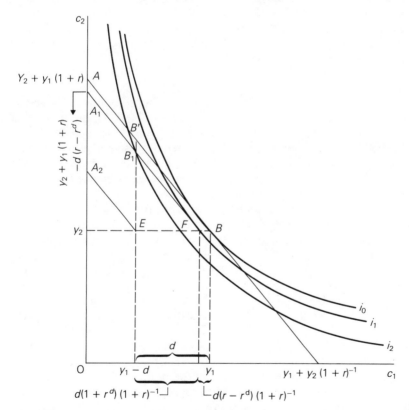

Figure 4.3

welfare which is given by the movement from the indifference curve i_0 to i_2, and thus is equivalent to a tax in the amount $\overline{FB}$.

The forced loan reduces the individual's net worth at the market rate of interest by $\overline{HB}$; that is, $d(r - r^d)(1 + r)^{-1}$. This is another reason for the existence of an element of taxation in addition to that which was found in the case above in which $r^d = r$: namely, that the forced loan prevents the individual's current consumption from exceeding $y_1 - d$. The lower the rate of interest on the forced loan, the larger the fall in the individual's net worth and hence the larger the size of the tax element.

A forced loan d carrying a rate of interest $r^d < r$ may be seen as the combination of an explicit tax in the amount of the induced fall in the individual's net worth $d(r - r^d)(1 + r)^{-1}$ and a forced loan at the market rate of interest r in the amount $d(1 + r^d)(1 + r)^{-1}$. In the current period the government would also obtain an amount of money d $(= d(r - r^d)(1 + r)^{-1} + d(1 + r^d)(1 + r)^{-1})$ from the individual and repay him $d(1 + r^d)$ in the next period. As a result of the explicit tax in the amount $d(r - r^d)(1 + r)^{-1}$, the individual moves from the indifference curve i_0 to i_1 in figure 4.3, and with the forced loan $d(1 + r^d)(1 + r)^{-1}$ he moves from i_1 to i_2. If $r^d = -1$, there is no loan element in the operation but simply an extraordinary straight tax in the amount d, and the budget line in figure 4.3 would then shift from AB to A_2E.

Even in a situation in which the government announces that the forced loan pays interest at the market rate of interest, the individual may distrust the government and expect not to be fully redeemed, and may identify the forced loan, totally or partially, as an explicit tax. The same happens when the maturity period and/or the interest rate conditions are not clearly specified at the issue date. Denoting by γ the individual's degree of perception of the explicit tax[4] $(0 < \gamma \leqslant 1)$, the purchase of a forced loan certificate for the price d is viewed by the individual as a mixture of straight tax in the amount γd and a forced loan $d(1 - \gamma)$ at the market rate of interest. It is easy to see that, from the individual's viewpoint, this case is equivalent to a forced loan in the amount d carrying a rate of interest $r^d = r - \gamma(1 + r)$.

It is easy to reverse the analysis and consider the case in which the forced loan pays interest at a rate r^d higher that the market rate of interest r. The opportunity budget line will move parallel to the right by the vertical distance $d(r^d - r)$, but for a liquidity-constrained individual the loan may still embody a tax element. This is the case when the rate of interest on the forced loan is lower than the rate r_1^d underlying the budget line A_1B_1 in figure 4.2: the highest indifference curve attainable by the individual is lower than the curve i_0. On the other hand, the forced loan will embody a subsidy element rather than a tax if it carries a rate of interest higher than r_1^d: the individual will then attain an indifference curve higher than i_0.

We have assumed so far that the individual is quite unable to borrow, even at a rate of interest higher than the rate r that he can earn on his savings. In the case of the forced loan at the market rate of interest depicted in figure 4.1, the result would remain unchanged if the individual could borrow but only at a rate $r^d \geqslant (\overline{EB'}/\overline{ED} - 1)$: B' on indifference curve i_1 would continue to be the best attainable position. However, the individual will experience a smaller reduction in welfare if he is able to borrow at a rate r^d such that $(\overline{EB'}/\overline{ED} - 1) > r^d > r$: the budget line will kink at point B' but to a slope lower than $A'D$, so that utility is maximized at a point of tangency located on an indifference curve higher than i_1.

Wealth-constrained Lenders

Let us now consider the case of an individual constrained only by his total wealth. A non-negotiable forced loan at the market rate of interest does not affect the optimal combination of current and future consumption, as the effective opportunity budget line does not change. Such a type of forced loan leaves the individual's welfare unchanged and thus there is no tax element. The loan results merely in a shift in the composition of the individual's wealth.

If the forced lender holds liquid assets that may be easily replaced by debt certificates, he can maintain the level of current consumption by adjusting the composition of the positive side of his balance sheet. In general, such replacement is easier in respect of financial assets (currency, bank deposits, bonds and stocks) than of tangible assets.

If the forced lender is able to borrow against future income at the market rate, he can maintain his level of current consumption by offsetting the debt certificate with an increase in the negative component of his wealth. The ability of the individual to borrow depends on his capacity to satisfy the collateral requirements, on the restrictiveness of the credit policy and on the development of the hire purchase system.

The analysis made so far shows that the individual's adjustment in the level of his current consumption and in the composition of his wealth are interdependent. The maintenence of current consumption in the case of a forced loan implies a simultaneous decision with regard to the substitution of debt certificates for other assets or to the increase in the negative component of wealth. The ability to make these operations and the conditions involved will affect the individual's decision concerning his level of current consumption.

The above analysis of the microeconomic implications of a non-negotiable forced loan paying interest at the market rate shows that such a loan contains a tax element for some lenders but not for others, as recognized by Shoup (1969, p. 425). No tax is imposed on those lenders whose optimal behaviour is simply constrained by total wealth. For those lenders who are also subject to a binding liquidity constraint, the forced loan contains a tax element that increases with the amount that they are required to lend and with their marginal rate of substitution of current for future consumption.

If the forced loan carries a rate of interest $r^d < r$, the wealth-constrained lender experiences a welfare loss as a result of the decrease in his net worth. The tax element equals the reduction in the individual's net worth at the market rate of interest $d(r - r^d)(1 + r)^{-1}$, the same amount as if the forced loan certificates were negotiable; and thus direct measurement is possible. What may be difficult to know is whether an individual is constrained by his total wealth alone.

If $r^d > r$, the wealth-constrained lender will attain a higher utility level; for him, the forced loan contains a subsidy element that is measured by the increase in his net worth.

4.3 EQUITY ASPECTS

The distribution of the forced loan among individuals involves an equity problem inasmuch as it may impose a tax burden on the lenders.

Whenever the forced loan certificates are negotiable, the tax element is, for any lender, equal to the reduction in his net wealth, which can be directly measured; so equity in its distribution involves no further difficulties than those of the distribution of a straight tax. But if the debt certificates are, as usually happens, non-negotiable, then in practice it may be very difficult to solve the equity problem adequately owing to the impossibility for the decision-maker to determine the exact amount of implicit tax falling on some lenders.

As shown above, in the non-negotiable case, the tax element is supplied by the reduction in net wealth only for individuals who are constrained by total wealth alone. Although it is impossible to know exactly which individuals are in that situation, their income and net wealth levels are the crucial determinants. The high-income and/or high-net-worth individuals have a greater ability to borrow or to substitute the debt certificates for other assets. Thus, given the prevailing credit policy and the development of the hire purchase system, it does not seem difficult to reach a satisfactory approximation by postulating a level of income y^* and a level of net non-human wealth w^* and defining as consumers not affected by additional constraints all those whose current disposable incomes (before the forced loan) are $y_i \geq y^*$ and/or whose net non-human wealth is $w_i \geq w^*$.

Hence, if it is intended that the burden of the forced loan should fall entirely on the group of non-liquidity-constrained individuals and this satisfies the prevailing equity criteria, then its equitable personal distribution raises no greater difficulty than that of an explicit tax. The real difficulty in ensuring an equitable personal distribution of the forced loan arises whenever the prevailing equity criteria require that the wealth- and liquidity-constrained individuals also purchase debt certificates. For these individuals, as seen above, the tax element is larger than the reduction in net wealth, but its size is impossible to measure because it depends on the marginal rate of substitution of current for future consumption. Thus, given a certain personal distribution of a forced loan, it is not possible to know the distribution of the implicit tax burden with income or wealth. It is also impossible to determine a forced loan distribution that will be consistent with a certain desirable tax distribution according to income or wealth. Therefore, when issuing a forced loan the government 'is operating in the dark' (Shoup, 1944, p. 129: 1969, p. 426), as it does not know the amount of tax that it is imposing on the liquidity-constrained lender: it may be too much or too little according to the prevailing tax equity criteria.

If it is assumed that an individual with net wealth $w_i \geq w^*$ also has current income $y_i \geq y^*$, then a forced loan carrying a rate of interest r^d and distributed proportionally to current incomes implies a regressive tax element when a liquidity-constrained lender is compared with one who is simply constrained by his total wealth. To avoid such regressivity, the forced loan would have to be distributed progressively with current incomes, or the debt certificates would have to pay a higher rate of interest to the liquidity-constrained individual. But once again, it is impossible to be accurate as to the degree of progressivity of the forced loan distribution or the interest rate difference between the lenders which will ensure a given non-regressive tax distribution. However, it can be asserted that, if the loan pays the same rate of interest to all lenders, then the regressivity of the tax element can be avoided by distributing the loan progressively only if its rate of interest is lower than the market rate: otherwise, the tax element is zero or negative for the wealth-constrained lender while it is positive for the liquidity-constrained lender.

The comparison between two individuals belonging to the liquidity constrained group is not clear cut. However, it is most likely that within that group a forced loan levied as a percentage of current income paying interest at a rate r^d implies a regressive implicit tax burden. In general, individuals with lower current incomes are also able to borrow less against future income and have fewer assets that can be replaced by forced loan certificates; in addition, they are likely to have a stronger preference for present over future consumption.

Assuming that the progressivity of the personal income tax reflects the desirable equity pattern for marginal taxation, the conclusion that may be drawn from this analysis is that the equity of a non-negotiable forced loan carrying a rate of interest r^d requires (1) that its distribution be more progressive than the personal income tax for income levels $y_i < y^*$ and as progressive as the personal income tax for $y_i \geq y^*$,[5] and (2) that $r^d < r$.

The ability to substitute debt certificates for other assets or to borrow against future income depends also on the individual's net non-human wealth, the distribution of which may differ significantly from that of the current incomes. In fact, an individual with current income $y_i < y^*$ may hold an amount of net wealth $w_i > w^*$ and vice versa. Thus, equity of a forced loan is achieved more effectively if its distribution is based simultaneously on the prevailing rules for the distribution of the personal tax and for the wealth tax.[6] For example, the individual may be required to lend an average of the amounts that would result from using the personal income tax and the wealth tax as guides for distributing the forced loan.

It is often suggested that, through a forced loan, a government may impose on the lower income groups an implicit tax element larger than would be politically acceptable as a straight tax. The underlying assumption seems to be that individuals have a lower perception of the tax element in the forced loan than of an explicit tax of the same amount. In the case of a forced loan, the tax is imposed on the lender who is involved in an operation in which he surrenders present money against a promise to be repaid with interest in the future. This is a factor that may point to tax illusion.

However, other factors favour the perception of the implicit tax element: i.e. the compulsory nature of the loan and the realization by individuals that it prevents them from achieving the desired level of current consumption; the knowledge that the rate of interest on the forced loan is lower than the market rate, if such is the case; the eventual delay in the delivery of the certificates representing the claim on the state; and a distrust of the government and its economic policy.

Thus, the degree of illusion about the tax element in a forced loan is not likely to be higher than it would have been with an explicit tax. It is even plausible that it will be no higher than in the case of some types of straight taxes – such as a consumption tax. This idea is corroborated by the very unfavourable reactions to forced loans that have occurred in several countries, which suggest that governments have underestimated the individual perception of the implicit element of taxation.[7]

4.4 EFFECTS ON CONSUMPTION

Forced loans are usually justified by governments as an effective instrument to reduce private current consumption. So it is of interest to examine how far forced lenders reduce their consumption and increase savings. This question can be easily considered drawing on our previous analysis of the forced loan in a two-period model of intertemporal consumer behaviour aiming at measuring the size of the implicit tax element.

Suppose that the forced loan replaces a voluntary loan of equal amount. Since we are concerned with the effects that result from the compulsory character of the loan, it may be assumed that the individuals do not anticipate the future debt service taxes. The question of the anticipation of the future tax liabilities arises whether the loan is forced or not.[8]

Consider first the case in which the forced loan certificates are non-negotiable and pay interest at the market rate. As we have seen in section 4.1, for those lenders who are constrained by their total wealth alone, current consumption remains unchanged; they do not have to save more than they would have done otherwise and thus, as far as this type of lender is concerned, it is completely wrong to identify the forced loan with compulsory saving.[9]

It is only for lenders who face a binding liquidity constraint that the forced loan implies a cut in current consumption (and an increase in savings) equal to the amount that they are forced to lend to the state. For them, forced loan means in fact forced savings.

In between these two types of lenders there are those who, in the absence of the forced loan, are constrained by their total wealth alone but, with the issue of the loan, have to move to a position where the liquidity constraint becomes binding. They have to cut their current consumption, though to a lesser extent than the amount they are forced to lend, because of their limited ability to make adjustments in the composition of their wealth, which depends crucially on their levels of income and net wealth. If the legal obligation to purchase public bonds falls only on the high income groups and/or those with positive net wealth, the forced loan cannot affect current consumption significantly.[10] As Shoup recognized (1944, p. 131), it is only when it falls mainly on the low income groups and those with negative net wealth that the forced loan will reduce current consumption significantly.

Therefore the conclusion is that a non-negotiable forced loan paying interest at the market rate, which for equity reasons exempts the low income groups or requires them to lend only a small proportion of the amount requested, cannot reduce current consumption significantly. Equity and a reduction in consumption are clearly conflicting goals in such a forced loan scheme.

Now suppose that the forced loan carries a rate of interest r^d, lower than the market rate r. For a genuinely liquidity-constrained individual, current consumption continues to fall by the amount that he is forced to lend when $r^d = r$. A lower rate of interest implies a larger tax element but not a higher decrease in consumption. For those wealth-constrained individuals who, as a result of the forced loan, become liquidity- as well as wealth-constrained, current consumption falls by less than the amount of the loan and for most of them by the same amount as when $r^d = r$. For a forced lender who is constrained by total wealth alone, there is now a decrease in the level of his current consumption as a result of the reduction in his net worth $d(r - r^d)(1 + r)^{-1}$. However, the reduction in consumption cannot help being a small fraction of the amount that he is forced to lend, particularly if the rate of interest on the loan is non-negative, because the fall in net wealth cannot exceed $dr(1 + r)^{-1}$ and is limited to one period.

Thus we conclude that, for a given personal distribution of the forced loan, the induced decrease in current consumption will be higher if $r^d < r$ than if $r^d = r$, but not significantly higher (assuming that $r^d \geqslant 0$). Therefore the above assertion that the forced loan can reduce consumption substantially only if it falls heavily on the low income groups and those with negative net wealth still holds. Hence, the conflict between equity and reduction in consumption remains basically unchanged when we consider the case in which $r^d < r$. However, since that is positive and proportional to the amount they are required to lend, a given decrease in aggregate current consumption is consistent with less inequity than when $r^d = r$.

The conflict between equity and reduction in current consumption can be mitigated only by adopting a forced loan scheme in which different rates of interest are paid to different lenders. For example, if the reduction in consumption goal requires the forced loan to be distributed proportionally to income, then (1) it should pay interest at rates that decline as the individuals' incomes increase, and (2) those rates should be lower than the market rate of interest for the wealth-constrained lenders so that they bear a positive tax element and at the same time contribute to the achievement of the decrease in consumption. Yet it is not possible to be precise as to the degree of variability of the interest rates with lenders' incomes, consistent with a specific equity standard, since the rates of interest that should be paid to the liquidity-constrained individuals in order to achieve a given distribution of the implicit tax burden depend on their marginal rates of substitution of present for future consumption, which are unknown.

Let us consider a wealth-constrained individual A and a liquidity- as well as wealth-constrained individual B with current incomes $y_1^A = 1000$ and $y_1^B = 500$. Assume that the government issues a one-period non-negotiable forced loan with the aim of reducing consumer spending, levied as 10 per cent of current income.

If the rate of interest on the loan is the same for both lenders, say 0 per cent while the market rate of interest is 10 per cent, the decrease in net wealth and the tax element for individual A is 9.1, i.e 0.91 per cent of his income. He will cut his current consumption by a fraction of 9.1.

Individual B has to cut his current consumption by the amount that he is forced to lend, i.e. 50. His reduction in net wealth is 4.55, but the size of the tax element is larger because he is prevented from maximizing his utility at a point of tangency, as we have seen above. The implicit tax element on B, then, represents a higher proportion of his current income than that of A. This regressivity with income can be removed, without changing the fall in the level of current consumption, by raising the rate of interest paid to B. This would shift upwards the effective budget line of individual B, thereby reducing the magnitude of the tax element to a fraction of his current income deemed desirable. The required rate of interest to be paid to B depends on his preference for current over future consumption.

If the forced loan certificates are negotiable, although carrying a rate of interest r^d below the market rate r, the decrease in current consumption is for all lenders solely the result of the reduction in their net wealth.

For an individual constrained by his total wealth alone, the decrease in consumption is the same as in the non-negotiable case, and thus the conclusion that it cannot help being a small fraction of the amount that he is forced to lend continues to hold. The decrease in current consumption by a liquidity-constrained lender is, however, much smaller than in the non-negotiable case. He will quickly sell the debt certificates he was forced to purchase and reduce his consumption by the excess of the price paid over the price obtained in the market, i.e. $d(r - r^d)(1 + r)^{-1}$, while he would have had to cut his current consumption by d in the non-negotiable case.

Thus, the conclusion is that the reduction in current consumer spending is lower if the forced loan certificates are negotiable rather than non-negotiable, for the same rate of interest and the same personal distribution. On the other hand, a negotiable forced loan cannot have a strong negative effect on current consumption whatever its personal distribution, particularly if it carries a non-negative rate of interest.

Inasmuch as the substitution of a forced for a voluntary loan reduces aggregate private consumption and increases savings, in a full-employment model the market rate of interest falls and capital formation increases. In a Keynesian framework, the forced loan has a contractionary effect on aggregate demand and real output and improves the external current account: the rate of interest falls, thereby stimulating private investment, but not enough to offset the decrease in consumption.

NOTES

1   For an appraisal of the wartime experience of forced loans see Heller (1951)

and for a review of schemes introduced in more recent years see Prest (1969).

2   See Shoup (1944, 1969); Holzman (1957); Prest (1969); Young (1973).

3   The non-negotiability may result not from a legal imposition but from the delay in the delivery of the certificates that can be negotiated on the market.

4   The degree of perception of explicit tax will tend to be higher if the distribution of the forced loan among individuals is linked directly to an existing tax, e.g. if the forced loan base is the amount of personal income taxes paid by individuals. The delay in the delivery of the debt certificates is another factor that favours explicit tax perception. Heller (1951, p. 121), referring to the English experience during the Second World War of a forced loan under the form of a personal income tax refundable after the war, says that 'taxpayers generally failed to differentiate sharply, if at all, between the compulsory-loan and straight-tax components of their gross liability.'

5   This implies that, in relation to the income tax liabilities, the distribution of the forced loan should be progressive for tax amounts $t(y_1) < t(y^*)$ and proportional for $t(y_1) > t(y^*)$.

6   The forced loan issued in France in June 1983 was levied as 10 per cent of the households' liabilities in personal income tax (above a certain amount) and in wealth tax.

7   See Shoup (1969, p. 426, n. 19) and Prest (1969, p. 43). In 1976 the Portuguese government had to abandon the idea of issuing a forced loan.

8   It is assumed that the degree of capitalization of future tax liabilities does not depend on the compulsory or voluntary character of the loan. This may not be correct: the degree of capitalization is likely to be higher when the loan is forced, owing to a higher degree of awareness of the issue of the debt and a lower public debt illusion. Yet the capitalization issue may still be relevant if the rate of interest on the forced loan is substantially different from that on a voluntary loan. On the capitalization of future tax liabilities implicit in government borrowing, see Cavaco-Silva (1977, 1982).

9   The term 'forced savings' when referring to a forced loan has been explicitly rejected by several authors. Shoup (1944, p. 126) writes: 'the usual forced loan proposal carries no provision that the taxpayer must save to make the loan.' Along the same lines, Prest (1969, p. 28) writes: 'although governments can legislate for schemes of compulsory lending, it is not normally within their power to legislate for *net additions* to the annual flow of saving.' Also, Heller (1951, p. 116) points out that compulsory saving is much more comprehensive than compulsory lending, 'not merely requiring the taxpayer to lend a given sum to the government (which leaves him the opportunity to dissave or reduce other forms of saving to meet the loan obligations) but requiring that a specified amount out of any given income should be saved, i.e. added to his total assets'.

10 According to Young (1973), forced loans in Israel in the period 1964–9 affected the composition of wealth rather than the level of consumption both in the short and the long run.

5

On the Cost Disease and its True
Policy Implications for the Arts

HILDA BAUMOL AND W. J. BAUMOL

5.1 INTRODUCTION

The cost disease of the performing arts seems to have become a mainstay in the arguments of those seeking public support in a surprisingly broad range of geographical arenas. Its logic has been mastered thoroughly by those who rely on it to help their cause. Yet, at least two misunderstandings seem widespread, and both of these weaken the case for public support of the arts. In this paper we seek to clear up these misunderstandings.

Specifically, the first of these is the judgement that the cost disease analysis must necessarily presage a grim future for the live performing arts and perhaps for quality of life generally – in short, just what is to be expected from a discipline justly dubbed 'the dismal science'. We will show, on the contrary, that the cost disease phenomenon inevitably means that society can expect to be able to support arts ever more generously and effectively while simultaneously increasing its consumption of material things – if only society chooses to do so.

The second of the misunderstandings with which this paper concerns itself is the view that when, as has often happened during periods of inflation, cost per performance or cost per attendee rises more slowly than the general price level, the cost disease is (apparently) cured, or is at least in remission, so that deceleration of public support may become appropriate. On the contrary, we will show that there is good reason to believe that in such periods the disease is not in remission but is, rather, suppressed, and that its suppressed variant threatens even more serious harm to the arts than its overt form. In short, when the disease assumes its suppressed form, that is no signal for friends of the arts to relax their efforts. Instead, it becomes appropriate for them to work even harder to provide adequate resources for the artistic activities they desire.

5.2 THE COST DISEASE: BRIEF SUMMARY OF THE ANALYSIS[1]

Since the cost disease is central to the analysis of this paper, it is necessary to review the nature of this malaise of live performance. Eighteen years ago, one of the authors of this paper and William G. Bowen, now president of Princeton University, showed that the performing arts are predestined to be the victims of a cost disease which condemns the cost per live performance, be it *Hamlet, The Barber of Seville* or a rock concert, to rise at a rate persistently faster than that of a typical manufactured good. An illustration will help clarify the reason. Compare what has happened to the cost of producing a watch with the cost of a musical performance over the centuries. There has been vast, labour-saving technical progress in watchmaking, which is still continuing, But live violin playing benefits from no labour (or capital)-saving innovations – it is still done the old-fashioned way, as we want it to be.

Towards the end of the seventeenth century a Swiss craftsman could produce about 12 watches per year. Three centuries later that same amount of labour produces over 1,200 (non-quartz) watches. But a piece of music written three centuries ago by Purcell or Scarlatti takes exactly as many person-hours to perform live today as it did in 1684.

What do these figures mean? They mean that, while one has to work just about as many hours to pay for a ticket to an opera today as one would have in similar jobs 300 years ago, the cost of a watch or any other manufactured good has plummeted in terms of the labour time we must pay for it. In other words, because manufactured goods have benefited from technological advance year after year while live performances have not, almost every year theatre and concert tickets have grown more and more expensive in comparison with the price of watches. This phenomenon has been called 'the cost disease of live performance'.

The message is simple. Prices of manufactured goods do not rise as quickly as those of concerts, dance or theatrical performances because manufacturers benefit from labour-saving innovation while the performing arts do not (to any large extent). This is another way of saying that cost per attendee or per performance must rise faster than the average price of other things; arts budgets therefore must rise faster than the economy's rate of inflation, which is simply the average increase in the prices of all the economy's outputs.

5.3 THAT BENEFICENT COST DISEASE[2]

It is almost impossible to tell the cost disease story without giving it the aura of a tragedy. What a dismal failure it seems to foretell, one in which every major ingredient of the quality of life is gradually priced out of the market by its irresistibly, remorselessly growing costliness. It suggests a barren society where the arts have been reduced to uncompensated amateur activities – without museums or libraries, with little education, vestigial garbage removal and even vanishing police protection. Indeed, there is a danger that society, misled by appearances, will resign itself to such a future, and that by its resignation it may bring about just these dismal circumstances that it could so easily avoid. This may well be a course on which we are already embarked, as a glance at deteriorating municipal services surely suggests.

Yet its inevitability is all a matter of misunderstanding. To those who understand the logic of the cost disease analysis this bleak future is presaged by the exponentially rising budgetary resources that will be required to prevent it. To others, the grim prospect seems to be approaching because of a mysterious acceleration of the budgetary demands of the services, which seem every year to require more money, in real terms, even as their quality deteriorates visibly.

Where in this unhappy prospect are there any rays of hope? We will show now that there is more than a mere ray. Properly interpreted, the moral of the cost disease analysis is sanguinity embodied. It tells us that humanity can have even more of everything – more manufactured goods, more municipal services, more arts activity – if only it chooses to apportion its resources in a manner consistent with this goal of growing abundance in every field.

A moment's thought confirms that, in a world characterized by the cost disease, this must be true. The disease originates from the fact that, even though there is *some* productivity growth in the stagnant services, it is significantly slower than productivity growth in the remainder of the economy. But a society whose productivity is growing everywhere, albeit in some areas more slowly than in others, obviously will be able to afford to consume constantly more, and certainly will not be forced to consume less and less. It has the means to enjoy more of all outputs, or it may instead choose to devote all of its increased productive capacity to a selected smaller group of items; but that is a decision to be made by society as a whole. The cost disease had created the illusion that society can no longer afford many things it used to be able to obtain. But the opposite is in fact true. A society beset by the cost disease can each year afford at least a bit more of each item it obtained the year before. It *can afford* more and slightly better endowed artistic activity each successive year, despite the rising real cost, and more manufactured goods as well.

A simple example brings out the sort of range of options to society that must inevitably go along with the cost disease.[3] Table 5.1 describes the output bundles from which a hypothetical economy can choose at a future date after unbalanced productivity growth of the sort that

Table 5.1 *Hypothetical arts and services scenarios, 1984 and 2008*[*]

(Prices: 1984 = 100)

	(1) Nominal GNP	(2) Real sevices cost	(3) Nominal services cost (trillions)	(4) Real arts activity	(5) Nominal arts activity	(6) Mfg	(7) %increase in Mfg over 1984
1984	1	0.25	0.25	0.0025	0.0025	0.75	—
2008 Constant services and arts output	2	0.25	0.50	0.0025	0.0050	1.50	100
Constant shares of total output	2	0.40	0.80	0.004	0.008	120	60
Doubled services and arts output	2	0.50	1.0	0.005	0.01	100	33.3

[*] Assumes constant 3 per cent per year rate of growth of productivity in manufacturing, zero growth in productivity in stagnant services, constant input quantities, wages and prices increasing at a rate of growth of manufacturing productivity.

engenders the cost disease has had a substantial period in which to manifest itself. For the sake of simplicity, we shall begin our hypothetical history with a GNP of £1 trillion, 24 per cent of which consists of stagnant services whose productivity is not growing at all. The remainder consists of manufactures whose productivity is growing at a steady 3 per cent per year compounded, so that with a given bundle of input flow output will double approximately every 24 years. Arts expenditure is assumed throughout to be 1 per cent of the outlays on the stagnant services. Wages and other primary resource prices are assumed to reflect productivity and hence to rise 3 per cent per year. Produced items are taken to be supplied competitively so that their prices correspond to their costs as determined by the prices and productivity of their inputs.

The first row in the table, the one labelled '1984', shows the assumed initial state of affairs. The interesting phenomena manifest themselves in the three rows labelled '2008', corresponding to three of the options open to society under the circumstances posited: (1) constant services output, which assumes that society will devote the same absolute volume of inputs to the arts and the other stagnant services that they did in 1984, so that with zero productivity growth their activity levels will remain absolutely fixed; (2) proportionate output growth, which assumes that society will choose to expand these activities strictly in proportion to manufacturing output; (3) doubled services output, which assumes that society will provide enough resources to the arts and the other stagnant services to double their 1984 activity levels.

The first thing to be noted is that, even in the most modest constant services output scenario, in nominal terms the required budget for the arts and other services in 2008 will have doubled from its 1984 value (columns (3) and (5)). Instead of £0.25 trillion, the services' budget will have risen to £0.5 trillion, and the arts budget will have gone up from £0.0025 to £0.005. This is because input prices will double in 24 years, and with no increase in productivity and constant outputs these budgets must, consequently, double.

Under this scenario, manufacturing output must also take a great leap, increasing from £0.75 trillion to £1.5 trillion. Thus, the doubling of outlays on the services can hardly be taken to constitute much of a real burden upon society.

Case 2 represents a less conservative goal for the arts and other services. Now the economy transfers to them a quantity of resources sufficient to permit them to expand their real outputs in strict proportion to manufactures. Nominal outlays on the services generally and the arts in particular must rise to £0.8 and £0.008 trillion, respectively.

Nevertheless, the transfer of resources to the services causes only some moderation in the outpouring of manufactures, which now rise only 60 per cent above their 1984 levels (columns (6) and (7)).

Society can afford even more ambitious service (and arts) outputs. For example, it can double them both from their 1984 output levels (last row of the table), thereby necessarily quadrupling their required

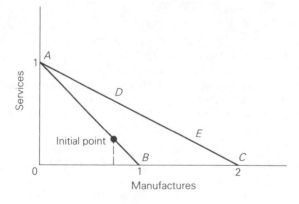

Figure 5.1 *GNP Growth and expansion of the service and manufacturing sectors*

budgets while still enjoying a quadrupling of the output of manufactured goods.[4]

The same example can be used to demonstrate the sort of fiscal illusion that the cost disease analysis is intended to expose. Suppose that by the year 2008 society increases the outlays devoted to services, including the arts, by 60 per cent, from £0.25 to £0.4 trillion. Since on our assumptions the prices of the services must have doubled, this means the real resources devoted to them will have fallen (in 1984 prices) from £0.25 trillion to £0.20 trillion. Yet the overall price level will have risen only 11 per cent, since the prices of manufactures will be constant, and with the resources devoted to manufacturing having gone up from £75 to £80 trillion in 1984 prices and productivity having doubled, manufacturing output must rise to 160. Hence, the 2008 price level must be

$$\frac{2(20) + 1(160)}{20 + 160} = 111$$

Thus nominal outlays on the services will have risen 60 per cent i.e. *by more than five times the rise in the general price level*,[5] and yet the quantity of services supplied will have fallen by 20 per cent from its initial level of £0.25 trillion in 1984 prices. No wonder the public will be driven to fear that it cannot afford to keep the supply of the services at their initial level, much less undertake any expansion in the resources devoted to them.

But, as we have seen, this conclusion is quite wrong. Here let us choose our words with care. We are saying that an implication of the circumstances that produce the cost disease is that it will actually be possible to expand significantly the resources devoted to the arts and the other services. The public *will be able to afford* to do so, and to experience substantial increase in the creature comforts they enjoy at the same time. But to say that they can afford it is not the same as saying they ought to do so. That is a judgement no economic analysis can entitle us either to make or to deny. All that we can say in good conscience is that society should be kept from making a negative decision, that is a decision to cut back on the arts and the other services contributing to the quality of life, solely by the misapprehension that it cannot afford to do otherwise.

Put in another way, fund-raisers who have used the cost disease as one of their arguments for ever increasing support may well profit by studying what has just been said here; for it permits them in good conscience to carry a banner inscribed with the motto, 'Yes, you can afford it!'

5.4 THE COST DISEASE AND INFLATION

Since the cost disease was described in 1964, arts administrators throughout the world have argued that, because performance budgets must inevitably rise faster than the general price level, increases in support that merely match the economy's price level must condemn the arts to decline and deterioration. So long as the data continued to show that *real* costs per performance or per attendee were indeed continuing to rise as predicted, all seemed well in the continuing relationships between the funding agencies and the recipients of their support. However, when recent data revealed some cases in which such costs were falling behind the inflation rate, more than one such group underwent feelings of panic and betrayal. The reliable old cost disease law had failed them. What had gone wrong? Or, rather, had something unexpectedly gone *right* for costs in the arts?

As a matter of fact, nothing has gone wrong with the cost disease model's predictions. Neither is there any reason to believe that matters have improved in any way for the costs of performance. There are two reasons why a slowdown, and perhaps even a decline, in real per-unit costs should have been, and were in fact, expected.

First, as we have seen, the cost disease is a manifestation of the *relative* lag in productivity growth in performance. Performance suffers because manufacturing productivity habitually rises so rapidly and pulls wages up with it. But in the 1970s, for reasons that are in some dispute, productivity growth in manufacturing slowed down to a crawl in almost every industrialized economy. Thus, the engine that triggers the cost disease virtually ran out of fuel during that decade.

Second, even the earliest study of the cost disease of the arts (Baumol and Bowen, 1965) indicated that, while for well over a century orchestral cost performance had *almost* always risen faster than the general price level, there was one persistent exception: periods of inflation. During each of the brief postwar inflations that the United States experienced before the Second World War, the rise in cost per performance consistently fell behind the general price level. Though we have no clear-cut evidence, our hypothesis is that in such periods the public resists increases in outlays on the arts which exceed the growth in the price level to the degree typical of uninflationary periods. Since in the performing arts expenditures must, in the long run, adjust themselves to receipts, cost per performance then lags as a matter of economic necessity. Whether this explanation is or is not valid, the fact remains. Experience has shown that in inflationary periods cost per performance does not necessarily rise faster than the general price level.

Thus, both the record of the past and the logic of the cost disease analysis should have warned us (and did) that the symptoms of the cost disease may become more moderate or may even (temporarily) disappear altogether during an era like the present.

5.5 ON THE SUPPRESSED FORM OF THE COST DISEASE

The important implication of the preceding explanatory hypothesis about the lag of real costs in inflationary periods is that the cost disease forces performing groups to find ways to sublimate the problem – to trade off increasing costs for money-saving changes in the way they conduct their activities. We shall now provide a convincing illustration of this phenomenon. One obvious way to suppress the cost disease is to cut down on the number of artists the performing organization has on its payroll. In the theatre, the obvious way to do this is to produce plays that call for smaller casts. Figures 5.2, 5.3 and 5.4 show what has happened to the proportions of plays and musical comedies, and to the cast size of all plays (except musicals), produced by the Broadway theatre for roughly five-year intervals since 1946. The almost perfectly steady decline was sufficient to cut the average cast size *in half*, from the 16-person figure with which the postwar period began.

We are convinced that this is but one dramatic example of a very pervasive phenomenon which is unfortunately very difficult, if not impossible, to document quantitatively. Major orchestras and opera houses have surely reduced the frequency with which they make use of outside soloists and star guest performers. Smaller budget orchestras

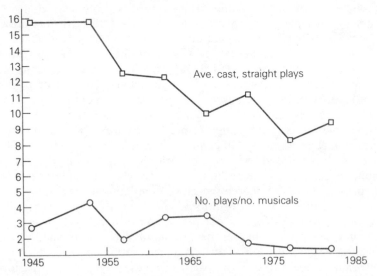

Figure 5.2 *Cast sizes, and ratios of straight plays to musicals, Broadway theatre, 1945–83*

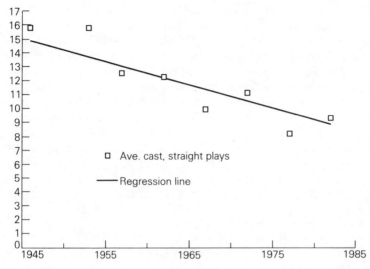

Figure 5.3 *Average cast sizes in straight plays, Broadway theatre, 1945–83*

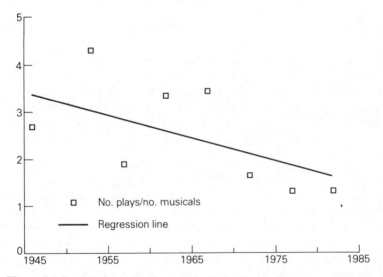

Figure 5.4 *Ratios of straight plays to musicals, Broadway theatre, 1945–83*

and theatres have probably cut expenditures on rehearsal time. In theatres and opera houses it is our impression that there has been a rise in the frequency of use of single sets, which eliminates the need for scene-shifting stagehands. Surely the gradual replacement of the three act–six scene play by those requiring a far smaller number of scene changes is an indicator of this phenomenon.

All of this boils down to the obvious choices relating to the cost disease. There are two different ways to live with inflation: either raise the price, or debase the product. In the performing arts, 'coping' can take the form of escalating real costs per attendee and raising real ticket prices. Or, instead, these obvious responses to the disease can be surpressed, and its virulence channelled into other consequences which many will consider still more serious – restrictions on the sorts of plays that can be produced (large-cast classics becoming economically unsustainable), cuts in the number of rehearsals, less expensive performers, larger theatres, safer programming and other reductions in the economically feasible range of artistic options. It is thus responsible for the phenomenon that has been referred to as the artistic deficit.

Clearly a disease whose symptoms are camouflaged in this way is not a disease that has been cured. In sum, even if real cost per attendee or real cost per performance rises more slowly than expected, or even (for a while) fails to rise at all, that is no justification for a withdrawal of support by the agencies that help to fund the arts, or for a relaxation of fund-raising efforts.

5.6 CONCLUDING COMMENT

We see, then, that two basic misunderstandings about the nature of the cost disease have impeded its utility to those responsible for funding the arts. The first of these is the illusion that the analysis implies a growing inability of society to maintain the funding that is required if the quantity and quality of performance activity are not to be eroded. What has been shown here, on the contrary, is the firm implication of the cost disease that the sources that are responsible for its occurrence also automatically provide the resources that can serve as its antidote or even its cure. Inability to pay the rising costs of the arts is simply not a valid excuse for starving the arts in a society destined to grow increasingly affluent because of rising productivity.

The second misunderstanding of the cost disease corresponds to a rather insidious threat to the viability of the arts which has been called the 'artistic deficit'. This has served to camouflage the cost disease, but may actually be one of its most serious manifestations. It restricts the opportunities to experiment, limiting the character of plays and the content of musical programmes to those that offer the promise of being viable financially. It involves the cutting of corners in terms of quality of performers (when their high salaries threaten budgets), in terms of rehearsal time, and in terms of freedom to utilize more costly options when appropriate, such as large casts or multi-set plays. The evidence here is still highly incomplete, but such evidence as there is indicates dramatically that the threat is very real.

Those who provide support for the arts must surely not ignore this threat and must take its financial demands into account in planning their funding targets; otherwise there is danger that they will find themselves underwriting a body of activities the quality of whose product ever decreasingly deserves the attention of the community and even the inadequate resources they are absorbing.

The moral is clear. In periods when real cost per attendee is rising, increasing funding of the arts may be required to sustain their health. But when cost per attendee falls, increased funding may be more urgent still!

NOTES

The authors are grateful to the Starr Centre for Applied Economics, New York University, for its assistance in the preparation of this paper.

1 Readers who have heard the cost disease story repeated ad nauseum are avidly urged to omit this section.
2 The substance of this section draws heavily on Bradford (1969).
3 The reader will recognize that the logic of the argument is perfectly general and in no way depends upon the particular numbers that happen to have been chosen for our illustration.
4 It is easy to show that, under the circumstances postulated, society could increase the resources devoted to the services to 250 per cent of their 1984 levels without suffering any diminution in manufacturing output. The general situation can be depicted diagramatically (figure 5.1). We have implicitly assumed away any diminishing marginal rate of transformation between the services and manufacturing and have selected output units so that the initial $MRT = 1$. Thus the initial production frontier is that labelled AB. The initial point is that labelled on AB. With a doubling of productivity in manufacturing, the frontier shifts outward to AC. It is clear that any point on the new frontier that falls on line segment DE, above and to the right of the initial point, constitutes a feasible increase in both manufactures and services.
5 In general, if the share, k, of the stagnant services remains constant and wages keep abreast with the constant growth rate of productivity in the remainder of the economy, then the price level at time t will be

$$p_t = ke^{rt} + (1 - k)$$

where r is the difference between the growth rate of productivity elsewhere and that in the stagnant services. Then, with a constant level of service activity, the growth in its cost relative to the growth in the price level over its value in period 0 must be

$$\frac{(e^{rt} - 1)}{p_t - 1} = \frac{(e^{rt} - 1)}{k(e^{rt} - 1)} = \frac{1}{k} > 1.$$

6
The Unwithered Welfare State

THOMAS WILSON

6.1 INTRODUCTION

In the United Kingdom the central objective of the various public services, loosely grouped together as 'the welfare state', has been to provide protection against poverty. It has, therefore, been reasonable to ask whether there is really a continuing need for such protection on so large and wide a scale; for with real incomes raised by rising output, it has become easier for private families to make their own provision. To quote from a well-known pamphlet published some 23 years ago by the Unservile State Group,

> There is not much point in talking of individual freedom and responsibility to those who live in fear of want. But if poverty is abolished, if income and wealth can be equitably distributed, if economic fluctuations can be mitigated, then individuals are in a situation where, potentially at least, they can plan their own and their children's future, and where it is less necessary for them to rely upon the State.... The true object of the Welfare State, for the Liberal, is to teach people how to do without it. (Peacock, 1961)

It could be inferred from these remarks that expenditure on the various welfare services should decline in real terms, and should do so even more markedly when expressed as a fraction of gross national product.

It need scarcely be said that this was a statement of aspiration rather than prediction. In the event, the welfare state, far from withering, has displayed vigorous growth at a rate over-topping that of national output. Although the boundaries of the welfare state are not clearly defined and are often disputed, we can obtain a reasonably good indication of what has happened if attention is confined to cash transfers, to health service and the personal social services and to education. Total expenditure on these items was about 13 per cent of GNP at factor cost in 1951; by 1973 it was 20 per cent; by 1981, 27 per cent.

There is nothing unique about the British experience in this respect.

In the continental countries of Western Europe, expenditure is usually higher relative to GNP than in the UK, in some cases substantially so. In the United States the ratio is lower but is nevertheless about 20 per cent. Even in Australia, where social security is highly selective, the figure is close to 20 per cent. We must, then, enquire into the reasons for these developments. In part, the explanation has no doubt been the empire-building propensities of those responsible for the provision of these services, but there are other reasons as well, which shall be mentioned shortly.

Whatever the explanation of past trends, it is beyond all doubt that this relatively fast growth of welfare expenditure must, at some stage, be halted. If projected indefinitely, the growth rates of modern times would ultimately so swell the total for welfare expenditure as to absorb the whole of the gross national product! Or if we direct attention to total government expenditure, of which social expenditure is an important component, simple extrapolation suggests that, for the seven major OECD contries, this total would absorb the whole GNP by roughly the middle of the next century! (HMSO, 1984).

Although the above is merely an idle exercise, it is one that forces us to recognize the obvious need to call a halt sometime. *What can still be debated is whether that time has yet come.* The UK government maintains that it has; other bodies insist that it has not. For example, the TUC has recently advocated a substantial rise in public expenditure, in particular on the welfare services, and has sought to support this demand by pointing out that we still spend proportionately less on these services than do a number of other countries – countries that have nevertheless had a better growth record than the UK. The controversy can be expected to continue, for it reflects differences in value judgements, differences in apprehensions of the facts of a kind that cannot easily be resolved and, to some extent, differences in the respective sectional interests of those who express these conflicting views. It is not a controversy that will easily be settled. There are, however, strong grounds for directing attention to some basic issues that must affect the answer:

1 What are the objectives of policy? What is public expenditure on this massive scale intended to achieve?
2 What are the most economical means of achieving these objectives?
3 To what extent may changes in policy that would otherwise appear to be desirable within this context be constrained by the need to allow for (a) undesirable side-effects or (b) commitments already made, which it would be morally improper or politically inexpedient to set brusquely aside?

6.2 OBJECTIVES OF POLICY

When Charles Carter set out recently on a search for the objectives of public policy, he found that the path he was following was by no means as well-trodden by politicians and civil servants as anyone less familiar with the conduct of public affairs might be inclined to suppose. Thus he was forced to observe: 'What is not clearly defined cannot be assessed: you cannot measure the fulfilment of a policy if you do not know what it is intended to fulfil' (Carter, 1984). Clearly, it will not do simply to list the activities for which official bodies are responsible, although this is often done. To explain that the purpose of a roads programme is to build roads can hardly be said to be of much help in assessing its effect on the public good!

When a more searching assessment is made, conflicts of opinion are bound to emerge. Varying weights will, therefore, be attached to various objectives of policy, whether these are expressed in broad outline, which is as much as can be attempted here, or are set out, as might be done, at greater length and in more detail.

Protection against Poverty

Protection against poverty has already been described as the primary aim of the welfare state, at least in the UK. It is sometimes suggested that those who support the provision of assistance for this purpose do so simply because they fear that they themselves may one day be in need of it. No doubt this is one explanation, but it is by no means the only one. Common observation leads to the contrary view that many supporters of such measures, even strong supporters, have clearly no reasonable ground for any such personal fear. In any case, it is quite improper, methodologically, for economists to commit themselves to so narrow a view of human motivation as is done in some theories of public choice. Utility functions are not to be regarded as simply independent: interdependence is also a factor. To make the point less pedantically, motives are mixed.

If protection against poverty is really the basic purpose of the various welfare services, those services would appear to have failed quite lamentably. According to the statistics frequently published, and, it would seem, widely accepted, poverty persists on a massive scale in the UK, notwithstanding the vast expenditure on the welfare state. Worse still, the steep rise over the years in real expenditure has not apparently prevented a *growth* in the number of families designated as being in poverty. Furthermore, it is not only the welfare state but the affluent society as well that appears to have been unsuccessful in removing the blight of poverty.

This is a failure that would seem at first glance to be peculiar to the UK; for poverty has declined sharply over the years in the United States, and in continental Europe the poverty problem is far from being the central preoccupation it is here. How is this to be explained? Have we been particularly inefficient in the use of such massive resources? That we have been wasteful is not in doubt; but many other countries have adopted policies that, for the achievement of this particular objective, must be deemed still more wasteful – consider, for example, the graduated pension schemes of most continental European countries, where benefits are related to previous incomes.

There may however be another explanation. The term 'poverty' needs to be defined, and we must set out how we propose to measure its incidence. To this we shall return below.

Redistribution of Income

The provision of benefits in cash and kind usually, though not invariably, implies transfers from those who are currently better off to those who are worse off before the benefits are received.

The adverb 'currently' is of some importance. Let us, for a moment, sacrifice realism to simplicity of exposition and suppose that everyone has paid on a genuinely actuarial basis for any benefits received. In these circumstances, the 'redistribution' taking place would be no more than that which occurs under any private insurance scheme. Even with transfers financed on an unfunded, pay-as-you-go basis, the transfers from cohorts of younger working age to those who are elderly and less well-off could be made in turn for successive cohorts without there being transfers *within* each cohort. The fact remains that the transfer system, like the tax system, is commonly regarded as a way of reducing horizontal inequality over time. Certainly, it will not do simply to say that people can be, and should be, left to make provision for their own needs *on the assumption* that the vertical distribution of income has been rendered satisfactory, unless one explains how this condition would otherwise be achieved. If benefits were to be cut, is it assumed that there would be an increased use of other redistributional methods, so that the net effect would be distributionally neutral? Or is redistribution acceptable? As usual, there are value judgements here, but there is an obligation to be explicit.

Graduated Income Replacement

This was, of course, a central feature of German pensions from the outset and most countries have followed this course including, latterly, the United Kingdom. The important exception at the moment is Australia.

Let me say at once that in my opinion there is no adequate reason to enforce a graduated benefit scheme. The state could, of course, offer to *provide* such benefits, *unsubsidized*, for those who chose *voluntarily* to obtain them in this way; but at present, compulsion is used. Moreover, there is much compulsion and tax bribery behind private occupational schemes. Official and private schemes together have a marked effect on life-cycle expenditure which should not be passed over as though no explanation or justification were required.

Increased Expenditure on Education, the Health Services, Housing, etc.

The reasons given for this intervention may be (1) externalities (e,g, in education); (2) a paternalistic concern that families may devote less to such purposes than a proper regard for their own good would entail; and (3) a feeling that 'common citizenship' requires certain benefits to be freely available to all, in particular education and the health services. This last point – a version of what James Tobin terms 'specific equality' – is one that individualists have difficulty in appreciating. It should not be dismissed out of hand for that reason, but its full implications need to be pursued and examined. If free access to such services is accompanied, as it need not be, by the monopolistic prohibition of private provision, or by the fiscal penalization of such provision, the total use of the service in question may be reduced and the burden on the Exchequer increased.

Defenders of the provision by the state of such merit goods – or 'simulated public goods', as I prefer to call them – may ask whether critics of such measures really maintain that, as a consequence, excessive resources are being devoted to these purposes. To this, the proper reply is surely that one does not know. It may be that *more* would be spent, rather than less, if greater freedom to spend were permitted. For there may be reasons for believing that supply is restricted – not, of course, because monopoly theory can be crudely transferred to the public sector, but rather because taxpayer resistance may be set a tighter limit than would be set by the market.

Not only may varying weights be attached to these different objectives by different people, but conflicts may be experienced. For example, insistence on a free supply of health services, education, etc., may inhibit an increased supply of graduated benefits. More generally, the pursuit of these objectives is necessarily subject to constraints arising from: (1) side-effects that interfere with other aims, e.g. the possible effects of benefits on incentives to work and save, and (2) existing commitments which cannot simply be set aside without regard either to fairness or to political prudence.

6.3 CASH TRANSFERS AND TAXATION

In developing these points in the rest of the paper I shall confine attention to cash transfers and taxation and neglect the issues raised by benefits of a particular kind, with one exception: assistance with the costs of housing.

A recent publication by the Institute for Fiscal Studies begins with the bold assertion that 'Social security is"another British failure"'(Dilmot, Kay and Morris, 1984). Although the authors are not explicit, the use of words would seem to imply that our failure is worse than that of most other countries. This indeed, would seem to be an inescapable inference. But there is another explanation which lies in the use of terms. In the United States, the number in poverty has fallen relative to a *static* poverty level; in the UK the poverty level – conventionally taken as the scale on which means-tested assistance in cash is provided – has roughly doubled since 1948 for short-term beneficiaries (the unemployed and the sick) and has gone up to about two-and-a-half times its old real level for pensioners. Until the late 1970s the poverty level, or levels, rose over the trend by rather more than gross earnings. On this basis, with 'poverty' given a severely relativistic interpretation, *a rise in the real standard of living of the lower income groups is not in itself allowed to have any effect on the number in poverty: that number can be affected only by a shift in the distribution of income in favour of the lower income groups.*

This is the procedure that is now followed almost universally by UK investigators. It is, in my view, grossly misleading. Due weight must indeed be accorded to the concept of relative poverty, but the improvements that have occurred in the standard of living deserve more than the perfunctory aside usually accorded to them. It would have made for greater clarity of thought if, like the Americans, we had had a static poverty line. It need not have been an operational poverty level – it is not so in the United States. Nor should it have been represented as a measure of 'absolute' poverty. It could have been used quite simply as a bench-mark, as a device for monitoring change in what is after all a rather important variable.

There is another reason why the number in poverty has been made to appear so large. This is because income to which the poverty test is applied is sometimes taken to include all benefits with the exception of the means-tested (supplementary) benefit. The poor are therefore those who are *entitled* to this means-tested benefit, not those still poor *after* deducting the number who have received it. The poverty index has thus become an index of selectivity. This procedure is so insular, and surely so eccentric, that it would be a dubious use of time to try to explain its intricacies to an international audience. It may suffice to underline the warning that statistics relating to the number in poverty in the UK must be interpreted with great caution. This is not to deny that there *is* genuine poverty and genuine hardship, which have grown worse in recent years with the rise in unemployment.

The objectives outlined in general terms above clearly require sharper definition. That need is very apparent with regard to the meaning of 'poverty'. Yet it is one that cannot be met by providing a fully objective and scientific definition of the poverty line – even for one country, even over a short period of time. It is true that Professor Minford seems to hold a different view, for the lower of the safety nets proposed in a recent paper is described as a 'true minimum', which must '... exclude all items not necessary for survival, otherwise the system becomes hopelessly expensive' (Minford, 1984). It is hard to know how, even if it were thought desirable, this subsistence level would be assessed. Most people, I believe, accept the view that poverty is necessarily relative to a particular society at a particular period. Adam Smith himself saw this clearly enough and gave various illustrations, of which I shall quote only one:

> Custom ... has rendered leather shoes a necessary of life in England. The poorest creditable person of either sex would be ashamed to appear in publick without them. In Scotland, custom has rendered them a necessary of life to the lowest order of men, but not to the same order of women, who may, without any discredit, walk about bare-footed. (Smith, 1964 p. 870)

Relatively, yes. We should certainly expect a more generous interpretation of poverty in a richer community. It does not follow that the *standard of living* of the lower income groups is, therefore, of little interest! Nor does it follow that the poverty level, or the whole range of cash benefits, should rise in line with rises in gross average earnings. Yet that is broadly what happened to UK benefits in payment over the trend between 1948 and roughly the second oil crisis in 1979. This occurred, it should be observed, not as a consequence of public debate leading to a statutory obligation to index in this way, but rather as the cumulative consequence of successive discretionary changes – a remarkable example of the working of an 'invisible hand' in government! In the United States and in Sweden, pension payments were indexed for prices rather than earnings; but the fact that these benefits were earnings-related meant that in these countries too the effects of rising earnings were reflected over time, though more gradually, in rising benefits.[1] (There were also some discretionary changes in these two countries.) In a number of European countries, benefits – or at all events, pensions – were both earnings-related and subsequently indexed to gross earnings. Here we have one of the principal explanations of the continuing growth of social expenditure.

In the United Kingdom, the practice of indexation was radically altered by Labour government legislation which came into force in 1978, and later by the Conservatives in 1980. All benefits in the UK are now linked to prices only. In other words, we now have benefits that are *static* in real terms, including static poverty levels. As a consequence, the gap between benefits and earnings has begun to widen, especially in the case of short-term benefits, received mainly by the unemployed.

I propose to lay some stress on the importance of indexation, because this crucially important issue has been somewhat overshadowed in recent public discussion in the UK by proposals for changing the structure of the social security system. Structural changes may indeed be required, but we must set then firmly in perspective. It is particularly important in this connection to distinguish between static and dynamic effects – between the immediate effect when some change is made and the implications of this change after some years have passed.

In the UK a great deal has been said of late about the need for a complete overhaul of social security. The changes proposed may take various forms, but I shall simplify by distinguishing between two broad groups of proposals. The first seems to reflect regret that we did not choose to follow a different path in the past, and finance the benefits from funded schemes, particularly for pensions. Furthermore, advocates of this practice feel that we should still adopt it. There are various ways in which this might be done. Pensions could be provided by private institutions, or by the state itself on an unsubsidised basis; or they could be available from either source with the choice left to individuals. Minimum contributions would in all cases be compulsory, anything above the minimum being voluntary. These benefits would be actuarially based, and the use of the term 'insurance' would now be entirely proper. There would also be a poverty net, but it would be quite unrelated to social insurance.

What advantages would accrue? The fact that contributions were compulsory would imply that choice was limited as with any basic flat-rate scheme – and necessarily so. The emphasis in some proposals would seem to be on a full or partial privatization of the source of supply, a different point. The accumulation of large funds would have a big impact on capital markets and rates of return – and would incidentally greatly facilitate nationalization if any government so wished, as Crossman saw clearly enough when he was making proposals for a UK complementary pension some 20 years ago.

In the present context we need not, however, involve ourselves too deeply in the debate about funding and pay-as-you-go. A resort at this stage to funding benefits already provided is simply not feasible, because the working population would have to pay twice over – once as contributions to their own funded benefits and once as pay-as-you-go transfers to those already retired (or who will retire in future years), for whom no fund has previously been accumulated. When a pay-as-you-go scheme has been in existence for several decades, there is no going back. New schemes are a different matter; hence the urgency in the UK of doing something about our fairly recently adopted (1978) scheme for the provision of earnings-related pensions on a pay-as-you-go basis.

The second line of approach is quite different. It does not reflect any vain wish to be able to start all over again but advocates instead a thoroughgoing reform of the present complex arrangements by integrating the social security system and the tax system. Thus it is held that, by means of a negative income tax or, its close cousin, a tax–benefit scheme, the following advantages could be achieved.

1 Administrative costs could be reduced by substituting a single net payment (positive or negative) for the current two-fold arrangement by which benefits are paid and are subsequently assessed for taxation.
2 The benefit system and the tax system have evolved in different ways with little attempt at consistency. Integration would, of necessity, mean harmonization.
3 The efficiency of the whole system would be raised by restricting the provision of net positive benefits to those in need of them instead of providing benefits to rich and poor alike, as is done under the non-selective social insurance arrangements. (It will be observed that this recommendation is dramatically opposed to the 'Back-to-Beveridge' or 'New Beveridge' recommendations, which would have entailed the virtual abandonment of selectivity.)

The first of these claims – the saving in administrative costs – needs much more detailed investigation and assessment than it appears to have received so far. It would certainly be quite absurdly unrealistic to suppose that the Inland Revenue could simply assume the new duty of providing positive benefits as well as extracting negative ones (i.e. taxes). It would be better able to do so in the case of benefits that are long-term and that do not attempt to assess the special 'needs' of individual families – as is done in the provision of assistance with housing, etc. But it is precisely these highly selective benefits that are so costly to administer, compared with the unselective, standardized social insurance benefits. There may indeed be a strong case for greatly simplifying such special benefits and relying more fully on cash payments designed to cover nearly all contingencies. But this simplification could be achieved whether or not there was a negative income tax or tax-benefit system.

The fact that benefits have to be provided at once when a family qualifies would pose problems for the Inland Revenue. Moreover, 'availability for work' has to be – or ought to be – established, in appropriate cases. There is the further very considerable complication that reasonably accurate tax returns would have to be extracted from the very income groups that are said to fail, from lack of information or lack of initiative, to claim fully the selective benefits at present available to them.

What we have to contemplate, then, is a mammoth department embodying most of those branches of the Department of Health and Social Security that deal currently with social insurance and means-tested benefits. Would there be a net saving? It should be conceded that, *in principle*, the answer ought to be in the affirmative, but the assessment of its likely importance is a different matter.

It may be maintained, however, that, whatever the final verdict under this first heading, there ought to be a clear improvement under the *second* heading – the removal of inconsistencies between the benefit system and the tax system. For example, the Department of Health and Social Security imposes what is, in effect, an income tax on earned income (the national insurance contribution), but its structure is quite different from the Inland Revenue's income tax. It is also reasonable to say that the tax exemption limit should be at or above the 'poverty' level at which, for families in similar circumstances, benefits are paid. This condition is in fact satisfied for some families but not for others. Would amalgamation lead to the removal of such anomalies? There are problems to be met that are by no means merely administrative. In order to remove the difficulties that *are* administrative, close coopera-tion between the different divisions of the vast new synthesized department would be required. If, however, this could be achieved, would it not be possible to obtain better cooperation without the amalgamation of the tax and benefit systems? The query is all the more relevant because housing and labour market problems – and these are very important as well as very complex – would in any case require the cooperation of additional departments.

We now turn to the third reason for advocating amalgamation, which is the one that has received most emphasis: that net transfers would then be confined to those who really need them. By contrast, the existing system is said to be wasteful.

The point can be conveniently illustrated by means of a diagram used by Beckerman and Clark (1982), which is reproduced as figure 6.1. D is explained by the fact that for some people the coverage provided by benefits is incomplete and that others do not take up fully the benefits to which they are entitled. It is *possible* that a national insurance tax (NIT) or tax–benefit scheme would help in reducing D; it is however C, and to a much lesser extent B, to which attention is particularly devoted by the proponents of such schemes. What are the orders of magnitude involved? It may be illuminating to look at some figures for expenditure on benefits corresponding to these categories. The following estimates are from Dilmot, Kay and Morris (1984) and are expressed as

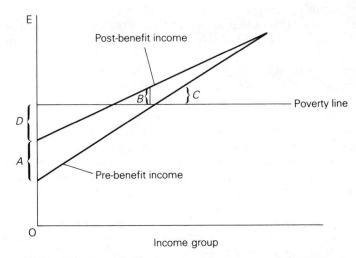

Figure 6.1 *Families are ranked by income with poorest on the left. (The linearity is merely for convenience of drawing.)*

$A + B + C =$ *total expenditure on benefits*
$A + B$ *= amounts received by pre-benefit poor*
C *= amount received by those not initially poor*
$A + D$ *= pre-benefit poverty gap*
D *= post-benefit poverty gap*

percentages of total expenditure on cash benefits:[2]

1 Received by pre-benefit poor (corresponding to $A + B$)   66%
  of which:
  (a) Proportion of expenditure needed to lift poor out of
      poverty (A) 54%
  (b) Excess (B) 12%
2 Received by those not initially poor (C) 34%

Account must be taken of the fact that some of the poor (D) were left in poverty. It is estimated that an additional 5 per cent or so of actual expenditure would have been needed in order to take them into account. If this is deducted from (2) above, the 'excessive' expenditure on benefits was 29 per cent.

Now let us recognize that it would be highly undesirable to have a system that was strictly concentrated on raising the poor to the poverty level; for when that point was reached, there would be a 100 per cent cut-off which would be damaging to incentives to work and save. There must always be some smoothing – some compromise between conflicting objectives. This means some expenditure on families in category B and even in category C. Moreover, it must be emphasized that these estimates relate to gross income before tax. In the UK all benefits, with the admittedly important exception of child benefit, are included in assessments for liability to tax. An element of selectivity is therefore already implicit in the existing system when benefits and taxes are taken together. It would, of course, be quite possible to introduce a more rapid tapering-off as gross income rose. This could be done in a tax–benefit system – or, indeed, by introducing tapering rules more generally into the existing system. Behind any procedure of this kind lies the assumption that more progressive taxation should be levied on that part of income that is derived from social benefits than is thought to be appropriate for income derived from other sources.

The effects of an interesting tax–benefit system have been estimated by the Institute for Fiscal Studies (Dilmot, Kay and Morris, 1984). It is claimed that about £5½ billion could be saved by adopting the scheme they have in mind, which provides for selectivity by category – age, employment, etc. – and by size of income. Now, £5½ billion is a large sum and, obviously, well worth saving if the constraints allow this to be done. But the greatest part of this saving comes from the basic pension and child benefits, by making both subject to an incomes test. If, as I myself believe, we cannot simply disregard the reasonable expectations of pensioners and must therefore exempt the basic pension from subjection to a severely progressive withdrawal rate, the saving will be reduced by something like one-third to two-fifths.

Let us, however, assume that £5½ billion could be saved, and let us set this in perspective. It is equivalent to about 15 per cent of cash benefits. By way of comparison, real expenditure on social transfers rose by 29 per cent between 1978–9 and 1983–4. The main explanation was the rise in unemployment, but, even if this is left out of account, real benefits rose by nearly 10 per cent over five years – and this under a government that was seeking to restrain the growth in public expenditure.

This rise since 1979 occurred notwithstanding the fact that, over these years, wage indexation applied only marginally. But consider the effect of wage indexation in the past when, moreover, real wages were rising more rapidly. Let us recall that short-term benefits per beneficiary – i.e. benefits to the unemployed and the sick – have roughly doubled in real terms since 1948 when our whole system was reformed: long-term benefits – pensions – have gone up to about two-and-a-quarter times their initial level. Suppose now that a NIT or tax–benefit scheme had been the model adopted in 1948, but that indexation had been the same. Expenditure would still have risen steeply. As a perentage of GNP, it would be only slightly below the figure actually reached with less selective arrangements.

Let us direct our attention to the familiar diagram illustrating a simple form of NIT (figure 6.2). This is usually presented only in static terms. But what is assumed to happen over time? Presumably there is to be

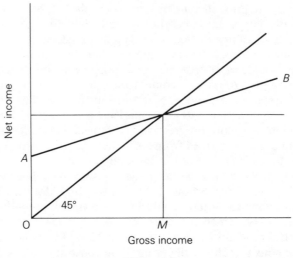

Figure 6.2

indexation for price changes so that the diagram can be translated into real terms, subject to the usual vagaries of indexation in practice. If, however, wage indexation were to be applied, then, with rising real wages, *AB* would also rise in real terms – would, in fact, have doubled or more than doubled since 1948.

To say all this is not, of course, to reject out of hand the case for structural change with greater emphasis on selectivity. But, to sum up, account must be taken not only of the administrative difficulties of combining a social security system with a tax system, but also of the constraints imposed by past commitments and by the need to have regard to the damage done to incentives by too heavy an emphasis on selectivity.

Finally, as we have just seen, these proposals for structural change are often presented only in static terms, although the problem is largely dynamic. A simple diagram will illustrate. In figure 6.3, *AB* is the old system, *CD* the new. The saving of *BC* may be appreciable, but the *slope* of *CD* may be no less than that of *AB*. This is a matter that has received far too little attention.

6.4 CONCLUDING COMMENTS

It is my contention that, if the growth in the cost of benefits relative to GNP is to be reduced, the arrangements for indexation must not be overshadowed in this way by proposals for structural change. What should these arrangements be?

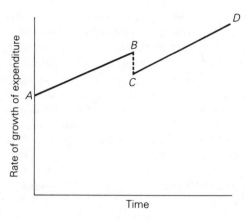

Figure 6.3

1 Price indexation would, I think, be almost universally supported today. It is important, of course, to use the *right* price index, and it would appear that this has not been done in the UK. It has been maintained that benefits are, in fact, *lower* than they would be if, with other things equal, a more appropriate index or indices had been used over the years.

2 Wage indexation in the UK in the past was to gross average earnings, and was carried out erratically without any statutory commitment for most of the period after 1948. Benefits are now adjusted only for prices, but there is a loose government commitment to raise real pensions when times improve. In a number of continental European countries, there has been an explicit link to earnings – a link now, I believe, disconnected in the German pension scheme, where discretion was always retained. Much concern has, of course, been caused by this indexation in France as the recession has deepened.

If, then, there is to be wage indexation at all, should the link be to *gross* earnings, the nearly universal practice in the past, or to *net disposable* earnings? Surely to the latter, although it is important to observe that fiscal drag in the tax system will not have the same effect as in the past – at least not in the UK.

If, however, the dependency ratio – the ratio of beneficiaries to workers – is rising, then indexation in per capita terms may not be appropriate. It may be wiser to relate total benefits to the total wages and salaries bill. This proposal raises some complicated questions which cannot be pursued here.

3 The third possibility is that the real poverty level and real benefits should be raised over time, in recognition of the relativity of standards, but by less than the growth in average real disposable income. Of course there are value judgements here, and of course views will differ with

regard to this issue – as with regard to so many others. This does, however, seem to be the right approach for those who would like to see a check to the relative growth of the welfare state. There is no question of its withering away. Indeed, it is clear that most people would not wish to see it wither away. (Milton Friedman himself has not gone as far as that.) Withering, no: pruning, yes. If that is the objective that commends itself, then the most important single means of achieving it may, over time, be the choice of the right formula for indexation.

With benefits rising less than earnings, there would be increasing scope for the exercise of self-help – which Beveridge himself regarded as evidence of self-respect. It is much to be regretted that greater weight was not given to considerations of this kind during that long period of strong and steady growth and high employment. Unfortunately, that was the very time when people in the UK fell into the habit of describing any and every hardship as evidence of 'social deprivation'. But conditions have changed again. Growth has been severely retarded, and mass unemployment has returned. In the Unservile State Paper to which I referred (Peacock, 1961), full employment was stated very clearly to be a condition for a decline in the need for welfare benefits. That condition is no longer satisfied. Moreover, one of the most striking features of the situation today is the conflict of interest between the employed and the unemployed. If this conflict were likely to be prolonged indefinitely, it could have some bearing on the proper choice of indexation.

It is scarcely necessary to add that unemployment on the present scale greatly affects the fiscal position. But it may be worth recalling the statistical fact that the rise in expenditure on unemployment pay alone between 1979 and 1983 was comparable to what might be saved, on realistic expectations, by introducing a NIT or tax–benefit system. And this takes no account of the associated loss of revenue.

It would be natural to follow on from here by discussing the extent to which the welfare state itself is one of the several factors contributing to the persistence of high unemployment. We should then have to direct attention not only to the disincentive effect, now somewhat reduced in the UK, but also to the effect of the employers' payroll tax, which distorts the composition of factor inputs. If it is politically impossible to get rid of this tax in a social insurance scheme, we may then have a strong argument for general budget financing – financing, that is to say, from a budget that does not include such a tax.

If I were to try to pursue these matters further I should, however be displaying a total and unforgivable disregard for the 'welfare state' of those readers subjected to this paper. No doubt I have caused it to wither already: if I now go on I may be guilty of complete defoliation. I must stop before that happens.

NOTES

1 In Sweden this was true only of the second and third-tier pensions, for the basic pension was flat rate.
2 The poverty line is taken as supplementary benefit cash payments *plus* average housing costs, which are fully met by the state.

7

Public Policy Aspects
of the Economics of Ageing,
(or The Economics of Dependence
Revisited)

ALAN WILLIAMS

7.1 PROLOGUE

During recent years attention has been increasingly directed towards the economic problems expected to arise in this country as a result of the increase that is foreseen over the next 30 years both in the number of elderly people and in their proportion to the population of working age. That opening sentence is not really mine, though it could well have been. Nor is it from the recent official HM Treasury Green Paper (HMSO, 1984) entitled *The Next Ten Years: Public Expenditure and Taxation into the 1990s*, though again it could well have been. No, that opening sentence is in fact the opening sentence of Paish and Peacock's (1954) *Economica* article entitled 'Economics of Dependence (1952–82)', which forms an excellent launching pad for the theme I want to develop in this essay, namely that the economics of dependence is still too dominated by narrow public finance issues, and needs to be emancipated from public sector accountancy in the same manner that public sector economics generally has emancipated itself, i.e. by starting from a more explicit welfare economics base.

The objectives of Paish and Peacock (henceforth PP) were more limited than this. Bewailing the lack of any properly worked out official demographic projections that would enable them to forecast the ratio of workers to non-workers in 1982, and the change in the real burden of transfers per worker that was likely as a result of demographic factors, they set about the task of (1) producing the demographic forecast and (2) applying some crude economic assumptions about the costs of maintaining each dependent person in order to estimate the broad orders of magnitude involved. Their broad conclusion was that:

the cost of educating and maintaining the non-working population (excluding wives of working husbands) at a constant cost per head will rise by an average of about $\frac{1}{2}$ per cent per annum for the next thirty years. This rate of increase is considerably less than the average of $\frac{3}{4}$ per cent per annum by which output per head of working population has risen during the past forty years .... Any serious problems which may arise in the financing of the support of non-workers will therefore be attributable, not to the mere change in the age distribution of the population, but to increases in the cost of education and maintenance per head of the non-working population, and/or to shifts in the responsibility for financing this expenditure, especially in the direction of the state. (Paish and Peacock, 1954, p. 286)

PP then went on to examine this last factor, again having to build up from scratch the basic data on the distribution of the relevant services by dependency group, admitting defeat in certain key respects (such as the allocation of social services expenditure between the working and non-working populations). They eventually came to the view that:

Allowing for the shortcomings of this comparison, there does not seem to be much doubt about the fact that in the future there will be a marked shift towards state responsibility for financing the expenditure designed to maintain the non-working population. Thus, while there may not be a 'resources problem' ... it seems fairly certain that there will be a 'transfer problem'. (Paish and Peacock, 1954, p. 293)

They then went on to consider some proposed solution to this transfer problem, concerned mainly with reducing the cost of pensions (e.g. by raising retirement ages, or by increasing contribution rates to reduce the call on general taxation), on which they took a rather guarded view. Instead they opted for 'measures which, by increasing the rate of rise on the national income will enable the country to bear its increasing burden with greater ease'. (p. 298); this led to a final paragraph, which in summary said:

As soon as we look at pensions policy, not with the object of securing an immediate saving of money, but with a view to encouraging as many as possible to work as much as possible for as many years as possible, the way is open for a number of possibilities in addition to those suggested earlier. One of these ... is to pay pensions to all who are past the present retiring ages, whether they are working or not, at a gradually increasing rate, reaching a maximum at the end of five years ... the indirect effects of the higher output and of the consequent rise in real national income might well make the experiment a profitable one even from the strictly budgetary point of view. (Paish and Peacock, 1954, pp. 298–9) [1]

It is tempting, with the benefit of hindsight, to go over the PP data, assumptions and conclusions to identify where they were 'right' and where they were 'wrong', but there is little point in that kind of exercise unless it helps those who later embark on a similar enterprise to do better. One such is John Ermisch, whose recent book, *The Political*

Economy of Demographic Change (1983), surprisingly makes no reference whatever to the PP work. *Sic transit gloria mundi.* But while Ermisch goes into a lot more detail than PP and has better (though still incomplete) data with which to work, he signally fails to pull together the diverse threads of the problem in the concentrated, single minded way that PP had done 30 years earlier. The recent Treasury paper referred to earlier does not help much either, since it is more of a political manifesto than a serious analytical study, informed by the view that:

> There will be some who will argue that it makes little sense to consider, still less decide upon, public spending totals without a clear idea of the implications for individual programmes. The government believes that such thinking has been largely responsible for the upward drift of public expenditure over many years. It is necessary to turn the argument round the other way, to decide first what can and should be afforded, and then to set expenditure plans for individual programmes consistently with that decision.(HMSO, 1984, p. 13).

So there is still plenty of scope for some latter-day PP to fill this gap – as, indeed, there still will be at the end of this essay, for it is not a task on which I intend to embark in the present context.

My ambitions lie elsewhere, namely in exploring more carefully the distinction that PP drew between a 'resources' problem and a 'transfer' problem, and developing it in a manner that leads to a rather different view of current UK policy on the care of the dependent population than that which informs present policy. The key element is the view one takes of the role of the household (and particularly of non-employed women) in the economic system. Current orthodoxy regards the household virtually as a 'free good' when it comes to providing care, rather as the physical environment was regarded in the economics of the firm prior to the development of environmental economics and its integration into the main corpus of economics. It is time the same was done for the economics of the household, and, although that challenging task will not be attempted here, I will sketch out a line of thinking that would, I think, be more compatible with that perspective than with current orthodoxy.

Quite understandably, PP did not tackle this broad issue, since they already had quite enough on their plates coping with the estimation problems involved in the task they had set themselves. I suspect, however, that they must (even then) have been uneasy about the treatment of households in their exercise, because initially they counted all married women as dependants, but then they modified this position so as to exclude from among the 'dependants' all married women whose husbands were still working. This group (about 10 million in a population of 50 million) was then subdivided into appproximately two equal-sized groups. The first sub-group comprised those who were participating in the labour market, who (with downward adjustment to whole-time-male-equivalent) were then counted as workers. The other subgroup (the non-employed wives of working husbands) was left in limbo, its members being neither workers nor non-workers! It is perhaps, no wonder that a recent 'Briefing Paper' from the Family Policy Studies Centre (Henwood and Wicks, 1984), concerned 'the needs of a rapidly ageing population and the challenge this represents – especially for the families of elderly people', is entitled '*The Forgotten Army*'! If my own essay were to sport a second subtitle, it would have to be 'The Economics of the Forgotten Army'.

7.2 A DIFFERENT PERSPECTIVE

PP did not explicitly define what they meant by 'a resources problem' and a 'transfer problem', but by implication it is clear that these concepts are concerned with the following questions:

1 *The resources problem*: Will net national product increase fast enough to enable the *extra* resources needed to support the dependant population to be found from the *extra* net national product that will be available (i.e. without encroaching on any existing use of net national product)?
2 *The transfer problem*: Will public expenditure rise at such a rate that the proportion of personal income taken in taxes will increase to a level that is unacceptable either on grounds of equity or on grounds of efficiency (i.e. owing to disincentive effects)?

The well-known weakness that national income accounting does not include household production is the key defect with the first of these definitions, and the restriction of the transfer problem to being a purely public sector phenomenon is the key defect of the second. It is these defects that I want to examine closely in what follows.

To do so I want to go back to some more fundamental ideas, and start from the proposition that the prime task facing public intervention in today's advanced economies is to enhance the length and quality of life of the citizenry, and to ensure that such enhancement is shared equitably among them, Unfortunately, this fundamental view of the objectives of public intervention too readily gets translated into the narrower view that the objectives are the maximization of GNP per head and the reduction of inequalities in the distribution of income and wealth. We too readily accept this narrowing of our vision, even though we know quite well that GNP fails to include a great deal of valuable output (and consumption) that takes place in society (e,g, within the families or household), and that inequalities in income and wealth are only part (though an important part) of the sources of inequality in society – another important part, for example, is unequal access to public goods and services, and yet another is lack of tolerance for minority groups.

If we return to the more fundamental way of looking at things, and ask ourselves what are the elements that contribute most to the enhancement of people's lives (both quantitatively and qualitatively), then a basic list would include command over adequate nutrition and shelter, a secure environment, and access to a wide range of rewarding experiences. The security of the environment should here be interpreted to include not only the protection of life and property, but also the confidence that in misfortune (e,g, illness or injury, bereavement, marital breakdown or unemployment) support is there to palliate its immediate effects and to speed the subsequent process of rehabilitation or readjustment. Similarly, among the 'rewarding experiences' to which people should have access is that of socially worthwhile and personally satisfying work, and also the opportunity to use their non-working time to participate in a variety of activities which draw as fully as possible on the cultural and recreational heritage of the society of which they are a part (which, ultimately, must be the whole human race). All this should be seen as part of an individual's 'consumption stream', and any 'public intervention' that generates such benefits must in this sense be seen as 'productive', since it adds to the value of 'consumption' in the society in the same way as do food, clothing, fuel, housing, etc. Since such public intervention typically occurs outside the market, we face severe practical difficulties in actually measuring its value (even if we believe market prices to be adequate for measuring the value of marketed goods), but this should not lead us into the trap of ignoring it (which implies assigning it zero value).

So let us look more closely at the 'social services' against that background. To concentrate on the resource-using side of the problem, I take the term 'social services' to *exclude* social security (i.e. to exclude all public interventions that simply redistribute cash), but to *include* all goods and services provided by the public sector for individuals where access, or entitlement, is determined mainly by criteria other than willingness or ability to pay at the point of utilization. Free health services, social work support, education, etc., are obviously social services within this definition, and heavily subsidized housing or transport for specifically designated groups of people may also be so regarded; but, in general, public utility enterprises will not be (because they operate mainly through markets), nor will agricultural or industrial subsidy programmes (since they are directed to 'businesses' rather than 'individuals', though I recognize that in the case of support for small farmers this is a rather fine distinction!)

I would now assert that all social services are, in principle, *productive* in the fundamental sense explained above, and that they should be seen as 'producing' consumption possibilities just as do the manufacturers of television sets. We still have to decide whether or not they do so *efficiently*, of course (i.e. whether, at the margin, the value of the benefits outweighs the value of the resources used), but this is equally true of the manufacture of television sets. Indeed, I would go further and argue that for allocative efficiency we must also ask, at the margin, whether, say, a child's lifetime consumption possibilities would be enhanced more by access to better schooling or by access to better television; for in principle, in the context of public policy, both are to be judged by the same criteria.

In my ideal world the success or failure of all public interventions (and all private actions) would be judged by their effects on the present value of the future stream of consumption possibilities open to the members of the society. If this is increasing, then the society exhibits 'growth', and if it is not, then it is a 'stagnant' society. So let us imagine a society that is devoting more and more of its resources to social services that extend the length and quality of life of its elderly population, who themselves, let us assume, produce nothing that gets measured in GNP. What would we observe within the present conventional wisdom, and how would we discuss the issues involved?

What we would observe is a demographic shift with an increasing ratio of 'dependent' to 'working' population, with increasing taxes levied on the latter group to set free resources for the former group to consume. Thus we shall be told that the crippling 'burden' of supporting the elderly is reducing the growth rate by forcing the (non-productive) public sector to take resources away from the ('wealth-producing') private sector. Indeed, this 'stigmatization' of social services as 'non-productive' even seems to spill over into the publicly financed education sector, which is similarly seen as being parasitic upon the 'wealth-producing' private sector (the implication being that television sets are wealth but teachers are parasites). The essence of the problem here is that we do not accord the same recognition and status to human capital formation as to physical capital formation, except when we have occasion for concern about the size or quality of the labour force, implying that we value 'human capital formation' only as a source of work effort to be bought and sold in the market.

To counter this perverted way of thinking, those who practise it must be challenged to define clearly what they regard as 'wealth'. I suspect that the typical answer will boil down to the assertion that 'wealth' is the capacity of society to produce marketable goods and services, as if that were the main objective of human existence; whereas I see such production merely as one of many instrumental mechanisms for improving human welfare (and a less and less important one as a society gets richer). I therefore think it very important to recognize that, when we talk about 'growth' or 'stagnation', we relate these terms to the value of the future life chances open to our citizens, and *not* to narrow and misleading concepts such as GNP. If we are able to do so, not only will we see the role of social services in a different light (as 'productive' as well as 'redistributive'), but we might even see growth where those with a narrow and distorted vision see only 'stagnation'.

7.3 WHO CARES?

So let us turn to the relevance of all this to the economics of dependence in the UK for the *next* 30 years or so. One of the currently proposed solutions to the transfer problem is to rely more heavily on 'community care' for the elderly, for the mentally ill, for the mentally handicapped, etc., because it is believed to be both 'better' and 'cheaper' than relying on the welfare state. Whether or not it is 'better' I will not explore further here, but for anyone interested in the problems of measuring the relative effectiveness of such options there is a burgeoning literature (see especially DHSS, 1983), which points out how difficult it is to make that judgement with any confidence. I want to concentrate here upon the resource problems associated with that particular solution to the transfer problem, and in particular, to address the following issue: Is greater reliance on the informal support system costless, and, if not, in what sense might it be regarded as a more costly alternative than providing more formal support and letting public expenditure rise as a consequence?

In tackling this question I shall initially adopt what seems to be the current UK Treasury position, namely that the main resistance to increasing public expenditure lies in the disincentive effects of taxation, and their consequences for growth, since there is clearly no physical shortage of the real resources needed to provide the required extra care (it is mostly labour, and over the next 30 or 40 years amounts to less than half a million people at the very outside, which is a small fraction of the current numbers who are registered unemployed, or who have withdrawn from or have not been allowed to enter the labour force, who probably number about 4 million in all). As the 1984 Treasury Green Paper says,

> It is likely that there will be an increase in employment in those sectors, especially in services, that are already labour-intensive, where output grows relatively rapidly, or where there is scope for growth in relatively low productivity occupations .... Higher output growth would of course imply a quicker decline in unemployment. (HMSO, 1984, p. 28)

So the scenario over the next decade is clearly one of reducing unemployment, rather than facing a labour constraint. The main emphasis of the Green Paper is upon the tax burden, and upon its 'consequences for incentives and growth' (p. 17), so I propose to work through that line of agument within my framework, in which it is to be assumed that caring for the dependent population is going to be done by somebody or other, and the point at issue is simply, By whom?

As is well known, the alleged disincentive effects of taxation have proved notoriously difficult to document empirically on any but a negligible scale, and there are good reasons in principle why this should be so. Moreover, if the additional taxes were levied on goods and services that are complementary with leisure, they may well have positive effects on the supply of effort. But even if we assume that the additional taxes are all levied directly on earned income, then, from a recent report (Ashworth, 1982) of both survey and econometric evidence on the elasticity of supply of labour in the UK, assuming an equiproportional impact on income and substitution effects, the net effect would be an elasticity of about 0.1. If taxation had to be raised by £1,000 million for the public sector to provide all the extra care required, this would represent a reduction of 0.06 per cent in personal disposable incomes (at 1981 levels – though by 2021 it would be a much smaller fraction). With a labour force of about 25 million, this implies a maximum disincentive effect equivalent to about 15,000 employees.

But consider now the alternative scenario, in which an equivalent amount of extra care is provided by the informal sector. This is not a simple equivalence to establish, because informal care has public expenditure costs too, so it is the amount of informal care that has to replace formal care to generate a net saving of £1,000 million that has to be estimated. If we concentrate on the elderly, which is both the largest group and the one likely to grow most in size, then each person kept out of hospital saves about £4,700 per annum, or, if kept out of a residential home, about £800 per annum (Maynard and Smith, 1983); so there is a rather large range of possible numbers to play with, depending on which parts of the formal sector get the most relief from the expansion of the informal care sector. Let us work with each extreme assumption in turn. To generate £1,000 million of net savings by not providing additional hospital care, about 210,000 additional old people would need to be cared for in the community. To do the same simply by keeping them out of residential homes, 1.25 million would have to be so transferred (which is about half the total increase in the total population aged over 65 even according to the government actuary's (HMSO, 1984) upper variant population projection!). But now consider the effects on the labour supply of households of having either 210,000 severely disabled or 1.25 million moderately disabled people to look after.

An Equal Opportunities Commission survey (1980) observed that 25 per cent of carers of the elderly had given up work or lost or altered the number of hours worked as a direct result of caring for elderly dependants. Similar, or larger, orders of magnitude have been found

(Baldwin, 1981; Hirst, 1985) for people caring for the severely disabled non-elderly. Even if we conservatively assume that only 15 per cent full-time equivalent workers are lost, this will represent 31,500 members of the workforce, or roughly twice as many as from the maximum disincentive effect of the taxation 'saved'. For the 1.25 million less severely disabled elderly in the alternative scenario, even a disincentive effect as low as $2\frac{1}{2}$ per cent would generate comparable magnitudes. It therefore seems most likely that this particular 'solution' to the transfer problem can be justified on the stated grounds of adverse effects on distribution and growth.

But although this calculation casts serious doubt on the validity of current policy (even within its own terms of reference), I am really not at all happy with the context within which that argument has been conducted, because it is still too deeply rooted in the notion that the role of the household is primarily as a source of labour for 'the market', and not as a productive unit in itself. This view seems even more surprisingly to underlie the recent survey book by Clark and Spengler (1980), which claims to 'provide a conceptual framework for the economics of ageing' yet hardly mentions health and social support systems, and is almost exclusively concerned with market-related phenomena. If we accept the 'different perspective' offered earlier in this paper, we have to consider the costs borne by informal carers other than those that show up in their withdrawal from the labour force. These costs are of two kinds: the material resource costs that caring entails (housing space, extra heating, lighting, etc.) and the costs in terms of the quality (and length) of life of the carers (e.g. loss of leisure activities, loss of contact with friends, marital difficulties, persistent anxiety and physical exhaustion). These have been well documented in the literature (Equal Opportunities Commission, 1980; Nissel and Bonnerjea, 1982; Finch and Groves, 1983; Levin *et al*, 1983; Parker *et al*, 1984) but are even more difficult to put an order-of-magnitude figure on than the earlier phenomena on which some heroic estimates were offered. What does seem clear is that

> stress influences outcome in terms of the duration of informal care ... where carers had been experiencing a high level of strain the surviving elderly people were more likely to have been placed in permanent institutional care, even when the carers had wanted to go on caring ... Moreover, the mental health of those who had continued to care had declined while that of those whose relatives had died or entered long-term care had improved. (Parker *et al*, 1984, pp. 67–8)

Thus, a policy of relying on the informal sector to provide any extra care is essentially a policy of letting these costs fall where they may, without any clear knowledge as to the magnitude of the costs. It is, however, not at all implausible that those mainly at risk (PP's 5 million non-employed married women?) would each be prepared to pay £200 per annum in extra taxation to avoid that risk (if *all* households paid it, it would be about £60 per household per annum, or about a 1 per cent increase in current tax levels), although this loads the comparison by relating the costs of the levels of care required in 30 or 40 years' time to 1981 income and tax levels. If real incomes (and absolute tax levels) doubled by 2021, these 'burdens' are obviously halved in relative significance.

7.4 CONCLUSION

Where then do we stand with the proposed solution of relying on the informal sector to deal with the 'transfer problem' imposed by the future burden of caring for the dependent members of society? My conclusion is that, in order to think clearly about this policy issue (and others like it), one needs broader definitions of 'the resources problem' and of 'the transfer problem' than those used by PP 30 years ago. I suggest the following candidates for consideration:

1 *The resources problem*: Will the productive capacity of the system (which embraces public and private production, including in the latter the non-marketed 'production' that goes on within households) increase fast enough to enable the extra resources needed to support the dependent population to be found from the extra capacity that will be available (i.e. without encroaching on any existing use of that capacity)?
2 *The transfer problem*: Will the mechanisms by which the needs of the dependent population are met be so adjusted as to minimize the welfare losses involved, which implies a concern for both the total opportunity cost and its distribution? (In this context, 'opportunity cost' should ideally be measured in quantity and quality of life expectancy.)

This broader formulation leads one naturally towards a rather more sophisticated cost–benefit approach to the evaluation of public policy proposals than that offered in the recent Treasury Green Paper, for it raises the possibility that, just as it is not possible to determine the net inflationary or deflationary effect of a set of budget proposals by looking at the overall size of the resulting budget surplus or deficit, so it is not possible to determine how much public expenditure we can afford without considering how the total is made up. After all, £1,000 million spent on caring for the elderly raises rather different considerations of 'affordability' than £1,000 million contributed to the EEC's Common Agricultural Policy.

Roughly ten years after the 1954 PP paper, Peacock published an article on 'Economic Analysis and Government Expenditure Control' (Peacock, 1963), in which he wrote: 'it seems sensible to advocate that the Treasury should initiate discussions and offer advice on the ways in which checks on efficiency might be devised using economic analysis' (p. 12). My view is that, in the social services field, the Treasury nowadays should be *seeking* rather than *offering* such advice! But I can agree with his next statement, which was that 'what is required is a closer examination of *alternative* methods by which a given aim can be carried out ... even if no precise guide to action can be given, the logical framework imposed in discussion of financial estimates by economic analysis would improve decision-making.' However, the *nature* of the economic analysis has, of course, to be appropriate, and I recommend a return to the broad vision provided by welfare economics and the abandonment of the narrowly focused tunnel vision of market economics which seems to dominate current Treasury thinking on these important issues of social policy.

NOTES

I owe special thanks to Stephen Birch in the preparation of this paper, since he did a great deal of the digging out of data and computational work which led me to the views now encapsulated in section 7.3. In this work he was ably assisted by Eileen Sutcliffe. At a more general level, my thoughts have been considerably influenced by the work of Ken Wright above all others, but latterly also by the work of Jonathan Bradshaw and his colleagues at the Social Policy Research Unit in York, on whose work I have also drawn heavily.

1   Since Peacock is now more heavily involved in the pensions issue, but now in the context of mass unemployment and the tremendous growth in occupational pensions, it will be interesting to see whether he still sees the problem in this light, and whether the 'transfer problem' is now interpreted to include that generated by private pensions as well as by state pensions.

8

Public Funding of Universities: Effects on Economics I Students

KEITH LUMSDEN AND ALEX SCOTT

8.1 INTRODUCTION

Although some notable economists have gone further than just to argue that universities should not be in the public sector, and although five of the top six US universities are private, no major university, including the private ones, exists today without some form of government support. However, the government and the universities, not surprisingly, seldom agree on the correct level of government finance for universities and the deployment of resources within universities. What makes these disagreements highly subjective is the absence of output prices to indicate priorities and the lack of an incentive structure within universities to encourage the efficient use of resources. This paper reports on efficiency issues relating to one aspect of university activities: the teaching of the beginning economics course.

Outside the Oxbridge system there exists a consensus on how to teach beginning economics. The typical student is expected to attend two or three lectures and one tutorial per week, read some assigned texts, and complete one or two essays per term. Not only is this model generally accepted in existing institutions, but it was also adopted by the new universities created during the 1960s and by the polytechnics, which were largely staffed by academics who had gone through the conventional university system. Among the reasons why this teaching model was generally accepted is that academics believed it to be efficient; given that it was based on many decades of unrecorded experimentation, and that it had been passed on in the oral tradition, it was reasonable to presume that this particular model had survived while others had fallen by the wayside. A second possible reason for its acceptance is that it may have been in the interests of suppliers to adopt this model. This is not inconsistent with efficiency; indeed, the theory of competition and concomitant efficiency conditions are based on the self-interests of suppliers. However, since the suppliers of university courses are in many respects local monopolists, self-interest is not a sufficient condition for efficiency.

There are two reasons why observers of the university system might question the efficiency arguments. First, the communications revolution produced no change in beginning economics courses; the Open University, a significant departure from existing practices, and one for which empiricism suggests substantial gains in cost effectiveness (Lumsden and Ritchie, 1975; Lumsden and Scott, 1982), had few takers of its innovative teaching techniques in the conventional sector. Second, educational research results kept stressing that students do not learn well by 'hearing' or 'seeing'; they learn by 'doing', and by receiving fast feedback on how well they are learning, given their study habits. In the bulk of beginning courses there was not much 'doing', and the traditional feedback mechanism was slow, inefficient and often confusing.

Why is it that a profession that prides itself on its research standards is apparently quite unscientific in its major activity, namely teaching? This is especially true in beginning courses, most of which consume large amounts of departmental resources. The answer may well lie in the 'self-interest of suppliers' argument. But how does self-interest make itself manifest? Suppose a lecturer invents a black box which is a perfect substitute for the live teacher in his course; it is 'perfect' in that student learning and satisfaction with the course do not decrease. The incentives for the innovative lecturer to use the black box are increased research and leisure time. However, if the departmental head, concerned with equity rather than efficiency, insists on the set quota of class contact hours, the incentive for any individual to innovate disappears. Why not share the black box with all members of the department? The answer is obvious: the department becomes a prime candidate for reductions in staff members. Thus, implicit tacit agreements become formalized within and between universities; staff–student ratios emerge as 'desirable norms', teaching practices become fossilized, and a structure emerges in which efficiency criteria are largely ignored.

The black box example is, of course, extreme. Black boxes do not exist, but grey boxes certainly do, and it is only in the relatively recent past that departments and institutions, finding themselves increasingly beset by resource limitations, are turning to these grey boxes. Since the mid-1970s the Esmee Fairbairn Research Centre has been conducting a research project attempting to assess the efficacy of innovative teaching techniques in beginning economics courses (Lumsden and Scott, 1983). This paper reports on some of the findings of that study, which have implications for student admissions, design of examinations and methodology of economics education research.

Selection of University Candidates

The cutbacks in resources for higher education by the government in 1982/3 led to increased competition for university places. Many departments responded to this excess demand by raising entry requirements. For a variety of reasons, departments typically aim to attract and admit the 'best' possible candidates, where 'best' is normally judged by performance at A level.[1] In several faculties, primarily the scientific, engineering and medical, the entry filter specifies subjects as well as number and class of A-level pass. In economics the principal filter is number and class of pass, with only a few institutions specifying either economics or mathematics as an entry requirement. Should economics follow the 'hard' sciences and specify A-level economics and/or mathematics as admission prerequisites?

The debate on the impact of school economics on university performance in the subject can be traced at least as far back as the late Lord Robbins's presidential address to the Royal Economic Society nearly 30 years ago (Robbins, 1955). Robbins voiced concern over two issues. First, he expressed a personal opinion that economics was not a suitable subject for study at school; he felt that the type of economics that could be taught to young students was a simplified distortion of the subject. Second, he felt that, even if economics were a suitable subject for school study, there was a high opportunity cost to students taking it. In particular, he felt that, while universities coped well with students who had never studied economics prior to university they could not cope with students who were deficient in basics such as the English language; the comparative advantage of schools lay in teaching basic skills.

Whatever the truth of Robbins's statements, economics has grown to be one of the most popular subjects taught at A level, and by the late 1970s ranked third among males and tenth among females in number of A level presentations; it is now firmly established as a major school subject. However, the current state of knowledge on the contribution of A-level economics to performance in university economics courses is 'thin' at best, though it is an area where many academics hold strong personal opinions based on casual empiricism (Wall, 1982). Some single-institution studies on the impact of A-level economics on university performance exist (Harbury and Szretern, 1968; Button and Fleming, 1982); the only large-scale studies that address these issues use scores on multiple-choice examination questions as a measuring rod of economics comprehension (Attiyeh and Lumsden, 1971; Lumsden, Attiyeh and Scott, 1980). This study attempts to overcome some of the shortcomings of past research.

Does the Form of the Examination Matter?

Many institutions have experimented with different forms of examination during the past two decades. The A-level boards have introduced multiple-choice questions, data response questions and interpretations, while many universities have introduced multiple-choice questions to complement the standard 'five essays out of twelve' approach. There is no agreement as to whether these developments have led to increased efficiency in the ranking of students because there is little hard evidence on the relationship between different types of examination. The benefits and costs of different methods of assessment to the institution are fairly obvious; good multiple-choice questions are difficult and expensive to produce but are cheap to grade and are free of problems of marker comparability; essay-type questions are cheap to produce but expensive to grade, and the problem of marker bias is expensive to eradicate.

This paper presents evidence on the statistical relationship between different forms of examination and their impact on the rank ordering of students.

Can Student Motivation be Measured?

A major drawback of much past research has been the implicit assumption that students wish to maximize their performance in the subject. However, since beginning economics is studied by a substantial student body whose objective is to maximize the probability of passing the course, the notion that 'more efficient' teaching methods will be associated with higher levels of performance is clearly suspect. The student whose objective is to pass the course will use a more efficient teaching method to economize on his time and effort rather than to increase his examination mark. Similarly, the 'better' student may not always perform better because examination marks are not the appropriate argument in his welfare function. This paper reports on student opinions of what their objectives are in the course.

Disaggregated Research

Most research in this field has been based on the experiences of single institutions. The advantage of single-institution studies is that much more information on the students can be collected; the disadvantage is that the results may not have general applicability. This paper presents both aggregated and disaggregated results, and these suggest that the results obtained from single-institution studies must be treated with considerable caution.

8.2 THE DATA SOURCE

During the academic year 1979/80 over 2,500 students studying first-year economics in ten universities, six polytechnics and one business school participated in a research project, the aim of which was to attempt to assess the efficacy of innovative teaching techniques in basic economics. A necessary condition for taking part in the project was that participating institutions had to agree to set a common examination, or part thereof, as their degree examination. The common three-hour final examination, which yielded several measures of output, consisted of twenty multiple-choice questions (ten micro and ten macro) to measure knowledge of concepts and simple to intermediate applications, one problem or case to measure complex applications and analysis, and one micro essay and one macro essay to measure synthesis and evaluation.

The form and content of the final examination were determined by a committee including representatives of each participating institution. To avoid any misunderstanding concerning examination content, detailed sets of course notes were provided to participating institutions. These notes, which reflected an advisory board consensus on which fundamental concepts should be included in any course purporting to teach basic economics, served as the basis of all the examination questions. A major innovatory feature of the common final, designed to produce a consistent measure of output, was the lack of choice of questions. Some institutions agreed to set the complete common final, others to include part of it as an obligatory section of their own final. Those institutions that could not agree to the obligatory nature of the common final were excluded from the analysis.

Table 8.1 *Number of Students Sitting Different Parts of the Common Final*

Output measure	No. of students
Micro essay	1,935
Multiple-choice	1,740
Case	1,254
Macro essay	1,629
Multiple-choice	1,483

Table 8.1 sets out the number of students who sat each part of the common final under examination conditions. A total of 1,032 students sat all parts of both micro and macro, i.e. the complete common final.

In addition to setting the common final examination, the participating institutions collected data from students on their personal characteristics, including their A-level performances, and their opinions of the course and teacher; the latter has been analysed to provide information on effective teaching (Lumsden and Scott, 1984).

Agreement to set the common final was a necessary but not sufficient condition for generating a usable set of marks. Clearly, the multiple-choice test scores introduced no marker bias; to ensure that marker and institutional biases did not occur in the case and essay marks, all papers were collected and regraded by a single experienced academic; the marks that he produced were used in the analysis without any alteration. Table 8.2 shows the degree of consistency between the marks of the regrader and the originals as revealed by the 28 correlation coefficients.

Table 8.2 *Correlation Coefficients between Regrades and Original Marks*[*]

Range of correlation coefficients	No. of correlations
0.40–0.59	9
0.60–0.69	12
0.70 and greater	7

[*] All correlation coefficients were significant at the 99% level.

The consistency of the regrader also came in for scrutiny. A random sample of 180 scripts was drawn and regraded; the correlations between these and the subsequent regrades were: case 0.94; micro essay, 0.77; macro essay, 0.84. In addition, there was no difference between the means of the regrades and the subsequent sample, and no evidence that there had been a significant change in standards during the protracted period of regrading.

The use of the common final overcomes many of the limitations of past studies. First, the measuring rods of economics comprehension are of three different types; second, they were administered under examination conditions; third, student numbers in the study were sufficient to include many variables in regression analysis without encountering degrees of freedom constraints; fourth, the results are not subject to the possible biases arising from using only a single institution.

8.3 THE EMPIRICAL FINDINGS

Selection of University Candidates

The mean scores (and standard deviations) on the different measures of output of students with and without A-level economics are reported in

Table 8.3 *First-year Performance of Students with and without A-level Economics*

Output measure	With A-level economics Mean	N	Without A-level economics Mean	N	t
Micro-essay	48.7 (16.2)	670	44.3 (18.3)	992	5.1[*]
Multiple-choice	7.2 (1.6)	571	7.0 (1.6)	855	1.9
Case	30.8 (27.1)	487	33.9 (26.2)	666	−1.9
Macro-essay	46.4 (17.1)	508	41.1 (20.1)	862	5.2[*]
Multiple-choice	6.0 (1.7)	451	5.6 (1.9)	789	3.8[*]
Total multiple-choice	13.0 (2.8)	451	12.6 (3.1)	789	2.3[*]

[*] Significant difference at the 95% level.

table 8.3. The scores of the two groups on the 20 multiple-choice questions corroborate previous findings; students with A-level economics perform statistically significantly better than those without. The difference is concentrated mainly in the macro section of the test, the difference on the micro part not quite meeting the 95 per cent criterion using the t-test. This finding parallels the results of an earlier study (Attiyeh and Lumsden, 1971) in which students with A-level economics starting first-year university economics courses scored higher in multiple-choice tests than those without; the superiority of scores was also significantly greater in macroeconomics.

The difference between the two groups on case marks is not statistically significant. The distribution of the case marks is bimodal because a considerable proportion of all students did not grasp the main point of the case and many were awarded scores close to zero. This is reflected in the very high standard deviation in relation to the mean. Given such a distribution, this element of the final examination is excluded from further analysis.

Differences in the essay marks are striking. Students with A-level economics do substantially better in both micro and macro essays at 10 and 13 per cent respectively. The fact that the effect is not confined to multiple-choice questions is a new finding.[2]

Mathematics is often regarded as a complementary subject to economics, and a few departments give an important weight to A-level mathematics when selecting entrants. The impact of adding the criterion

Table 8.4 *First-year Performance of Students with and without A-level Economics and Mathematics*

Output measure	With both A-level economics and maths Mean	N	With neither A-level economics not maths Mean	N	t
Micro-essay	47.8 (16.3)	316	44.7 (18.6)	385	2.3*
Multiple-choice	7.3 (1.6)	291	6.6 (1.6)	292	5.3*
Macro-essay	45.5 (17.0)	242	41.8 (20.0)	309	3.7*
Multiple-choice	6.2 (1.8)	218	5.2 (1.9)	278	6.0*
Total multiple-choice	13.4 (3.0)	218	11.7 (3.0)	278	6.3*

* Significant difference at the 95% level.

of A-level mathematics to that of A-level economics is shown in table 8.4. The differences between the two groups on both parts of the multiple-choice test are much larger than those found in table 8.3. The scores on all 20 multiple-choice questions corroborate earlier findings (Lumsden, Attiyeh and Scott, 1980) that the gap between those with A-level economics and mathematics and those with neither is much greater than the gap between those with A-level economics only and those without A-level economics; the difference is 15 per cent compared with 3 per cent for students with only A-level economics. The coincidence of A-level economics and mathematics identifies a group with a considerable advantage in multiple-choice tests in economics.

However, the essay results reveal the opposite. The difference between the two groups is reduced in relative terms (although still significant at the 95 per cent level). On the micro essay, the difference between those with and those without A-level economics was 10 per cent; adding the criterion of A-level mathematics reduced this to 7 per cent. On the macro essay the difference for the former group was 13 per cent, and this was reduced to 9 per cent. This suggests that any learning spillover or filtering effects associated with the combination of economics and mathematics are confined to the multiple-choice part of the examination.

Those who are convinced that good mathematicians also make good economists may find food for thought in this result. At first-year level good mathematicians do not appear to make good literate economists, a conclusion probably reached already by many non-mathematical economists.

The differences between the means of the various groups of students with and without A-level economics and mathematics are indicative of causal relationships. However, other student characteristics may influence performance; for example, there may be systematic differences in the amount of study time devoted to the course by different groups of students. Using each measure of comprehension in turn as the dependent variable, multiple regressions were carried out in which the explanatory variables related to student charateristics (sex, age, number of A levels, native English speaker, general aptitude), student input (amount of time spent in class, amount of time spent studying), whether an economics major, objective in the course (maximizing mark or just pass), opinion of teacher, whether the student had A-level economics, A-level mathematics or both. The multiple regressions are reported in table 8.5 along with the means of each variable.

The *F*-statistics indicated that the group of variables used in each regression was significant at the 99 per cent level. Although the coefficients of some variables were large in relation to the mean of the dependent variable, the R^2 values were low, as is common in educational cross-section regressions.

Table 8.5 *Multiple Regression Results: Examination Performance as a Function of Student and Course Characterstics*

	(1) Mean	(2) Micro essay	(3) Macro essay	(4) Micro mult.ch.	(5) Macro mult.ch.	(6) Total mult.ch.
Student Characteristics						
Sex (Male = 1)	0.66	− 3.00	− 2.82	0.20	0.25	0.52
		3.3	2.6	2.3	2.2	3.0
Age	20.6	0.14	0.10	0.01	0.03	0.04
		1.1	0.7	0.9	1.8	1.7
No. A levels	2.93	1.28	− 0.95	0.11	0.17	**0.35**
		1.6	1.0	1.4	1.5	2.0
Mean A-level grade	2.81	1.23	**1.86**	**0.22**	**0.30**	**0.51**
(E = 1, ..., A = 5)		1.9	2.2	3.4	3.2	3.4
Scottish Examination Board	0.43	− **12.64**	− **17.60**	− 0.37	− 0.16	− 0.37
		2.7	3.3	0.9	0.3	0.4
No. of Highers	5.04	**1.68**	**2.05**	**0.14**	**0.20**	**0.36**
		2.8	3.1	2.5	3.0	3.5
Mean Higher grade	3.69	**2.65**	**3.01**	**0.24**	**0.25**	**0.48**
		3.8	4.0	3.7	3.3	4.1
Non-English speaker	0.04	1.48	− 5.13	− **0.48**	− 0.53	− **1.01**
		0.6	1.9	2.2	1.8	2.2
AH5 score	34.02	0.08	− 0.16	**0.03**	0.60	**0.06**
		0.8	1.2	3.2	1.3	2.9

cont.

Table 8.5 cont.

Study habits

% lectures attended	92.64	**0.14**	**0.20**	0.00	0.01	**0.02**
		3.1	3.2	0.1	1.7	2.3
% tutorials attended	87.35	0.00	0.01	0.00	0.00	0.00
		0.00	0.4	0.9	0.5	0.00
No. hours studying	4.70	− 0.29	− 0.51	− 0.02	− 0.06	− 0.10
		1.4	1.6	1.0	1.8	1.9
More time on economics than other subjects (yes = 1)	0.38	**3.14**	1.98	0.02	− 0.01	0.07
		2.8	1.2	0.2	0.0	0.3
Economics major	0.41	− 1.72	0.02	0.09	− 0.07	− 0.17
		1.8	0.0	0.9	0.6	0.9
Course goal (just pass = 1, ..., maximize mark = 5)	3.82	**1.72**	**2.67**	0.09	**0.17**	0.22
		3.2	3.7	1.8	2.3	1.8

Opinion of teacher

Opinion of lecturer	3.54	0.69	1.37	0.00	0.09	0.15
		1.1	1.6	0.00	1.0	1.0
Opinion of tutor	3.51	0.89	− 0.76	− 0.04	0.09	0.03
		1.6	0.9	0.8	1.0	0.3

A-level economics and mathematics

A-level or Higher economics	0.40	**5.02**	**5.58**	0.23	**0.63**	**0.92**
		3.9	3.5	1.8	3.8	3.5
A-level or Higher mathematics	0.55	− 0.59	− 1.47	**0.35**	0.29	**0.61**
		0.5	1.0	2.8	1.8	2.4
Economics + mathematics	0.19	− 1.89	− 1.37	− 0.27	− 0.39	**− 0.86**
		1.1	0.6	1.6	1.8	2.5
Other economics courses	0.05	**5.82**	3.78	**0.48**	**0.56**	**1.17**
		3.0	1.7	2.6	2.3	3.0
R^2		0.08	0.10	0.09	0.10	0.13
F		4.7	4.8	5.1	4.4	4.4
N		1662	1370	1482	1240	1240
Mean of dependent variable		46.08	43.03	6.99	5.80	12.75

Notes

1 The means in column (1) describing the student characteristics relate to the largest sample, i.e. students doing the micro essay. The means for the other sample are similar because most students are common to all samples.

2 The t statistics appear under the regression coefficients.

3 The coefficients that appear in bold type are statistically significant at the 95% level. (For t values greater than 1.65 the coefficients are significant at the 90% level.)

A-level Economics and Mathematics

Of the sample, 40 per cent had taken A-level economics, 55 per cent A-level mathematics; just less than half of the A-level economics students also had A-level mathematics, i.e. 19 per cent of the total sample. Some 5 per cent had taken an economics course other than A-level or Higher; this included a wide range of courses in further education.

The impact of having taken A-level economics is significant and large in absolute terms for all measures of economics comprehension except micro multiple-choice, which is significant at the 90 per cent level and is consistent in sign. It adds 5.02 points to the micro essay, 5.58 to the macro essay, 0.63 to the macro multiple-choice and 0.92 to the total multiple-choice. The coefficients range from 7 to 13 per cent of the means of the dependent variables. This is fairly conclusive evidence that students with A-level economics perform better at the end of the first year on most measures of economics comprehension.

The coefficient of having taken A-level mathematics is positive and significant for micro and total multiple-choice; the macro multiple-choice coefficient is significant at the 90 per cent level and is of similar magnitude. Since the regression has already taken into account several measures of student ability, in the form of number of A levels, mean A-level grade and AH5 score,[3] the general ability dimension of having A-level mathematics is partly captured already. It is possible that micro multiple-choice is the part of the examination that comes closest to mathematical type problems.[4]

A-level Qualifications

While no distinction is made between the English A-level examination boards, a distinction is made between students with A levels and those with Highers awarded by the Scottish Examination Board (SEB); this is because there are major differences in the two types of qualification. Students typically take Highers a year earlier than A level in a larger number of subjects, and the grading is on a scale A–C, compared with A–E for the A-level boards. The mean of the SEB variable indicated that 43 per cent of the sample had Highers. The average A-level student had three passes, and the average Higher student had five passes. The mean grade on A level was just below C, and the mean grade on Highers was just below B.

The number of A levels is significantly related to total multiple-choice score only, and the *t* statistics suggest a weak relationship with the other measures of output. There is a lack of variability in the number of A levels because the vast majority of non-SEB students in the sample had three A levels. The substitution of a dummy variable to capture the effect of having less than three A levels was not statistically significant. The mean A-level grade is positively related to all measures of economics comprehension except the micro essay, though the latter coefficient is similar in magnitude and is significant at the 90 per cent level.

The negative coefficients associated with SEB Highers students is due partly to the difference in the mean number of Highers taken and the higher mean grade arising from the restricted scale. The fact that the number of Highers taken is significantly related to all measures of output is probably due to the higher variability in number of Highers taken. As with A levels, the mean Higher grade is significantly related to output.

The regression coefficients indicate the trade-off between type of A level and overall grade; table 8.6 shows the effect on student performance for a department that increased the average A-level grade of its intake by an average of one grade compared with one that maintained existing grade standards but opted for candidates with A-level economics, *ceteris paribus*. These results suggest that, as far as

Table 8.6 *The Effect of Grade Level versus A-level Economics*

| | Increase in performance owing to: | |
| | Additional average of one grade (%) | A-level economics (%) |
Output measure		
Micro essay	1.23	5.02
Macro essay	1.86	5.58
Micro multiple-choice	0.22	0.23
Macro multiple-choice	0.30	0.63
Total multiple-choice	0.51	0.92

first-year final examination marks are concerned, there is a considerable trade-off between average A-level grade and having A-level economics. For example, the C average student with A-level economics will perform about the same in a multiple-choice examination as the average student without A-level economics (i.e. 0.92 compared with 2×0.51). For the macro essay the results equate a D average student (unlikely to be at university) with A-level economics to an A average student without economics (i.e. 5.02 compared with 4×1.23). These results, of course, do not imply anything about performance in subsequent years; there is some evidence (Lumsden, Attiyeh and Scott, 1980) that the multiple-choice advantage of first-year students with A-level economics persists in later years.

Does the Form of the Examination Matter?

The weight of academic opinion in economics is that there is a considerable overlap between essays and multiple-choice questions.

A good multiple-choice test in economics can measure a substantial part of student attainment but not all of it. In this respect, economics is somewhere between mathematics and history. The scores on good multiple-choice tests in mathematics correlate so closely with grades on other forms of examination that for all practical purposes the correlation can be regarded as 1.0. In economics, the correlation can be expected to range between 0.60 and 0.75. (Fels, 1970)

While Fels provided no empirical backing for his assertion, he is certainly not alone in his belief. In September 1981 the common final examination was studied by the 100 participants in a conference on new methods of teaching economics; they comprised 30 economists from universities and polytechnics, together with senior educators in other disciplines. The participants were allocated to 20 'teams', each of which had at least one economist member, and were asked to estimate the correlations between the different parts of the examination. The means

Table 8.7 *Estimated Correlations between Different Types of Examinations: the Views of 100 Educators*

| | Micro | | Macro | |
	Case	Essay	Mult.ch.	Essay
Micro				
Multiple-choice	0.60	0.55	0.75	0.49
Case		0.61	0.53	0.55
Essay			0.47	0.74
Macro				
Multiple-choice				0.57

of the estimated correlations of the 20 groups are shown in table 8.7. The means conceal a wide range of estimates from 0.2 to 0.83. On average, the educators fall just below Fels's lower estimate of 0.60, with 50 per cent of the groups coming within his 'expected range'. One characteristic of these estimates is the expectation of a higher correlation between multiple-choice test in micro and macro, and essays in micro and macro, than between different tests within the same subject area. The educators considered that there was a bigger overlap between test skill than subject skill.

The actual correlations between the different measures of output are shown in table 8.8. All of the actual correlations are lower than the estimates of the educators. Given the size of the sample and the fact that the measures were obtained under test conditions, there appears to be very little overlap between some of the methods of testing economics comprehension. The highest correlations are between similar methods of testing rather than between different methods of testing the same subject: the correlation between the micro and macro multiple-choice test is 0.43 and between the micro and macro essay marks is 0.54, both

Table 8.8 *Correlations between the Different Types of Examination*[*]

| | Micro | | Macro | |
	Case	Essay	Mult.ch.	Essay
Micro				
Multiple-choice	0.11	0.18	0.43	0.18
	1254	1332	1483	1483
Case		0.23	0.10	0.14
		881	1254	1032
Essay			0.19	0.54
			1211	1211
Macro				
Multiple-choice				0.26
				1483

* All correlations are significant at the 99% level.

of which are much higher than any of the other correlations.

Given that the correlations between the different forms of examination are relatively low, the regression results in table 8.5 throw light on whether the form of the examination affects students with particular characteristics.

Male and Female Performance

It has now become part of the conventional wisdom of research in economics education that females perform less well than males in examinations in beginning courses. This conventional wisdom has an empirical base drawn from different countries over the past 20 years. While the empiricism is robust, the foundation of the current paradigm is suspect. All the research results supporting female inferiority are based on multiple-choice tests. Three factors led to those tests being accepted as valid almost without question:

1 the high standing within the profession of economists involved in their construction;
2 the large samples of students tested to generate norming data;
3 the assumption of high correlations between multiple-choice tests and essay examination marks.

The finding of female inferiority spawned a series of inductive papers justifying the results on an *ad hoc* basis. The conflicting psychological literature, which argues that people who mature earlier have higher verbal learning rates, thus suggesting that females (who mature earlier than males) should perform better on essay examinations than males, was ignored or left as a puzzle.

> The puzzle surrounding the argument, however, is that most studies of achievement in introductory economics find that verbal Scholastic Aptitude Test (SAT) rather than quantitative SAT is more important in explaining success (Siegfreid, 1979)

According to the hypothesis, females should perform better in essay questions (verbal skills) than males and no worse on multiple-choice questions. On the multiple-choice tests, the results substantiate previous findings that females do significantly worse on multiple-choice questions in economics. However, the finding is reversed for essays and supports the psychological literature: males scored 3.00 less on the micro essay and 2.82 less on the macro essay. This is the first result that shows that females perform significantly better than males on economics examinations. The implications of this finding are that, for an examination to be free of sex bias, it should consist of approximately 50 per cent multiple-choice questions and 50 per cent essays.[5]

Non-native English Speakers

The 4 per cent of students who were non-native English speakers scored less well in multiple-choice questions and the macro essay; the coefficients are relatively large and reflect substantial differences in performance. The former result may reflect language difficulties also experienced and reported by UK school pupils in multiple-choice questions. The desire on the part of examiners for brevity in multiple-choice questions produces questions where a lack of understanding of a key word reduces a student to guessing the meaning of the question. The poor performance by non-English speakers in the macro essay, while not quite significant at the 95 per cent level, may reflect less familiarity with UK economic policies and institutions either studied in school or learned about in newspapers and magazines.

This finding demonstrates another instance where the form of the examination could place a particular group of students at a relative disadvantage.

Can Student Motivation be Measured?

Study Goal An implicit assumption made in much educational research is that students attempt to maximize their performance on examinations. However, it is possible that many students wish only to pass the course but not to maximize their mark since it is not their speciality subject. Students were asked the following question:

	Just pass				Maximize score
In the course, my study goal is to:	1	2	3	4	5

The mean of 3.82 indicates that, on average, students study for more than a bare pass; only 6 per cent of students chose the 'just pass' response; on the other hand, only 27 per cent responded that they were attempting to maximize their scores. Economics majors did not express a stronger desire to maximize their marks on the economics exam than non-majors; the means of the objectives of economics and non-economics majors were not statistically significantly different.

The coefficient of this variable is significant for both essays and the macro multiple-choice; the micro and total multiple-choice are significant at the 90 per cent level and are consistent in sign with the other coefficients. The magnitude of the coefficients suggests that course goal has a substantial impact on exam performance. The 'mark maximizer' (who responded 5) would score 17.56 ($4 \times (1.72 + 2.67)$) more marks on the two essays than the 'pass maximizer' (who responded 1); this amounts to 19 per cent of the sum of the means of the two essay marks. On the multiple choice the 'mark maximizer' would score 0.88 (4×0.22) more than the 'pass maximizer', i.e. 7 per cent of the multiple choice mean. The omission of student goal from past research undoubtedly contributed to the 'no significant difference' findings which permeate the literature.[6]

Economics Majors   This variable, which took a value of 1 if the student was majoring in economics (including joint honours degree programmes) and 0 if majoring in another subject, had a mean of 0.41, indicating that 41 per cent of the sample were economics majors. On all measures of output the non-significant coefficients indicate that the fact of being an economics major, having controlled for other student characteristics, conferred neither an advantage nor a disadvantage in examination performance.

Student Study Habits   Four variables yield information on reported student study habits, Students were asked for the percentage of lectures and tutorials that they had attended, the average number of hours spent studying each week, and whether this was the same, greater than or less than the time spent studying for other subjects. The sample attended 93 per cent of lectures, 87 per cent of tutorials, and studied 4.7 hours per week outside class; 38 per cent reported that, compared with other subjects being taken, they spent above-average time on economics.

The results suggest a fairly consistent relationship between student course inputs and performance. Attendance at lectures was positively and significantly related to both micro and macro essay and total multiple-choice scores. However, tutorial attendance was not related to any measure of output. The latter result has important resource allocation implications, since most beginning courses run large numbers of small tutorials which consume a significant proportion of departmental resources. In an attempt to estimate the marginal product of tutorials, two specifications of the input variable were used: total number of tutorials in the course, and tutorial hours offered per student. Neither specification generated a significant and positive regression coefficient, suggesting that there is no learning payoff to tutorials. In this reported regression, even the motivational aspects of tutorial attendance fail to produce a positive association with performance on any measure.

The interpretation of the results on study time is not obvious. While the coefficients for the number of hours spent studying are not significant at the 95 per cent level, three of them are significant at the 90 per cent level and all of them are negative. However, for the micro essay, the coefficient of the dummy variable indicating that more time was spent studying economics than other subjects was significant and positive. It is possible that the results reflect the difference between absolute and relative inputs: the less able students study more, but, given this, the higher their input to economics the better they perform; this can only be a tentative conclusion since the coefficients for relative time spent are not significant in four cases.

Student Opinion of Lecturer and Tutor   Students were asked to provide their opinion of their lecturer and tutor on a scale of 1 (poor) to 5 (excellent). The mean opinion of 3.5 in both cases indicated that on the whole students considered their teachers to be slightly better than average (denoted by a score of 3, the midpoint on the scale). There was no statistical relationship between students' opinions of lecturers or tutors and performance on any measure of output.

Disaggregated Research

Since many published results in economics education are based on single-institution studies with limited output measures as the dependent variable, it is of considerable interest to find out where the results that emerge from the sample as a whole vary from the single-institution results found by disaggregating the sample. Choosing one student characteristic – A-level economics versus no A-level economics – and the 11 largest institutions in terms of student numbers, the *t*-test was used to calculate the difference in mean performance between students with and students without A-level economics on the various measures of economics comprehension. The results are shown in table 8.9.

No clear pattern by institution emerged, the significant differences

Table 8.9 *Differences between Students with and without A-level Economics*

Inst. No.	N	Micro essay	Macro essay	Micro mult.ch.	Macro mult.ch.	Total mult.ch.
1	374	X				
2	220	X			X	
3	76	X			X	X
4	79					
5	67			X		
6	98			X	X	X
7	184	X	X		X	
8	180		*	*	*	*
9	63					
10	112	X	*		*	*
11	209	X	X			X

X   The difference between the means statistically significant at the 95% level.
*   This part of the common final not set.

being scattered in a seemingly random pattern between micro and macro and between multiple-choice and essay. In no institution were students with A-level economics superior on all measures of output; in two institutions for which all measures were available there was no difference between the two groups. These results suggest that there are strong institution-specific influences at work which can obscure the underlying relationship and further indicate the dangers inherent in generalizing results from single-institution studies using one measure of economics comprehension.

8.4 CONCLUSIONS

There seems little doubt that students who have taken economics as a school subject have an advantage, *ceteris paribus*, in examinations at the end of first-year economics courses in universities. Since other research, albeit based only on multiple-choice tests, suggests this advantage is maintained in subsequent years, a case can be made for conveying this information to pupil counsellors in schools.

The form of the final examination can introduce a significant bias into student rank ordering by sex; given the typical clustering of students around the 50 per cent correct mark, this implies that a pass or fail for many students can be affected by the type of examination set. For those universities currently using multiple-choice questions, the elimination of sex bias in examinations will be costless and will consist merely of altering the mix of the examination.

The allocation of teaching resources is more of an historical accident than the product of research into teaching efficiency. Since results suggest that the marginal product of beginning economics tutorials is zero, departments should not be afraid to adopt innovative technologies. Altering the labour–capital input mix is unlikely to affect student performance adversely. Scrapping tutorials, however, is likely to meet with considerable faculty resistance because of the vested interests of tutors. Tutorial-taking is typically a more pleasant way to fulfil contact hour requirements than preparing and giving a new course.

Finally, the results cast serious doubts on much past research in the field; many important variables have been ignored, samples have been biased, and the findings of many studies are institution-specific.

NOTES

1 The term 'A level' includes the Scottish Examination Board Higher Grade unless otherwise stated.
2 The results are not disaggregated by either A-level board or by grade of pass because, despite the size of the sample, disaggregation to grade by board produced insufficient data in many cells to perform meaningful statistical analysis.
3 General Aptitude and Student Age: the AH5 (Heim, 1968) is a measure of overall ability which is intended to discriminate among individuals in groups of known high intelligence, such as university students. The AH5 test comprises 72 questions of which 14 are numerical, 22 are concerned with word association and 36 with visual logic. It is not possible to identify common features in the AH5 and the multiple-choice test questions; none of the micro multiple-test questions require the manipulation of numbers, and only one of the macro multiple-choice requires the ability to add and subtract. Since other measures of student ability, i.e. number of A levels and A-level grade, are included in the analysis, it is an empirical issue whether AH5 picks up an ability level over and above that captured by those other measures. In the event, the AH5 coefficient was positive and significant only for micro and total multiple-choice scores; the effect is relatively small: an extra 10 points on the AH5 (29 per cent of the mean) is associated with an extra 0.3 of a point on the micro multiple-choice (4 per cent of the mean). The coefficient of the age variable was not significantly different from zero for any of the output measures. Thus, any advantage that a student may enjoy by being older disappears by the end of the first year. The lack of a statistically significant finding here may be due partly to the lack of variability in the age of students, as 90 per cent were aged between 18 and 23.
4 An interaction variable was included in the regression to control for the fact of having done both A-level economics and A-level mathematics. A positive and significant coefficient here would suggest that the effect of the two qualifications combined is greater than the sum of their individual effects. The coefficient is significant at the 95 per cent level for total multiple-choice score and at the 90 per cent level for macro multiple-choice; the fact that the coefficient is negative suggests that the joint effect of having A-level

economics and mathematics is not additive; i.e., the student with both does not score an additional $0.92 + 0.61 = 1.53$ points on total multiple choice compared with the student with neither. To use the interaction coefficient it is necessary to take into account that students with A-level mathematics score significantly more on the AH5, have significantly more A-levels and significantly higher A-level grade than those without A-level mathematics. The effect of having A-level economics and mathematics compared with having A-level economics only, taking the adjustments into account is as follows.

	A-level maths coefficient		Higher AH5, more and better A levels		Interaction coefficient		Net effect
A-level	0.61	+	0.53	−	0.86	=	0.28
Higher	0.61	+	0.79	−	0.86	=	0.54

The net effect of adding A-level mathematics to A-level economics is less than the sum of the individual regression coefficients. For A-level students the group with A-level economics and mathematics scored 0.28 more than the group with A-level economics only, compared with 0.61 points more had the effects been additive; for students with SEB Higher, the additional effect of mathematics is greater at 0.54 points.

5   Multiple-choice questions are of course not heterogeneous; neither are essays. In this particular examination the multiple-choice questions were relatively complex and the essays very broad. Whether the recommended proportions would hold for simple multiple-choice questions and narrow essay topics is an empirical issue.

6   Another potentially important variable is student attitude to risk; i.e., given their study habits, do students consider themselves to be risk-avoiders or risk-takers? Information was collected on this variable, but is not included in the regression because it is highly correlated with course goal; students who were mark maximizers also tended to be risk-averse.

9

The Efficacy of Macroeconomic Policy

MAURICE PESTON

9.1 INTRODUCTION

This paper is concerned with the two traditional questions of macroeconomic policy: (1) What is it that makes policy necessary? (2) What is it that makes policy desirable? The answers to be given to the questions are also traditional. The need within the mixed economy arises from market failure. Effectiveness depends on a capacity on the part of the authorities to supplement or enhance market forces. If there is no market failure, policy is obviously irrelevant. It is not surprising that economic theories predicated on the non-existence of market failure find no room for policy (see Peston, 1980, p. 77). What is much more interesting is the sort of theory in which market failure occurs but policy turns out to be ineffective, or effective only to some small degree.

If we ask ourselves how, in particular, policy used to be approached in macroeconomics, we can offer two sorts of answer. One is based on the notion of chronic demand deficiency. The private sector had a chronic tendency not to wish to buy full-employment output. It was the task of public expenditure (or tax cuts, if taxes were positive) to fill the gap. A second answer was to do with fluctuations in private expenditure. Sometimes demand would be too low, and on other occasions too high. In the former case public expenditure could be raised or taxes cut; in the latter, the settings of the instruments would be reversed. In general, both sets of ideas were brought to bear. Private demand fluctuated and was chronically deficient. Public expenditure could offset the fluctuations and fill the gap, or taxes could be manipulated to do the job.

There are three additional points to bear in mind by way of introduction. First, there was some discussion over the relative efficacy of fiscal and monetary policy. Second, pretty well the whole of the analysis of this subject, following the appearance of Keynes's General

Theory, concentrated on remedying problems to do with aggregate demand. Third, it was assumed that economic experience could be divided into two basic states: unemployment and inflation, or deficient demand and excess demand.

On this latter point, even with the recognition of the Phillips curve and the apparent need to choose between combinations of unemployment and inflation, the decision problem was not felt to be of overwhelming difficulty. A choice would have to be made, but the feasible set included pairs of inflation rates and unemployment levels which were all tolerably acceptable. We had not yet arrived at the issue of stagflation, i.e. where the feasible inflation rates and unemployment levels are singly or jointly extremely unattractive.

I have remarked that at a more fundamental level it was understood that the need for policy arose from market failure in one sense or other. Sticky prices, wages or the rate of interest gave rise to difficulties. While ultimately the Pigou or real-balance effect might guarantee the purchase of full-employment output, that was seen as a logical point, rather than one of any great practical significance, not least by Pigou himself (Pigou, 1943).

Excess saving at full employment could be interpreted as indicative of a future demand for consumer goods, warranting high investment now. The difficulty lay in translating such future demands into present commitments, i.e. another case of market failure. Once again, however, it must be said that suggestions such as this were more in the way of being intellectual jokes than serious empirical propositions.

What was appreciated early on (i.e. some 25 years ago) was that it was distinctly possible for fiscal policy to make things worse. In separate articles, and using quite different methods, both Friedman and Phillips made the point that fiscal policy could be destabilizing. Friedman's article was statistical in nature (Friedman, 1953), emphasizing the correlation between the instrument and the final target. Phillips was more formal mathematically, laying great stress on time lags. The two together may now be seen as giving rise to the key issues of 'signal extraction' and 'speed of response'. In a noisy world, in which governments are slow to size up the situation and slow to act effectively, it would be better to do nothing. (We return to these points below.)

9.2 A SIMPLE MACROECONOMIC MODEL

In order to discuss these matters it is useful to consider the following generalized model.

Aggregate demand curve: $Y_D = F(P, G, M, A)$ (1)

where Y_D is aggregate demand

P is the price level

G is an indicator of fiscal policy

M is an indicator of monetary policy

A is an exogenous shock.

We assume that G and M are independent of each other.

$F_P < 0$

$F_G, F_M, F_A > 0.$

Aggregate supply curve: $Y_S = H(P, W, T, B)$ (2)

where Y_S is aggregate supply

W is the wage level

T is an indicator of fiscal structure in so far as it influences aggregate supply[1]

B is an exogenous shock.

$Y_P, Y_T, Y_B > 0$

$Y_W < 0.$

(We shall treat both functions as linear approximations over some relevant range.)

We define full employment or maximum capacity output as Y^*. We do not assume that this is necessarily the output that would be produced by that level of employment corresponding to labour market equilibrium.[2] We also do not assume that labour market equilibrium necessarily occurs where the demand for labour as a function of the real wage paid by employers equals the supply of labour as a function of the real wage received by employees.[3]

If we take G, M, T, R and W as given, aggregate demand equals aggregate supply at some appropriate price level. This will give short-run equilibrium output Y. If goods and money markets are always in equilibrium, output will fluctuate around a mean level determined by $E(A)$ and $E(B)$. Its variance will depend on σ_A^2 and σ_B^2 (assuming cov AB is zero). This mean and variance will also, of course, depend on the values of the other variables and the coefficients, F_i and H_i.

An alternative general formulation is in terms of the rates of change of the variables and the appropriate elasticities:

$$y_D = f_1^- p + f_2^+ g + f_3^+ m + f_4^+ a$$ (3)

$$y_S = h_1^+ p + h_2^- w + h_3^+ t + h_4^+ b$$ (4)

In continuous equilibrium,

$$y = y_D = y_S.$$ (5)

From this we derive

$$y = \frac{h_1(f_2g + f_3m + f_4a) - f_1(h_2w + h_3t + h_4b)}{h_1 - f_1} \tag{6}$$

$$p = \frac{(f_2g + f_3m + f_4a) - (h_2w + h_3t + h_4b)}{h_1 - f_1} \tag{7}$$

$$y + p = \frac{(1 + h_1)(f_2g + f_3m + f_4a) - (1 + f_1)(h_2w + h_3t + h_4b)}{h_1 - f_1} \tag{8}$$

Accepting that inventory variations do allow firms to stabilize output and employment to some degree, let us now examine where, within this elementary analysis, policy enters. The usual answer is twofold:

1 Macroeconomic policy can affect the mean level of output and employment.
2 Macroeconomic policy can affect the variance of output and employment.

The analysis revolves around the following considerations:

– the absolute and relative sizes of the coefficients F_i and H_j;
– the closeness of Y to Y^*;
– the predictability of A and B;
– within a dynamic formulation, the speed of adjustment of G, M, etc.;
– additionally, in the dynamic form we can see directly some further possible meanings to be given to policy ineffectiveness:
  (a) from the supply side, h_1 may be close to zero so that aggregate supply does not respond to price changes;
  (b) from the demand side, $1/f_1$ may be close to zero so that aggregate demand is always dominated by the real balance effect;
  (c) the coefficients f_2, f_3 and h_3 may be close to zero;
  (d) the rate of change of either prices or wages may, themselves, vary to offset policy changes on the demand side.

Demand Management

In this connection it is worth emphasizing that in the standard treatment (certainly in that which was dominant in the literature up to the 1970s, and is still dominant in most textbooks) macroeconomic policy was about shifts in aggregate demand (see, for example Peston, 1982; Peacock and Shaw, 1971). Essentially, it was whether private demand needed to be encouraged by policy measures and supplemented by public demand to buy full-employment output. In addition, it concerned itself with policy offsets to private demand fluctuations; i.e., stability was an important objective.

There is a major point to be made here about alternative formulations of the stabilization problem. One approach sees the economy as fluctuating around a mean position which is one of full employment.[4] (That mean may itself have been influenced by policy.) A second approach sees full employment as a maximum (or virtual maximum); therefore, the mean position of the economy is less than full employment. This implies that the role of policy is to fill the gap between actual output and full employment. It is significantly different from the former because it then follows that, on average, the economy operates at less than full employment.

Let it be said immediately that each view is a possible one to hold. It is merely a matter of making different assumptions about the typical behaviour of firms and households which may be more or less plausible and more or less supported by evidence. In practice, it is not at all easy to see how one might decide between them. What must be said, however, is that policy discussion has moved in the last decade or so from the one to the other. For the most part, up to the 1970s macroeconomic policy was thought to be about maintaining full employment. Mistakes in the excess demand direction would add to inflation; mistakes in the other direction would cause a loss of output. Since then a number of (but not all) economists have defined full employment as a feasible mean path for the economy. They have then tried to analyse policy symmetrically about that mean, especially as far as output is concerned.

We shall return to this theme in due course, but it is worth stating now that the argument that follows tends more to accept the notion of full employment as a maximum. The result of policy error, therefore, will be that on average the economy is at less than full employment. It may then be inferred that the more successful is stabilization policy, the better will be the average performance of the economy. In other words, the mean and variance of the system will not be independent of each other.

Supply-side Considerations

While it would be a mistake to say that macroeconomic policy analysis took no notice of the supply side, it did not see problems of stabilization policy as being dominated by supply-side fluctuations. The aggregate supply curve was thought to give rise to issues of the following sorts.

1 The position of the curve might be unfavourable in the sense that in an open economy the real exchange rate led to a current account deficit. Attempts to deal with this via nominal devaluation could be offset by money wage changes based on a high degree of real-wage resistance.

2 There was a strong tendency for the aggregate supply curve to move

to the left, i.e. for P to rise relative to Y_S. This would be attributable largely to W rising. In a growing economy prices should be considered relative to the degree of capacity utilization; i.e., Y_S/Y^*. There could be independent cost push, together with a Phillips curve effect relating the rate of rise of W to Y_S/Y^*.

3 The full-employment output Y^*, defined as the maximum level of aggregate supply, was thought to be amenable to policy. Included in such policy might be macroeconomic measures to raise public and private sector investment.[5]

It was, perhaps, worth noting that it used to be believed that cost-push pressure to raise money wages would be eased by policies that increased the real rate of growth of the economy. While many of these would be more microeconomic in character, it was felt that the maintenance of a high degree of capacity utilization was itself conducive to fast growth. (There were economists who took the opposite view. They felt that the full employment targets of the 1950s and 1960s were excessive and inimical to growth.)[6]

Although a fluctuating aggregate supply curve was not seen as the cause of trouble, the need for policy was clearly related to the slope and the ease with which the curve itself might be shifted. A fall in aggregate demand would lead to a larger reduction in output and a smaller reduction in prices, the flatter the aggregate supply curve. This is the first condition that gives rise to the need for policy. If now the money wage fell, the aggregate supply curve would shift towards the right, causing output to move back towards full employment. A failure of the money wage to adjust downwards is the second condition giving rise to the need for possible intervention.[7]

Given a contractionary exogenous shock, price and wage sluggishness led to output falling and staying below full employment. A return to full employment would then depend on another expansionary exogenous shock. Alternatively, the offset must be provided by public policy. In other words, policy is needed to offset market failure.

Most economists accepted this formulation. This did not mean that they went on to advocate intervention, and especially not the form of intervention called 'fine-tuning'. Thus, there were always economists who felt that the way to deal with market failure was directly to improve the way goods and labour markets work. In particular, they saw price stickiness as arising from monopoly and oligopoly, and wage stickiness as arising from trade unions. They advocated competition policy to deal with the former, and control (even abolition) to cope with the latter. (This view is associated with, *inter alia*, Hayek, Robbins and Cannan.)

Other economists distinguished major from minor shocks. The latter were soon offset or reversed themselves. Intervention was required only to deal with the former. Above all, a large and persistent business downturn should be met by public works programmes and a lowering of interest rates. This was advocated as a way of dealing with the slump of the early 1930s even before the appearance of Keynes's General Theory. (It was also advocated by many economists who disagreed fundamentally with Keynes, and who thought that in more normal circumstances the free market worked as well as could be expected.)[8]

Where the lines between occasional interventionists, coarse-tuners[9] and fine-tuners should be drawn is hard to see. Suffice it to say that in the heyday of macroeconomic policy there were few economists who were against all active policy and equally few who felt that policy to deal with output and employment should be reviewed every day. (Interest rate and exchange rate policy did require continous revision in the relevant markets.)

9.3 AREAS OF DISAGREEMENT

Economists were, however, divided on other grounds. One obvious area of disagreement was between advocates of fiscal and monetary policy. There were also arguments about the dangers of intervention, between those who stressed the benefits of success and others who emphasized the risks of failure. Finally, there was a great debate on objectives, especially between those who saw an important choice between a higher degree of capacity utilization and a lower rate of inflation.

The first of these now appears rather peculiar. One reason is that there seems to be nothing fundamental about it. It is simply a technical matter (or an 'empirical' matter) whether variations in public expenditure have a more powerful, a more certain and a quicker effect on aggregate demand than do variations in the money supply. Given the appropriate empirical conditions, monetary policy may be the more effective instrument of fine-tuning, or fiscal policy may be, or a combination of the two. The association of fiscalism with interventionism either is trivial or masks something quite different in the policy debate.

A second reason is that it is now recognized clearly (and ought to have been 20 years ago) that fiscal and monetary policy are closely interwoven. The need to finance the public sector borrowing requirement influences the structure of public debt and, therefore, the money supply and the level of interest rates. Interest paid on the debt is public expenditure, and interest net of tax adds to public sector borrowing.

Indeed, the interconnection is so close that it turns out that what some so-called monetarists call monetary policy, the so-called fiscalists call fiscal policy. The obvious example is the 'helicopter money' experiment, which is correctly interpreted as an increase in transfer payments or a reduction in taxation financed by increasing the money supply.

The next area of discussion derives from the important early work of Friedman and Phillips already mentioned. Each of them points out that policy may destabilize even though the objective is to stabilize. The reasons may be that the scale of intervention or its timing is innappropriate. This means that, viewing policy as giving rise to a feedback from past states of the economy to present and future states, a stable system may be changed into an unstable one, or shocks which it is intended to be dampened are amplified. In other words, policy may move the economy further on average from its desired state or increase the variance of the economy around its average state.

Now, what is important to note about this view is that it does not state that policy is ineffective in the sense of having no effect, but rather that its effect is to do harm.[10] (We ought to add that there are those who claim that there are actual incentives to do harm. Thus, it is said that politicians will manipulate the economy for short-run electoral purposes despite the long-run damage that would result. That may well be true, but it should be remarked that this requires that the public either are irrational or are kept deliberately and unnecessarily in ignorance.)

On the general presumption that the risks of intervention are excessive, this is something that the interventionists themselves can recognize. Subject to the political point just made, they are as likely as their critics to recognize circumstances where changing the instruments is too fraught with error. They may be wrong on occasion, but it is not obvious that they will be persistently wrong. The contrary point must also hold; there will be other circumstances in which inaction may be more dangerous than intervention.

The conclusion to be drawn from the Phillps–Friedman caveats is not anti-interventionist: it is rather that crude and badly timed policy can do harm. To keep the instruments fixed is to avoid the risks of destabilization while forgoing the benefits of stabilization. Only if it is believed that stabilization comes from somewhere else does it begin to make sense to keep the instruments fixed. Otherwise circumstances must be analysed and the risks of inactivity compared with the risks of action.

The third area of debate was about objectives. This was so even though, at a superficial level, it appeared that disagreement was about means. In target and instruments terms it must be assumed that policy-makers have insufficient instruments, or that the instruments themselves are imperfect. Again, several interpretations are possible.

Recall that our simple model is a linear approximation. It is likely that, as we deviate too far from the level around which we have approximated, F_i or H_i tend to zero. In essence the true model is nonlinear, and significantly so for large deviations. This means that there are restrictions on the feasible range of Y_D, Y_S and Y (and for that matter P as well). If we add to that even the simplest dynamics, the feasible range of Y_t will depend on how far the policy instruments can be changed from their earlier values, and what the initial values of Y and P were. It is then obvious that a desirable state Y^* may be attainable only some time in the future. Alternatively, the more rapidly we reach it, the less rapidly we may reach a desirable price level, P^* (or rate of change, p), if at all.

Suppose now the coefficients F_i and H_i are themselves not fixed or known for certain, so that risk is muliplicative and not just additive. It is well known that there can never be a sufficiency of instruments in these circumstances. The problem is akin to that of portfolio selection, and for a given mean outcome an additional instrument imperfectly correlated with existing ones can lower the variance of some or all of the targets (see Brainard, 1967; Peston, 1982).

Lastly, the instruments themselves may not be completely under the control of the policy-makers. Experience has shown that even something such as public expenditure in current prices cannot be brought completely under control. Effective tax rates are hard to fix at predetermined levels. It follows that, for these and a wide variety of other reasons, the money supply can also at best be kept within a wide band, which itself seems to have a life of its own. And if nominal magnitudes are hard to control, real ones are even more difficult. More to the point, concentrating on one will leave the other drifting more.

All these limitations on the use of instruments make policy difficult, but not impossible. They do, however, remind us that the problem of choice of ends remains even within an otherwise optimistic policy world. In particular, a policy of full employment (unless that end is defined trivially) may be achieved only if a higher than entirely desirable inflation rate is accepted. Even with several fiscal and monetary instruments available, none of them may be able to uncouple the price level or the inflation rate from the degree of capacity utilization. There is not a shortage of instruments, but a shortage of effective or relevant instruments.

One way of summarizing where we have got to is to state that the theory of macroeconomic policy was based on the key proposition that market failure (and notably the behaviour of the labour market) created the need for intervention. Although policy was fraught with difficulty and likely to be imperfect, it was possible, through intervention, to raise the average degree of utilization of resources and to lower its variance. Weakness of the instruments and their being limited in number meant that this real advance was obtained at a cost in terms of inflation. Furthermore, in an open economy the need to balance the current account (if not to have an average surplus) over the medium or longer term, and the difficulty of achieving a real exchange rate that would allow this to happen, also caused real output to be lower than would otherwise be desirable. Economists differed in their judgement of the scale and frequency of intervention, and on the priority to be given to one end rather than another, but few favoured no intervention and no feedback from current events to policy. Having said that, most economists were optimistic about the position and rate of change of the aggregate supply curve. They did not predict that the effective cost of full employment was very high. Contrariwise, they did not predict that the unemployment cost of anti-inflation policy was high. In the UK the debate was about unemployment in the range 1.5–2.5 per cent of the labour force, and inflation rates of between 1 and 6 per cent.[11]

Before considering how the climate of opinion has changed, there are additional comments to be made. One is that economists were aware that the nature and existence of macroeconomic policy itself could directly affect private sector behaviour. They understood, for example, that (1) if the government announced its intention to maintain full employment and to adjust fiscal and monetary policy to achieve it, and (2) if people believed that intention and its efficacy, either *a priori* or as a result of experience, private expenditure might be higher on average and more stable. In other words, intervention would become less necessary in terms of both frequency of need and scale. They also understood that a policy of maintaining full employment, no matter what, implied that all upward movements in the aggregate supply curve (P being high for all Y/Y^*) as a result (say) of wage-push would be validated by raising the money supply and public expenditure in current prices. Thus, cost-push inflationary pressures might be exacerbated and the inflation rate might get out of control. This could be mitigated by a policy of fixed exchange rates, and by an implied threat not to validate all cost-push. But in both cases the theoretical point holds and was recognized: there could and probably would be a direct, rationalized connection between full-employment policy and the way the private sector behaved. There could even be the paradox that the discovery and announcement of full-employment policy would lead directly to the problem being transformed from one of unemployment into one of inflation. Therefore, most intervention would be to dampen down the system rather than expand it (see Peston, 1980).

A second point is that economists were aware that the evolution of the economy itself would affect behaviour. Households whose behaviour was limited by current income could be freed from that if they accumulated assets, particularly liquid ones. Examples of what could happen were the postwar consumer boom based on unspent wartime income, and the subsequent development of hire purchase and more general consumer borrowing to finance expenditure. The growing importance of consumer durables also changed the source of the shocks hitting the system so that variations in household purchases might rise in importance compared with those of business.[12]

Third, to go back to the subject of linear approximation, economists were not ignorant of the fact that the economy did not behave symmetrically about its initial position. It was easier to contract the economy than to expand it, so that the aggregate supply curve was a concave function. For the purposes of elementary teaching this might be represented as comprising two segments, a horizontal one up to full employment, and a vertical one thereafter. But this was no more than an expositional device. Economists were in little doubt that over a relevant range there would be some tendency towards diminishing marginal productivity of the variable factor; and in addition, its price would rise as more of it was brought into employment. There was no agreement, however, about how close to full employment all this occurred, and whether there might not also be a relevant downward-sloping segment of the aggregate supply curve. There was also disagreement about whether and in what sense the economy was on its aggregate supply curve. And all these issues were related to the debate about the behaviour of real wages over the cycle. On this last point it may be said that, even if real wages rise in the upswing, the aggregate supply curve can be upward-sloping; i.e., all that is required is that money wages rise more than prices.

If we go beyond the static aggregate supply curve to a more dynamic one relating the inflation rate to aggregate supply, a similar point holds. Attempts to raise output may be increasingly dissipated in a high inflation rate the nearer one is to full employment. Attempts to reduce the inflation rate may be dissipated in lower levels of output as the economy is moved in the reverse direction.

All these points of apologia are intended to lead to the conclusion that the established theory of macroeconomic policy was not so deficient as is sometimes suggested, nor were actual policy-makers ignorant of economics beyond the first-year level, or lacking in practical judgement. It is now necessary to point out where deficiences lay, and in what ways progress in the subject may be said to have occurred in the past dozen or so years.

Deficiencies and Recent Developments

Some are to do with comments already made. The connection between the fiscal position and the monetary position was not fully appreciated. This was so even after the key points had been made in the literature.

On money itself, there was the post-Radcliffe debate on the relative significance of narrowly defined money and broadly measured liquidity, together with the continuing argument over what was cause and what effect. Moreover, some economists who explored the consequences of varying the money supply could say that that was all they were doing. They were not claiming in addition that the money supply was easily controllable. In fact, however, until the 1970s, most of the protagonists in the debate cannot fall back on that position. Those who favoured a greater use of monetary policy thought that the money supply could be controlled by policy-makers, and most of those who opposed them did so on grounds of the ineffectiveness of the policy rather than the dubious nature of the instrument itself. It has taken the experience of the past few years to show what an elusive thing the money supply is, and how difficult it is to control.

In a way this is surprising, for quite elementary considerations should have given economists pause. The Keynesian motives for holding money can be satisfied by different things to be called 'money'. Elementary micro theory tells us that, in general, if something becomes scarce, something else will be substituted for it. Lastly, it has been a commonplace in banking studies for half a century or more that balance sheets are manipulated to thwart the authorities to some degree. All that has happened is that relevant institutions have proliferated and their operators have become more talented at asset adjustment and window dressing.

If asset theory in general, and the money supply in particular, are placed in an international context, the same point holds. The key ideas are not new. Keynes himself, despite the closed economy bias of the General Theory, was well aware of the international linkage of interest rates and the importance of capital mobility. Equally, his comprehension of the gold standard required him to perceive the connection between the current account of the balance of payments and the money supply. Moreover, even though these matters were neglected in much economic teaching and research, actual policy-makers could not and did not do so. At a minimum, they were aware of the fact that the domestic interest rate, unless capital were completely immobile internationally, could not be isolated from what ruled overseas, and also that short-term movements in the exchange rate would be influenced by international capital flows.

It must be agreed, however, that these topics have been explored more satisfactorily in recent years. Moreover, they have to be given greater weight if only because capital has become more mobile internationally, a consequence of the abolition of exchange controls, the expansion of multinational corporations and the increased sophistication of international financial institutions (see Dornbusch, 1980).

The same kind of comment can be made about recognition of international economic inter-dependence arising from trade flows. This too goes back a long way. After all, what does the international trade multiplier and the balance of payments constraint amount to if not that? Whether or not one regards purchasing power parity as a helpful proposition, it was never possible to neglect the connection between overseas and domestic prices, given the exchange rate (or to assume that the exchange rate could be held indefinitely if the domestic inflation rate differed from that ruling in the world at large). None the less, here too more openness of economies, and a clear understanding of the supply-push behind exports and not just demand-pull behind imports, have led to a change of emphasis. Apart from anything else, the era of floating (especially dirty floating) requires a reformulation of policy analysis, and due consideration must be given to interest rate and exchange rate volatility.

Now, there are several consequences of all this. One is an enlargement of the range of topics that economists need to concern themselves with. A second is recognition of the complexity of certain issues that had been thought to be rather simple. A third is an acknowledgement that economic policy-making itself has become more difficult. This last point relates to two more matters. They represent a resurgence of very old established truths: (1) the need for international economic and financial cooperation, and (2) the fact that the economy can get stuck in an extremely adverse state. On the latter, the parameters of the system can change adversely, providing objective grounds for pessimism where earlier there were equally strong grounds for optimism.

None of this can be doubted, but in saying that it is possible to overstress the errors of the past and the achievements of the present. Above all, it is possible to be far too pessimistic about the efficacy of macroeconomic policy. This is not to say that in the UK, for example, it will suddenly become easy to restore full employment without regenerating a very high rate of inflation. It is to say that policy initiatives exist which can improve on present circumstances and which were available earlier to avoid the poor performance of the past few years. At the very least, it must be said that we have gone from undue optimism to excessive pessimism.

It has not been established, either in the literature as a general theoretical proposition or in the actual economic systems that exist, that macroeconomic policy is ineffective with regard to the price level, or GDP, at current prices. At most, certain examples have been exhibited within which policy is neither necessary nor effective with regard to real output. But there is nothing new or original about that, since these models are of optimally self-adjusting systems. No one is likely to doubt that, if the economy works according to classical principles and does not deviate from full-employment equilibrium except for unpredictable random shocks, then macroeconomic intervention is irrelevant and unhelpful.

At a lower level, if the domestic price level equals the foreign price level and the domestic interest rate the foreign interest rate, policy measures that depend for their effectiveness on differences between home and foreign variables will fail. But that too is not new. Indeed, what is remarkable about these things is that the law of one price and perfect interest arbitrage do not seem to hold exactly, not even over quite significant periods of time. These are puzzles that need exploring further. But our inability to explain them satisfactorily does not lead validly to the conclusion that they do not exist.[13]

This last consideration holds *a fortiori* for policy itself. The useful outcome of the policy debate of recent years is the emphasis on the question, What is it about the economy that makes macroeconomic policy necessary and effective? We do not yet know the definitive answer to that question, and are, anyway, obliged to recognize the limitations of policy. It would be idiotic to go further and say that, therefore, policy is unnecessary and ineffective.

9.4 POLICY PROBLEMS RECONSIDERED

Let us, therefore, reconsider our initial elementary formulation of the policy problem (bearing constantly in mind its most misleading simplifying assumption, the closed economy). Let us also assume that we know what level of output or degree of capacity utilization corresponds to full employment. Given an exogenous shock such as a reduction in A, and with no change in the policy instruments, there exist a price level and an average money wage (in the simplest case, both below their initial values) that restore full employment. Alternatively, there exists a level of the instrument G (or M) that generates full employment for the initial price and wage.

The case for increasing G is that P or W does not fall sufficiently, if at all, or that these falls occur very slowly. Prices may not fall in the short run because the change in demand is regarded as transitory, soon to be reversed and dealt with by inventory variation, with the result that reductions in output and employment are expected to be temporary. Another possibility is that prices are fixed for periods of time of varying length because of contractual arrangements. In addition, falls in price are limited if variable costs, chiefly wages, do not change. Wages too may not change because of contractual arrangements. Again, if the exogenous shock is seen as transitory, temporary redundancies and reductions in overtime may be accepted as a more appropriate response. Lastly, if some workers are let go, the labour market does not work to enable them easily to undercut their fellows left in jobs, and certainly not in the short run. (There is also the point that Keynes noticed, namely how much weight workers place on the maintenance of relativities.)

Of these possibilities, a misinterpretation of the shock, in the sense of confusing the transitory with the more persistent, itself should disappear. To the extent that it does not, the government might help, as might various private economic agencies, by clarifying what has happened. In this connection it must be emphasized that, although we have expressed the shock as a typical macroeconomic indicator A, this covers coincidental falls in demand in several markets which together are of sufficient size to affect the whole economy and are disseminated through other markets in the usual multiplier process.

The analysis of what has happened in a form sufficient to influence individual behaviour in the current direction is not likely to be at all easy. While not rejecting the view that the government ought to help the economy to be more capable of autonomous adjustment, it is difficult to believe that the stabilization problem can be dealt with entirely by education and persuasion. The point holds even more strongly if the shock is something to be forecast. Public and private agencies make forecasts in varying degrees of detail, and with varying accuracy, on what is likely to happen to the economy up to a year or two ahead and why. Larger firms also make forecasts for their own purposes. It could well be that the government forecasts better than anyone else, although it is not clear that this must be so. If it is so, the argument above implies that these forecasts should be published, and efforts made to establish their credibility. Once again, however, it is doubtful that a firm concerned with the demand for its own products and its own cost curves will even begin to consider changing prices until it is confronted with evidence specific to itself.

On all of this, whatever the firm expects to happen to demand or believes has happened, it is constrained in price adjustments by its costs. In other words, it is limited by what its suppliers are doing, and all of them together are limited by wage costs.

In the labour market, the proposition that wage rates will be adjusted downwards because of a demand shock that is said to have occurred, let alone one that is forecast to happen, is even more far-fetched. The point must be reiterated that the overall macroeconomic shock is a term of art. Individual markets are hit to a greater or lesser degree by a fall in demand which is multiplied through the economy.

If, therefore, the new macroeconomics is based on the interpretative and forecasting ability of the private sector, assisted by the government, then, while its premises are not unattractive, its conclusions verge on the nonsensical. Like other forms of optimal adjustment theory, the information augmentation variety is a special case, of use to academics but lacking in practical force.

More serious is the suggestion that demanders and suppliers of goods and services (including labour) are aware of the sorts of shock that afflict the economic system. It will, therefore, pay them to write into their explicit contracts, or tacitly to assume in their implicit ones, arrangements for renegotiation in the face of, for example, falls in demand. To some extent, of course, this will happen, but again there are good reasons to believe that as a stabilization process it will be rather weak. For one thing, prices and wages are not specific to the firm as buyer, but the fall in the demand for its product is. The relevant recontracting may therefore be impossible, at least until the recession has spread far enough. There is also the moral hazard problem. The firm knows much more about the demand for its product than its suppliers do. They are always in danger therefore of being misled about what is happening in individual cases, and are more likely to agree to reconsider wages and prices when sales have actually fallen and unemployment has emerged.[14]

Another observation on the automatic adjustment process goes back as far as Fisher and Keynes. For most firms prices are set to cover costs already incurred and to make some profits. To cut prices first involves losses and possible bankruptcy, especially if the firm's liquidity position is impaired. But if money wages are cut ahead of prices, real wages will fall, causing effective demand to fall and the downswing to be intensified. This suggests that the free market way to recovery will be slow, faltering and in its initial stages perverse. To repeat the point, this is so no matter how economically sophisticated, well informed and rational people are (see Tobin, 1980).

There is one final, and quite decisive, argument in favour of intervention. This revolves around the proposition that the recovery process viewed by the individual firm and household involves a form of externality. On the face of it, a recession is always Pareto-non-optimal. There is output which employers and employees wish to produce and which they also wish to buy. Everybody can be made better off back at full employment and most people will actually be better off. That is the case for action. Consider now the feasible set of choices of a household or firm. In making its decisions, each may act independently of the other. Workers, in particular, may take no account of the effect on prices of a reduction in money wages, and will assume that others will behave in the same way. While the latter consideration may imply an advantage to individual wage-cutting by raising the person's employability, we have already pointed out that most sections of the labour market do not work in this way.[15] In these circumstances of slow reaction on the wage side, there will be similarly slow reactions on the price side. In sum, we have a non-cooperative game in which (1) each individual firm would cut prices if it believed that all other firms were going to do so and that wages in general were going to fall too, and (2) wage-earners would cut wages if they believed that all wages were falling, together with the general level of prices. In addition, collective bargaining is a non-cooperative game in which a lack of trust of each other dominates employers and unions. Because these assumptions are not made, the low level of activity persists. Eventually, some kind of recovery process will emerge, or a more beneficent shock will occur. In the meantime, action of a macroeconomic character is called for on the part of the authorities.

At a more practical and empirical level, I have indicated how the economic environment has changed to exacerbate the policy problem. There are two facets of this which I must now underline before concluding. The first relates to the behaviour of the money wage in a depression. It is now a characteristic of the UK (and of other advanced economies) that, even at high levels of unemployment, the rate of change of the money wage is 'high'. Indeed, compared with 20 years ago it is no lower than what was associated with full or over-full employment. The explanation of this adverse shift in the Phillips curve is usually given in terms of the rate of rise of prices. The cause is either inflation expectations, or a high level of core inflation based on past experience (Eckstein, 1981). Whether one or both positions are adopted, there is something disturbingly *ad hoc* about them. In particular, they fail to address the issue of scale, i.e. of so much unemployment and money wages continuing to rise rapidly.

It is apparent that, while a slack labour market may attenuate wage inflation, large numbers of workers can be available for work on nominal and real terms lower than those being received by their colleagues, but can be unable to substitute themselves for them. I have emphasized that there is something distinctly mistaken about the neo-classical version of the way labour markets work. Furthermore, the answer does not lie in any simple sense with the public sector or with trade unions. This is not to deny at all the enormous importance of both of these things (see Peston, 1984). But in the UK the excess wage pressure is occurring in the private, and to a considerable extent non-union, sector.

One explanation is palpably absurd, namely that the present level of unemployment corresponds to full employment (or overfull employment) (see Metcalf, 1984). This is not to say that the percentage unemployed corresponding to full employment as laid down in the mid-1960s must be fixed for all time. Changes in preferences, in institutions and the economic environment suggest that a larger unemployment percentage corresponds to full employment today compared with 20 years ago. But the evidence of willingness of the unemployed to take jobs and to accept lower real wages than could otherwise be the case indicate that, while a 1.5 per cent unemployment rate is much too low, 12.5 per cent is much too high.

Whatever the explanation, interventionist policy is limited in a way that is much more serious than 20 years ago. It is both more difficult for contraction to shake inflation out of the system, and for expansion to raise output and employment. Since in the first instance policy operates through nominal demand, what is being said is that an increase in nominal demand is dissipated excessively into prices, and a decrease in output. The position is precisely the reverse of what is required. (An interesting theoretical issue that needs to be raised here is whether the adverse supply response is connected with the nature of the demand increase, and if so why? As an example, consider the consequences of an increase in consumer spending. Will output in the short and medium runs behave any differently if this is caused by an autonomous fall in the propensity to save instead of a direct tax cut?)

Concern with the downward inflexibility and upward instability of the rate of rise of the money wage is what nowadays lies behind the analysis of incomes policy in its various forms. For the most part, discussion has been at an extremely simple level, concentrating on rather naive empirical tests of the effects of past policies on the one hand, and equally naive 'if only we had wage restraint' policy proposals on the other. But, as I remarked earlier, the past few years have seen the emergence of much more sophisticated approaches to the workings of labour markets. That work may in due course clarify what is possible in the incomes field, and provide a more effective policy instrument to associate with ordinary demand management.

The second policy constraint relates to the first, but arises in the international field. It used to be thought of the UK economy that too high a degree of capacity utilization and too fast a rise in nominal demand would cause a current account deficit, and make it impossible to hold sterling at its Bretton Woods par value. The new view with floating rates is that what happens is a rapid fall in sterling. This may be connected with a current account deficit, but equally it may not be. What matters may be an expected deficit leading to a capital outflow based on fears of depreciation in the future not offset by an interest rate differential. Alternatively, the fears of depreciation are based on an expectation of a higher inflation rate. This again may either have a direct effect on sterling or an indirect effect via an expected current account deficit. The inflation itself may be expected to arise from a money-financed government deficit resulting from the initial expansionary policy or from the labour market and the adverse Phillips curve. This latter phenomenon, in the minds of some economists, occurs because of workers' inflationary expectations derived from money supply expectations, derived in turn from the higher public sector borrowing requirement (PSBR). The number of plausible stories appears to be endless. But they all revolve around currency depreciation and capital outflows resulting from expansionary policies. In addition, if sterling is maintained in value by monetary stringency and a rise in interest rates, the expansionary effects of the policy (assuming this has come from the fiscal side) will be diminished.

The analysis of the interaction of current account, capital account and fiscal and monetary policy is characterized by a proliferation of models.

This is not necessarily a bad state of affairs in that it throws light on the different constraints to which these policies are subject depending on circumstances. Guidance is also provided, therefore, for the study of actual problems, and questions of significance are raised. Typical useful questions are (1) whether the country in question is small in the sense of taking world interest rates as given; (2) whether and to what extent interest arbitrage holds, and (3) whether the country's currency is a key currency in the sense of being used for trade, especially for trade between other countries, and in providing liquid balances to meet international precautionary and speculative motives. Increased emphasis is placed on forward and futures markets for currencies and on the term structure of interest rates. All of these matters have to be related to risk in international economic and financial transactions. In particular, the small country is not confronted with a fixed interest rate at which it can borrow limitless amounts. Instead, the marginal cost of funds to it rises because of some notion of increasing risk. For that reason it is important to note that arbitrage applies to marginal rates; i.e., it is the differential interest rate on marginal funds that would equate to expected depreciation (or the difference between future and spot rates) under perfect arbitrage.

Unfortunately, these marginal rates are not easily measured. As a consequence, much of the theory may be trivialized along the lines of 'No perceived profit opportunities will be forgone; therefore, perfect arbitrage must occur at the margin; therefore, interest payments made and received at the margin must differ from those actually quoted on average.'

This trivialization will be accentuated if the important concepts of 'confidence' and 'expectations' are used to fill all the gaps in theory and applications. If expansionary policy in one country at one time accompanies appreciation of the currency and in another country at a different time accompanies depreciation, it may be correct to explain this in terms of expectations or confidence.[16] But with no independent measures of these, it may also be vacuous.

It will be widely agreed that the introduction of the formal analysis of expectations into macroeconomics and the relationship between that and the explication of confidence represents an important advance in the subject. In addition, the distinction between transitory and permanent exogenous shocks and policy changes is surely a valid one. But at the purely theoretical level, all these are much more difficult ideas than some of those who use them realize, and their application in the present state of knowledge is dangerous. That is not to say that their use is to be banned or even discouraged, but that policy recommendations based on them should be accompanied by an economic health warning.

9.5 CONCLUDING COMMENTS

To conclude this paper, let us examine briefly the distinction between permanent and transitory shifts in policy, policy surprises, and the old issue of rules versus discretion. If, for example, tax rates are cut, this is taken to imply an increase in disposable income relative to current income. Thus the aggregate demand curve shifts to the right. The extent to which income rises depends on the slope of the aggregate supply curve. There will then be subsequent effects depending on (1) how the resulting public sector deficit is financed, and (2) whether the aggregate supply curve moves in the medium and the long term.

It may be postulated, however, that consumption is a function of disposable permanent income. Consumption will then rise more if the tax cut is thought to be permanent rather than transitory. Now, in economies where a tax cut requires a long and complicated legislative process, and in which the change itself may be specified *ab initio* as shorter or longer-lasting, the distinction being considered here may to some extent be observable. In other economies, where tax changes are made more easily, and in some cases require no serious legislative manoeuvres, it is much harder to decide whether a change is temporary or permanent. A government may in some cases announce that a particular change will be reversed on a particular date in the future. Even then, circumstances may cause it to renege on its promise. None the less, such policy moves do occur. The treasury may announce profits tax concessions for investment in a slump, but say they will be reversed two years later. No doubt this will have different effects on investment from the same concessions with no time limit attached.

But most tax changes are not of that sort. They are made and there is an attempt to justify them. The transitory–permanent distinction must then lie in the minds of firms and households. If it is important for behaviour, this must be via expectations. Private decision-makers must forecast the government's behaviour in future and act accordingly.

Such forecasting must be made on the basis of what the government says, its credibility, and its past behaviour (see Barro and Gordon, 1983). Attention must be paid to objectives, government assessment of circumstances, and the instruments it applies to deal with the gap between the actual and desired states of the economy. Considering the complexity of macroeconomic policy-making, especially in a parliamentary democracy, it is not surprising that little progress in this area has been made so far. The models that have been analysed and estimated have been simplistic in the extreme, but this does not mean that they are totally without interest. They may well be the first steps towards major advance in the future.

My concern here is less with how progress has been made or will be made, and more with the logical basis of what is being attempted. Suppose that (1) the economy is subject to exogenous shocks which are predictable to some degree; (2) the usual conditions for macroeconomic intervention hold, namely sufficient price and wage stickiness to cause the effects of the shocks to be multiplied throughout the economy, any automatic offsetting forces being limited and slow; and (3) the authorities commit themselves to a full-employment policy.

If this policy is believed, it is reasonable to infer that firms and households will base their decisions on the assumption that actual income and output will be those corresponding to full employment. This belief may arise analytically and directly from an understanding of what the policy-makers are up to (including some persuasion on their part); or it may emerge from experiencing how the authorities react to external shocks.

I have already pointed out that, as a result of these beliefs, the average level of economic activity may be greater and its variance less. But an expectation that the economy will typically be at full employment will not necessarily guarantee either that that condition will hold or that there will be a low variance around the mean state. To the extent that intervention is required, the government must actually engage in stabilization policies. Furthermore, the more successful it is, the more will real output, the price level etc., appear to fluctuate unpredictably about fixed means.

The logical problem is then as follows. A strong *a priori* belief in the efficacy of macroeconomic policy may cause the private sector to behave so as to limit the need for such policy, and in the extreme to cause it never to be required at all. If that belief is then taken to imply the irrelevance of intervention, will not the new belief emerge that, should a shock occur that requires offsetting, no such action will be forthcoming? Will private decision-making then revert to its pre-intervention assumptions?

The answer to this is that logically no decision-maker should postulate, in the case as stated, that a shock that needs to be offset can occur. In other words, he must stick to the belief that the private sector, having convinced itself that the government, being committed to act and therefore obviating the need to act, will never waver. It will always offset all predictable shocks – not by wage–price adjustments, which are not needed, but by basing all spending decisions on correct full-employment assumptions (taking into account a pre-announced public expenditure path).

The question that needs to be asked is, How stable is this *a priori* form of the credibility of policy, based on its never being used, likely to be? To put it another way, is it not at least possible that the government may actually have to pursue an active stabilization policy to substantiate its credibility? Firms and households will in the downturn react on the assumption that full employment will be restored rapidly, and as a result the downturn will not be strong. But for this to happen regularly the government must stimulate the economy.

If the government also commits itself to acting by rule, this makes its actions more effective, not less (cf. Kydland and Prescott, 1977). To say that it will predict actual demand, an elementary policy rule is: compare it with potential output, and vary taxes to bring the two closer together. To argue that such a policy works either by not announcing it, or by disguising it, or by occasionally not sticking to it contradicts the reasons why the rule was introduced in the first place.

It is to be inferred from all of this that the central questions of macroeconomic policy remain those that have been emphasized by critics of it. They are: (1) What kind of circumstances give rise to the need for that policy? (2) What are the preconditions for that policy being effective? These critics are also correct in distinguishing the impact effects of policy from the medium and longer-run effects, although there is nothing new in that. The need to distinguish transitory from permanent shocks and interventions is attractive but intellectually rather difficult to clarify, and even more difficult to apply in practice.

Above all, the notion that policy should be based on rules makes sense. What is mistaken is to assume that appropriate rules are simple. Moreover, if policy-makers are restricted to a class of simple rules, there is no reason to believe that these should contain no feedback element from contemporary forecast shocks.

The real point at issue concerns the dependability of government responses. Where the shocks are typical of those that have been experienced in the past, it may be inferred that both the government and the private sector will learn what is necessary, and each will come to rely on the other for a characteristic mode of behaviour (Bray, 1982; Townsend, 1983). Except in special circumstances, this reliance will help to stabilize the system, with both public and private sectors reinforcing each other. The government is ineffective not because its actions are surprising, but because they are not surprising.

In the more difficult but more interesting case where the shocks to the system contain an element of novelty, policy-making becomes more necessary because it must be assumed that the decentralized private sector will find it harder to work out a set of reactions that returns the economy to the most desired feasible state. The novelty may of course arise on the side of the government, which seeks to pursue new objectives, or to use instruments in a new way. Equally, policy-making itself becomes harder for the same reason. In one sense, what the goverment does will be news in that it is coping with novel circum-stances; in another sense, it will be as anticipated, i.e. it will endeavour to ascertain what is happening, will examine individual instruments to determine which needs to be changed, and will continue to aim at objectives such as full capacity and low inflation. I reiterate that it is the constancy of this response that helps the policy to work rather than hinders it.

NOTES

I am indebted to participants at the seminar and also to colleagues at Queen Mary College for helpful comments on an earlier draft.

1 The sort of effects T is meant to take into account are such taxes on employment as the national insurance surcharge.
2 In the case of men, for example, full employment might be defined in an institutional or sociological sense to mean availability of jobs for all men of normal working age who are neither disabled nor temporarily withdrawn from the labour force for education and training.
3 Quite clearly, in labour markets dominated by bilateral bargaining, equilibrium will be hard to define, and the outcome of such bargains on any occasion, or even on average, will not necessarily correspond to what is correctly to be called 'full employment'.
4 Typical of this is the approach based on the supply function first enunciated by Friedman, which was derived from the Phillips curve, but is now called the Lucas supply curve. It is worth querying whether the Lucas–Friedman supply curve makes sense, especially in the form in which it is usually presented. Actual supply differs from normal or full-employment supply as prices differ from expected prices. One explanation of this is simply error on the part of employers or employees. Another, or possibly the same, explanation is that they are surprised by the gap between expectation and outcome and react to it. In a stochastic world. however, there is nothing surprising about actual values differing from expected ones. It is, therefore, not at all obvious that such a deviation would lead to any adjustment in real behaviour.
5 It is entirely mistaken, therefore, to believe that supply-side economics is something new. It is nearly as old hat as demand management. What, after all, were the 1960s debates on raising growth rates about? It is not even true that the incentive effects of tax cuts have any novelty about them. What is and was in question is the effectiveness of supply-side measures, especially in other than the very long term.
6 Paish (1966) advocates in Ch.17 an increase in the margin of capacity unused from 3.9 to 5 per cent. This corresponds to a rise in average unemployment from 1.8 to 2 per cent. He says: 'If a large proportion of capacity is unused for long periods it may well be that the long-term rate of growth will be slowed down.... But the permanent maintenance of the small proportion of unused capacity suggested here would be more likely to increase than decrease the rate of growth' (pp. 331–2). The point is reiterated more strongly in Paish (1970, p. 92).
7 In dynamic terms, the relevant condition is diminished in the rate of rise of prices and wages. It should be emphasized that whatever rationale is put forward for price and wage stickiness does not necessarily carry over to stickiness in the rate of rise of prices and wages.

8   It is always worth recalling that Keynes was joined in his advocacy of public works by others, such as Henderson, Salter and Stamp. See Winch, (1969, p. 212). He also reminds us that Pigou took public works seriously enough as an alternative to wage cuts (Winch, 1969, p. 153). Note also Pigou (1944).

9   I am indebted to D. Currie (1982) for this expression.

10 It certainly was and is Friedman's judgement that intervention is likely to be damaging. Phillips, though cautious, was not an opponent of intervention, especially if due attention was paid to economic dynamics, notably the rates of change rather than just the levels of targets.

11 An example of the extent of optimism is provided by Paish (1966). He refers to 'Phillips' estimate that just over 2 per cent of unemployment is consistent with a rise in wage rates of $2\frac{1}{2}$ per cent a year (and therefore, no price inflation) ....' Happy days!

12 Reference must obviously be made at this point to Friedman (1958) and to Modigliani and Brumberg (1954). The relevance of all that from our point of view is that the marginal propensity to consume out of permanent income is very low, with the implication that the multiplier is also likely to be low. The result is that exogenous expenditure changes will not be significantly amplified as income changes, and also that government expenditure will not be amplified much, either. The significance of this result should not be exaggerated in that the preponderant part of a durable goods purchase counts as savings in permanent income theory. What is important is that Friedman was one of the first economists to stress the point that the value of the multiplier could be rather low.

13 Thus, the new macroeconomics viewed as a programme of criticism of the old macroeconomics is of considerable interest. A lot of important questions are posed that demand answers, and should not have been neglected. Acknowledging that is a far cry from accepting that the precise models and elementary theories examined by the new macroeconomists are valid or have much policy relevance. In particular, it is important to enquire why prices are sticky and why markets fail. But an inability to explain these phenomena satisfactorily does not imply that they do not exist.

14 The deficiences of implicit and explicit contract theory are well known and do not have to be re-examined here. In recognizing them, however, it is vital not to go to the other extreme and pretend that the problem does not exist at all. Above all, if unemployment and stagnation are Pareto-sub-optimal and price and wage inflexibility are part of the cause, it must be a central question of macroeconomics why such stickiness persists.

15 Of course, labour markets do not all work in the same way in all countries. It may be easier for workers in the UK than in the USA to defend themselves from competition from the unemployed.

16 The obvious example is that expansionary fiscal policy with tight monetary policy in the USA has led to real growth in that country accompanied by dollar appreciation. It does not follow that the same policy would yield the same results in the UK. Equally, the recent successes of the Swedish economy would not necessarily carry over without major reforms in the wage bargaining process in this country.

10

The Theory of Social Contract and the EEC

FRANCESCO FORTE

10.1 INTRODUCTION

Public choice theory is normally applied to individuals or their representatives dealing with issues of a central or a local government.[1] It has rarely been applied to the constitutional choices relating to the formation of a federal state (See Oates, 1972; Breton and Scott, 1978; and Wust, 1981), or of a 'prefederal union' (see European Commission, 1977). While research on the economics and politics of European integration is extensive, scant attention has been devoted to it in terms of public choice theory. Yet the 'social contract' (Breton and Scott, 1978), which in public choice theory is assumed to take place at the constitutional stage, with the constituents acting as contracting parties, is actually taking place among the governments of the EEC in order to enlarge (or not) and to deepen (or not) the existing union. The European Parliament did pass, by majority, a constitution in June 1984. However, since the Parliament has no legislative authority in this matter, it behoves us to examine EEC practice and to consider how social contract theory might be applied to this 'preferential union'.

10.2 HISTORICAL ANTECEDENTS

The contractarian constitutional stage in public choice theory is assumed normally to be an 'anarchic stage'. No state or public action exists prior to the constitution, so that in cases of total disagreement no public good could be supplied. The reality of national constitutions, however, has been very different. In the cases of the 1791 French Assemblée Constituante, of the Weimar Republic Constitutional Assembly and of postwar Italy, a state was already in existence and public bureaucracies were already providing public goods (or bads), levying taxes and exerting extended public powers under an existing legal system.

In many instances, the constitution was meant to set limits to the existing powers of the state. On the other hand, if no agreement could be reached on the supreme organs of the state, the risk of anarchy would have become real: and in the case of the French Assemblée Consituante, a prolonged period of bloody 'revolution' occurred, often resembling the Hobbesian state of 'bellum omnium contra omnes'.

For these reasons, a public choice consistent theorist would have disapproved of the application of a unanimity or a qualified majority rule. On the other hand, lack of agreement by a dissenting minority would have reflected some sort of Pareto optimality inconsistent with the 'liberal postulate'[2] that one would deduce from the contractarian approach (in a Buchanian and in a Harsanian, or in a Rawlsian or a Senian, world).[3] Indeed, one purpose of the constitution was to introduce (or reintroduce) constitutional liberties and parliamentary democracy while limiting arbitrary powers. Lack of agreement on the basic institutions would have brought Hobbesian anarchy, perhaps with a 'Hobbesian end', through a *coup d'état* of the existing bureaucratic powers.[4] In such cases, decision costs – as defined in the Buchanan–Tullock paradigm of the optimal decision rule – would be very large and would rapidly increase. On the other hand, external costs might decrease sharply in the initial range, for normal citizens.[5]

An historical case closer to the EEC contractarian constitutional situation may be that of the creation of the American federal state. The various American states, having acquired autonomy, were 'contracting' to form a sort of 'superstate'. In case of disagreement they would have retained their own army, police, justice, monetary and trade powers; though without that agreement a 'bellum omnium contra omnes' might have spread through an explosive mixture of economic and political interests, and (most importantly) the absolute Hobbesian (imperial) government might have been welcomed back by Americans torn by an excess of democracy, i.e. by an incipient Hobbesian anarchy.

In the case of the EEC, the constituents of the ten nations know very well that no possibility of a Hobbesian 'bellum omnium contra omnes' exists, since all of them adhere to the NATO pact, to GATT, to IMF, and now to an already irreversible free trade area – with some sort of government and parliament.

If the Philadelphia convention had not agreed to approve a federal constitution with a clear definition of the various powers of the federal government and of the states, the federation would not have been able to exert the vast functions given to Congress in the enthusiastic period following independence; i.e. to declare war, maintain an army and navy, appoint ambassadors, determine the standards of coinage, borrow money, make treaties, establish post offices and post roads – much more than a 'minimal state' in the Nozik sense.[6] If those federal powers were not clarified, consolidated and completed[7] and voting rules specified, an internal conflict could have easily developed, since the equilibrium was highly unstable.

A public choice theorist, while recommending a minimal majority principle on the basis of these Hobbesian risks, would have approved the idea that dissenting states could leave the new union before or early after the approval of its constitution thus enticing the majority to minimize the degree of 'coercion' or 'frustration'[8] of the minorities, allowing – as far as possible – a double regime of strong and weak union.[9]

EEC countries, while with varying degrees of interest in pursuing a broader and deeper European 'social contract', are all free from that vigorous Hobbesian factor of social cohesion which is 'fear' of instability, chaos and conflict. On the other hand, the powerful bureaucracies of the various national states are an inertial factor against European Union (EU), while the need to empower the government of the new American union was a driving force in favour of federalism.[10] Constituents, in the US case, were mostly members of the US assembly, while in the present EEC case the constituents are the delegates of national administrations. In the former case it was in the interest of the delegates to develop the union; in the latter case it is against their interests.

10.3 VOTING RULES IN THE EEC

In ordinary matters too, the majority rule contemplated by the Rome Treaty has been systematically weakened in EEC Council (since January 1966), on the basis of the so-called 'Luxembourg compromise', a statement invoking the unanimity principle in all cases 'involving very important interests of one or more nations' (EEC *Bulletin* no. 3, 1966). Even if originally approved only by the French, the Luxembourg compromise has been constantly adhered to; thus, the unanimity rule has been actually reintroduced in the EEC legislative process through a minority resolution!

It seems that the respect for the unanimity principle emerged tacitly, as a 'rule utilitarianism', obeyed by each country for the fear that its violation would justify reciprocal damaging behaviour. However irrational from the point of view of the citizens, it is quite rational from the point of view of bureaucrats – by nature risk-averters – and political leaders conditioned by them at the EEC (Council) level. 'Maximin' here implies a strong bias in favour of the status quo, i.e. existing national powers which are likely to be considered in the utility functions of both domestic bureaucrats and many national politicians.[11]

According to Buchanan and Tullock, at the constitutional stage the true rule of unanimity should hold and produce positive results, because

> agreement seems more likely on general rules for collective choice than on the latter choices to be made *within* the confines of certain agreed rules …. Essential to the analysis is the presumption that the individual is *uncertain* as to what his precise rule will be in any one of the whole chain of later collective choices that will actually have to be made … the individual will not find it advantageous to vote for rules that may promote sectional, class or group interests because, by presupposition, he is unable to predict the role that he will be playing in the actual collective decision-making process at any particular time in the future. (Buchanan and Tullock, 1962)

Breton and Scott (1978) refuse to 'make use of this general line of argumentation because it does not appear to us to be of help in understanding the role of the constituent assembly in changing the structure of the public sector'. This position seems plausible if, as in this approach, the focus is on 'reassignment' rather than on an *ex novo* constitution. The situation is similar for constitutional EEC negotiations. Assuming full mobility throughout the entire territory of the union, citizens choosing constitutional principles of EU applicable to their grandchildren might attach a limited weight to the interests of the country of residence. They might even have more concern for their present class interests than for their national interest.

But the assumption of 'full mobility' for the large majority of EEC citizens – ten countries with different languages and cultural backgrounds – appears unreal: national interests are to be expected to be persistent; and 'property rights' existing in the various countries cannot be expected to be 'impartially protected' by the various citizens.

The burden of national interests is even more pronounced for the EEC 'constituents', Bureaucrats of a given state *institutionally* represent the interests of their own country, even if they expect their grandchildren to belong to another country. They are motivated by the preservation and expansion of powers of their own (domestic) bureaucracy, in which they make their career (very few of them expect permanently to be members of the Eurocracy). Thus, they have no 'veil of ignorance' on their 'section, class or group interests'.

Utility functions of politicians normally include, as arguments, the expectation of re-election, and the preservation or maximization of power, prestige and related benefits. Political leaders negotiating EEC matters, being national leaders, are expected to 'bring home' either the best domestic result compatible with continued EEC membership, or the best EEC result compatible with some minimum domestic 'net gain'. In other words, they are expected to pursue a 'weak Paretian' criterion for their country.[12]

Now, both Olsson and Buchanan, through different paradigms, show that concentrated sectoral present interests exert a stronger pressure than interests diffused over space and time, in proportion to the utility of the proposed actions (see Olsson, 1965). Ministers of national governments running sectoral departments and pressed by domestic organized interests operating in that area exert a greater pressure than ministers representing 'general' domestic interests.[13] A sort of weak Paretian solution may thus emerge where the sectoral interests of each country obtain a net gain while each country or most countries – considering all interests – have a net loss, in terms of an hypothetical Kaldor–Hicks–Scitovsky compensation to the 'damaged'. In principle, one might improve the situation by bribing the prevailing interest groups to renounce the allocational distortions, while keeping the distributional benefits through other devices. But, ethical reasons apart, such a 'bribe' would not be accepted by the privileged because they would trade powers generating income for an income stream from a weaker source.

To sum up, we are not, as in the case of EU, in an Harsanian 'moral-value-judgements emphatical world', but in an Harsanian economic-man egoistically-utilitarian imperfect world, without Pareto optimality. The point, however, should not be overdone. Leaders of states and goverments, minded as political innovative entrepreneurs, may have a scope for advancing EU through the 'cooperative, positive game' that is made attractive by the very extent of the above-described deviation.[14]

10.4 ARGUMENTS FOR INTERVENTION

To develop this cooperative game under weak Pareto principles, those political entrepreneurs should approve some new *basic European* constitutional choice in order to set 'driving forces' for the positive game.

One of the 'basic choices' might be devolution of many ordinary decisions to bodies, such as the EEC Assembly whose members have an interest in expanding EU powers at the expense of domestic power, precisely as the US Congress had in the period of development of the American Union. Doubtless, sectoral interests are heavily represented in this Assembly, together with the various nationalities. However, while the influence of the different pressure groups will to a degree offset each other, the openness of the debate will help to increase the influence of diffused interests (see Becker, 1983).

Following Buchanan and Tullock (1962), one can have six possible typical orderings of 'social costs' of activities left to pure individualistic behaviour of private units or organized through voluntary contractual arrangements (*a*), carried on through public compulsory action, either national or local (b), or carried on by EU action (g). These activities may be classified as follows:

1 supply of goods and services and of their financing;
2 supply of market regulations;
3 supply of other regulations of social life;
4 supply of macroeconomic monetary, fiscal and income policies and institutions;
5 redistributions.

The possible orderings are:

  (i) $(a \leqslant b < g)$
 (ii) $(a < g < b)$
(iii) $(b < a < g)$
 (iv) $(b < g < a)$
  (v) $(g < a \leqslant b)$
 (vi) $(g < b < a)$

Obviously, these 'social costs' include the loss of potential benefits. Activities with no net benefit should not be chosen even if undertaken under the best-ranking solution.

As for the subsets (i) and (ii), the correct constitutional choice to be made by the rational European constituents would be to leave them in the private sphere of action unless a *clear case* can be made in favour of public action. The existing EEC constitution, indeed, already includes precise clauses in favour of the free market role – which is not equally assured by most of the national constitutions of the member countries. This difference is explained by the fact that benefits from European unification largely derive from the formation of a broadened competitive market. Existing governments are already huge (according to many, 'too big'); therefore to find room for the new functions of EU one should, whenever possible, shrink the size and scope of existing public activity to avoid the expansion of EU through an expansion of the public sector as a whole.

Much public regulation may be effectively replaced through regulations by private associations, with some limited compulsory coordinating role at the government level. In this framework the fact that European money (ECU) developing mostly as a 'private institution' appears as a rational choice. The EU proper function here could be in the area of coordination and guidelines.

There is a more insidious case: that in which a 'public supply' has been allowed, in the form of an assignment of a 'regulatory' function f in a given sector to the domestic government. Here, according to ordering (i) and (ii),the EEC should be left outside the picture. *However, for the reason already noted, one may conceive a full assignment to the EEC of 'deregulation' in the area of f.*

What should one do, however, if some activities that would be suited to private activity have been assigned to EEC regulations, as may be the case for some agricultural actions more suitable for the free market? If $a \leqslant b < g$ for, let us say, one out of ten countries, the unanimity rule will fail to achieve the optimal solution, unless liberalizing log-rolling (not easy in the present EEC corporatist atmosphere) can take place.

The constitutional problem to be solved is not only that of agreeing on the assignment of f to the EU, but also of agreeing on suitable rules of decision-making for the effective exercise of the assigned (deregulation) function.

Let us proceed to subsets (iii) and (iv). The main reasons for the assignment of functions to national or local rather than to new supranational governments appear to be: differentiation of preferences and competitive supplies in the area of public goods; diseconomies of scale of huge bureaucracies and closer democratic control; lack of entitlement of the higher government to exert functions implying extensive powers on persons and wealth; positive spillovers from other (assigned) functions; and the cost of change implied by devolution to a new government. Personnel redistribution, from a social contract point of view, should be precluded from the EU since, as noted, under the veil of constitutional ignorance, full mobility of future citizens of the various countries cannot be assumed.

Similarly, it is illogical, in a contractarian approach, to expose future generations to the risks of the burden of a public debt – even for capital expenditures – issued by the EU government, whose bequests of tangible benefits to the future EEC members are still too modest to warrant such an insidious entitlement to their wealth.

Given the dominant size of national budgets and the constitutional limits to EU budgets, and given the fact that public debt is constitutionally inappropriate to the EU budget, macroeconomic functions in the area of fiscal policy must belong to the member states. Nevertheless, given the large externalities of these policies, coordination by a EU authority would improve their results, thus improving the functioning of the Common Market.

As for defence, a EU vertical coordination contradicts the entitlement of national governments to this supreme tutorial function, which – as noted – cannot be removed through Hobbesian factors, since these have already caused a broader alliance. Horizontal coordination among the EU countries could, however, increase the effectiveness of their defence expenditures and of related technological spillovers to the a sector.

As for income policies, the case for some vertical coordination at the EU level is supported by the fact that they consist not only of instruments pertaining to the jurisdiction of domestic governments, but chiefly of choices of units that should compete in the unified EEC area.

Under the unanimity rule, as for its ordinary functioning, the EEC is certainly less dynamic than national (or local) governments. Unless EU decision-making is made more efficient, there is a presumption against the 'centralized' solution, both for the direct exercise of functions and for their vertical coordination.

In orderings (v) and (vi), assignment to the EU prevails over assignment to private units and domestic public powers. But since the budget must be balanced, either taxes are increased or expenditures are reduced. The room for EEC tax powers is clearly a matter for a EU constitution, where agreement *per se* is not easy.

There is, in addition, the question of the non-neutral status quo of the EEC budget, on which this finance has to be added.[15] Unlike the United States in the nineteenth century, the EU has to develop its appropriate functions in an age in which state and local governments have already expanded (and over-expanded) their activities to the highest levels. Reducing domestic public expenditure may be an extremely difficult operation. And as for reducing wasteful expenditures in the EEC, certainly one cannot hope to go very far through the unanimity rule. Furthermore, the existing distinction of obligatory and optional expenditures creates an asymmetrical situation.[16]

This is not the place to discuss in detail the assignment criteria that enable a 'pre-federal' government to perform activities of regulation and of provision of goods and services. The criteria include: externalities (or spillovers), economies of scale (for separable goods) and of systems (for the provision of goods and regulations with elements of interconnection), competition in innovations, and the net value of a political tutorship at this level (where the gross benefit has to be weighed against the loss of sovereignty).

Clearly, such activities as scientific research, higher education, European communications, environmental protection, etc., belong to the set of eligible EU functions. The Hirschman (1981) linkage paradigm illustrates this point most generally. The seminal reason of the EEC, as noted, is the creation of a common market, with the attendant benefits of free competition. But this creation produces a chain (or linkage) reaction in the ranking of b over g and also of private over public action. Thus, corrective interventions in weaker regions imperilled by the Common Market may be justified. Once a unified agricultural market implying trade diversion has been accepted, g expenditures to maintain its functioning have acquired a permanent status, even if not always a persuasive justification. Rules of the game for industrial policy at EU level are an obvious result of the linkage effect. A unified customs duties administration should follow from the very fact that the Common Market implies a customs union, if everybody (including the domestic bureaucracies) were loyal to this basic tenet.

For similar reasons, functions in the area of money would appear typically appropriate for the European union. However, given the links between monetary and fiscal policy and national autonomy here, the effectiveness and equity of a EU monetary policy is imperilled. Thus, the case for a true European Monetary Union is weakened. On the other hand, it may be very difficult to persuade the central bankers to release some of their discretion to a supranational entity, unless their association retains the ultimate powers in this area.

A summary of the discussion of the foregoing is given in table 10.1.

10.5 POSSIBLE CONSTITUTIONAL OPTIONS

There are several ways to minimize the risk of (country) anti-Paretian solutions while increasing the scope for Paretian gains:

1 a 'qualified unanimity' rule, when the unanimity principle is unavoidable;
2 a 'workable' qualified majority rule;
3 dividing the set of possible choices into subsets, applying different decision rules to different matters;
4 constitutional *limits* to the choices or their results;
5 constitutional *principles* to be observed in the ordinary choices.

The unanimity rule, at the European constitutional level, appears unavoidable, for a long period of time, because of the feebleness of the 'veil of ignorance' assumption. The unanimity rule may be needed also in some ordinary matters, where the dangers of exploitation of individual countries may be particularly important.

However, it seems useful to try to adopt some qualifications to reduce the inherent strictness of the principle. A 'social contract' positive approach may help in the task, leading to a smoother formulation of the Luxembourg clause. Let us consider the approach of Scanlon (1982).

Scanlon's contractarian criterion of 'reasonable refusal' (the RR principle) states that it would be unreasonable (ethically unjustified) for others to refuse to undertake a given choice or action if we, being put in their place and comparing the two positions, could not refuse. The essence of the RR principle is that it is better to find agreement on some common principle than on none at all, for *ethical* reasons. We may replace 'ethical' with 'utilitarian' if we expect gains from a societal progress, as it is in the case for a EU social contract; there are spillovers from the agreement on any common principle, because it enhances the sense of community, thus fostering new agreements.

If this is true, 'reasonable agreement' rather than 'benefits for every party' should be the true long-run Paretian criterion. RR is weaker than a pure Pareto criterion because it allows 'reasonable losses' for some party, while the pure Pareto principle implies that no party has to incur

Table 10.1 *Government Intervention: Summary of Possibilities*

	Non-market regulation	Market regulations	Supply of goods and services	Redistribution		Supply macroeconomic institution and regulation		
				Personal	Regional	Monetary	Fiscal	Become P.L.
Private actions	P	P	P	—	—	P	—	P
State and local govt. actions	P	P	P, C	P	P	P	P	P
European govt. actions	P	P	P, C	—	P	C, P	C	C

P   Provision of.
C   Coordination of.

a loss. In a 'rule utilitarianism' framework, one bears some losses with the expectation that others in their turn, in keeping with the RR principle, will agree to undergo reasonable losses for the 'common interest'.

While Scanlon halts at a qualitative level of comparison of losses and benefits of two social parties who 'exchange their place', it seems useful to elaborate a more articulated code of RR behaviour. If the loss of A is 'bearable' and the losses of B and C, arising from a veto by A, are individually no smaller, A should not be entitled to cast a veto. If the loss of A is 'unbearable' while the losses of B and C, caused by A's veto, are bearable, then A can cast a veto.[17]. If the loss of A is 'unbearable' and the lack of gains of B and C is larger, A still is entitled to cast a veto, since the *loss of gains* is more bearable than a *true loss* – unless B and C are so poor that it is 'unbearable' for them not to have some gains.

One may object that this seems arbitrary, because of the difficulties of country comparison and because of the vagueness of such concepts as 'bearable loss', 'large loss', inequality of wealth, etc. But practical considerations give content to a general rule like that of RR. The Luxembourg clause, for example, emerged through constant behaviour. The RR principles that I am now suggesting replace it may be viewed as its rationalization; according to the Luxembourg clause, a country is authorized to exert a veto whenever some of its important interests – according to its own appreciation – may be damaged. The RR principle tries to increase communication among the parties in order to render less vague the relevance of interests claimed to be damaged, and compares them with the interests of the benefiting countries in the hope of developing common principles.

Buchanan and Tullock's general solution for ordinary choices seems to be a uniform 'qualified majority rule'. However, a careful interpretation of their basic analysis shows that this 'monistic solution' does not follow from their paradigm: decision-making costs may be different for the various matters, as may transactions costs. In fairness, however, Buchanan and Tullock view external costs as more preoccupying than transactions costs; and a large part of their discussion is devoted to how consensus may emerge through log-rolling.

It is mostly from Wicksell's seminal contribution that one can derive arguments for a simple majority rule combined with various degrees of qualified majority principles. As for a union of states, there is, in respect to the standard paradigm, a complication arising from the fact that a 'majority' may consist of a majority of population and a majority of countries, unweighted or weighted for their incomes or their currency reserves and the like. Furthermore, a coalition of countries may be more persistent than a coalition of interests.

As for the Commission, the simple majority rule is adopted and the four large countries have no more than 2 of the 14 seats, while the other countries have only 1. Since the population percentage of the small nations is about 15 per cent, clearly, decisions might be taken here by an official majority representing a minority of the population.

As the Assembly is elected through the principle of 'one citizen–one vote', the devolution to it of given matters would automatically imply that, whatever majority rule is adopted, it will be the majority of the EEC population and not of the member countries. On the other hand, except for some budgetary votes, the simple majority is sufficient for Assembly deliberations – normally a simple majority of votes cast, exceptionally in the stricter version of the majority of its members.

The qualified majority scheme provided for the Council – six countries and 45 votes out of 75, with the four major countries having 15.9 per cent of the votes each – apparently protects important minorities from the costs of external effects. Since each larger nation has 10 votes out of a total of 75 and three of the small nations have 5 votes each, the countries-majority rule acts as a constraint on the 45-votes majority rule, ensuring that the four large nations cannot form a winning coalition with just one of the six small countries.[18]

The majority required to allow a veto power to a given country can be easily determined through the formula

$$V_m = V_t - (V_i - k) \tag{1}$$

where V_m is the 'required majority' as a percentage of total votes assigned to country i, V_t is the total number of votes and k is 1 vote. It follows clearly from this formula that, while a couple of large nations can never be exploited, any single large nation is potentially subject to exploitation, since each has 15.9 per cent of the votes, while the 'required majority' of votes of the EEC – let us call it $\bar{V}_m$ – is 71.5 per cent. Thus,

$$V_m = 100 - (15.9 - k) = 83.1 > \bar{V}_m$$

On the other hand, a group of four small countries, including the main three, could become an 'exploited minority'.

It should be added that sometimes the mere reliance on the population criterion does not seem appropriate. Thus, for a monetary union, votes should be distributed according to reserves, if one wishes to make sensible the qualified majority rule.

It is probably for these reasons that the Luxembourg clause has been tacitly approved, for all ordinary decisions of the Council, because of the fear of exploitation by both large and small nations.

Wicksell (1958) in 1896 distinguished four categories of issue in discussing the application of voting rules:

1 matters of ordinary legislation, where 'freedom of movement, of occupation, religion, research and of press … remain permanent

features of the civilized world', but a choice between mutually exclusive alternatives must be made;

2 public goods and the related taxes, which should be considered as their prices;

3 legislation having to do with disputable titles and privileges; .

4 expenditures for previously existing obligations, which should be met independently from the utility expected to be received by the country.

For categories 1 and 4 Wicksell holds a simple majority rule on the ground of the necessity for deciding and (for category 1 only) because of the fact that, at any event, the accepted principles of the 'civilized world' hinder oppressive choices.

For category 2, Wicksell maintains that an 'approximate unanimity' would be appropriate since only in this way is one assured that 'each individual would be certain that he would never be burdened with a larger share of the costs (of public expenditures) than he personally or his interest group had accepted through their representatives in the legislature'. Furthermore, the aggregate amount of public expenditure of each type will not exceed the cost that citizens individually are prepared to sustain, 'The practical realization of the principle of voluntary consent and unanimity, as I should like to call it, requires first that no public expenditure ever be voted upon without simultaneous determination of the means of covering their cost.'

Wicksell's 'approximate unanimity' runs from 3/4 to 4/5 and even 9/10. It is a 'qualified majority', derived 'from practical reasons', i.e. from the general interest to reach a fruitful conclusion through the voting procedures.

Quite different is the approach to category 3, which greatly affects the matters of distribution of existing property rights and incomes:

> If there are within the existing property and income structure certain titles and privileges of doubtful legality or in open contradiction with modern concepts of law and equity, then society has both the right and the duty to revise the existing property structure. It would obviously be asking too much to expect such revision ever to be carried out if it were to be made dependent upon the agreement of the person primarily involved. (Wicksell, 1958)

On the other hand, Wicksell believes that in these distributional matters one should 'proceed cautiously enough'. Therefore he concludes that 'it would be quite in order to make decisions of this kind subject to a more or less qualified majority, but such a rule would be a matter of preserving a certain desirable stability in social relationships.' Thus, here, the qualified majority rule must be conceived as a way to introduce a bias in favour of the status quo.

Following the Wicksellian classification, the vast area of legislation having to do with freedom of movements, occupations and trades, in which the EEC already has jurisdiction, should be brought under the simple majority rule. This legislative power could be directly exerted through EU regulations (i.e. 'true' laws of immediate application) rather than through 'directives' (i.e. laws setting the principles for national laws to be enacted to apply them); a matter of debate could be whether these choices should be kept to the Council, where the (simple) majority rule would mean a majority of the voting rights of the member states (and perhaps of states), or devolved to the Assembly, where the simple majority means a majority of representatives coming from different states. In support of retaining several of these norms to the Council is the argument that they have but a modest substantive legislative content, most being technical norms rather than 'laws' in the substantial meaning of regulation of subjective rights.

The Assembly could concentrate on normatively 'richer issues': could be empowered to enact, under the simple majority, legislation in general criminal law, the family law, the law of contracts, the commercial law (including regulation of companies) and private finance laws. Thus, the EU could become a reality in vital aspects, without 'budgetary costs'. Here legal preferences may cross national frontiers, and the parliamentary debate may help to get an advanced unified legislation with the broadest point of view. A qualified majority for category 2 of Wicksell's classification and the related link between specific expenditures and revenues fits perfectly with the bulk of the EU budget, since personal redistribution functions are not attributed to the EEC budget, nor could they be recognized in the foreseeable future. The citizens, more than the countries should be considered here to have tax prices.

Wicksell proposes a 'conservative' qualified majority principle for legislation involving the structure of property rights and incomes, i.e. distributional matters. The EEC has (and should have) competence in the area of regional redistribution through the Social Fund and the Regional Fund, to the benefit of *less favoured areas*. Here the Wicksellian pro-status quo rule should be applied 'in reverse', i.e. to preserve existing expectations of the regions that have been entitled to this European redistribution in order 'to preserve a certain desirable stability in social relationships' (as for regional solidarity).

Finally, Wicksell's category 4 is also quite appropriate in EEC matters: existing financial obligations, whether related to useful expenditures or not, must be met, and therefore agreement on the means of finance must be reached. This is, typically, the situation with an EEC budgetary deficit; it is not permitted by the Treaty (article 199), but if, for some irrational reason, it arises, it must be covered, because the Community is not allowed to issue debts and a respectable institution must honour its obligations.

Wicksell's classification is not exhaustive. The vast and diverse set of 'regulatory functions' such as those in the area of customs duties, trade, services, requirements for industrial and agricultural products and so on, minimum prices of agricultural commodities and other dirigiste measures that are crucial to EU problems is only partially covered by his category 1 relating to 'necessary legal choices' coming under the label of 'ordinary legislation' or general rights. However, it can easily be adapted to take care of the dual character of the regulatory activities, some being *necessary* legal choices, others only *optional*.

Customs duties, foreign trade restrictions, minimum and maximum prices and analogous 'optional' measures providing protection to producers or/and consumers should be assimilated to the supply of public goods and related tax prices. Even if their benefits do not flow through the budget, they impose analogous burdens to provide gains on which one should compensate the losers. The rule of 'approximate unanimity' of delegates or representatives of different countries should guarantee that they provide Pareto improvements and that some sort of compensation is actually paid to citizens and countries that, through specific measures, bear losses higher than the burdens. Parliamentary log-rolling should protect against bargaining among restricted interests and/or stalemates. But also, excess expenditures belong to the area of *necessary* choices, where a decision one way or the other must be taken. Here perhaps one could combine the qualified majority rule applied to the supply of goods with the principle of a growing domestic contribution to the EEC increasing expenditure imputable to a given country.

'Unanimity', as seen, is required by the Treaty to design the guidelines of coordination for stabilization policies, while a qualified majority is required to carry them on. This is a naive procedure, given the difficulty, if not the inconsistency, of the distinction between guidelines and specific actions in these areas. On the other hand, time-consuming procedures are not appropriate for macroeconomic policies. Perhaps one should scale down the scheme, requiring some income-weighted qualified majority both for the 'rules' and for the exercise of authority to implement or complement the macroeconomics rules. For some quick decisions, however, a simple majority may be preferable.

As for further progress in the area of defence and foreign policies, perhaps one could combine the Scanlon RR unanimity rule with an exclusion clause: those who are not interested in the agreement might be excluded.

The risk of exploitation or undesired choices may be reduced to 'reasonable' (in the RR sense) dimensions through the (Buchanan–Tullock) device of a two-layer system: constitutional constraints and guideposts and ordinary legislation operating within this framework or design.

The present system of approval of the budget requires a complicated qualified majority principle for so-called non-obligatory expenditures, a much simpler decision-making process for the obligatory expenditures,[19] and strict unanimity for new fiscal resources.

These requirements may be simplified, while keeping a qualified majority principle, if constraints to perverse or excessive country redistribution relating to fiscal revenues and expenditures and to protectionism are provided through a constitutional formula of fiscal correction. In addition to the increase in VAT assignment, other financial resources could be found to finance the EU budget if allocation reasons so suggest. Here, however, a 'constitutional limit' should be applied on the revenue side, in addition to the specified constraints on the expenditure side.

10.6 CONCLUDING COMMENTS

One might argue that, while boundary constraints can be easily introduced in a constitution (if agreed upon), it is foolish to impose constitutional constraints in the form of 'general guidelines'. Actually, several constitutions include emphatic and inane sentences with regard to fostering human and social progress, economic welfare and other general values. Articles 2, 6 and 39 (among others) of the Rome Treaty are typical examples of this tendency.

However, this need not be the case. Articles 100 and 101, on the harmonization of legislation against distortion of competition, are typical of general constitutional principles with a core of unambiguous operational content: the room of choice is constrained, in the first case, through the specification of a definite direction, namely the removal of obstacles to, and distortions of the Common Market, and in the second case through a 'procedural rule' setting forth an authority issuing corrections whenever domestic legislation distorts competition within the Common Market.

Because of these basic constitutional rules – substantive and procedural – the assignment to EU, under simple majority, of full functions of direct legislation in the area of regulatory power necessary to market functioning, as well as in other areas of Wicksellian 'ordinary legislation' having to do with general rights, corresponds to the Wicksellian concept of rationality in areas of *necessary choices* among alternatives in the framework of generally accepted principles.[20]

NOTES

1   At the constitutional level, obvious references are Buchanan and Tullock (1962), Harsany (1976), Rawls (1971), Sen (1970) and Sen and Williams (1982).

2 For this type of inconsistency see Rowley and Peacock (1975) and Barry (1983).

3 For Buchanan and Tullock, the liberal postulate appears easily derivable from their 'individualistic postulate'; for Rawls, it is pervasive of his list of 'primary goods'; for Sen, it is implied by his specific criticism of welfarism and Paretianism; and for Harsany, by his 'individualistic ethic' and his 'rule utilitarianism'.

4 The word 'bureaucracy' in the public choice lexicon includes also the army.

5 Politicians might sharply disagree about the *details* relating to the powers of chambers, of the head of state and his role and so forth, while ordinary citizens may be concerned only with *basic* options.

6 The post office and public debt, for example, go beyond the Nozikian minimal state (see Nozik, 1974).

7 In addition to the powers already given by the old Articles of Confederation, the Congress was given, by the new Constitution, the power to levy taxes, duties, imposts and excises, to regulate commerce with foreign nations and among the states, to pass bankruptcy and naturalization laws, and *'to make all laws which should be necessary and proper for carrying into execution the foregoing powers'*.

8 For this concept as applied to the assignment of functions to the various levels of government see Breton (1974, chapter 4) and Breton and Scott (1978, chapter 5).

9 The unpleasantness of this perspective for the larger states actually led to a 'great compromise', signed on 7 June 1787, whereby membership of the lower House was apportioned among the member states according to population whereas Senate seats were assigned equally two to each state. Another question of interest to weaker states concerned slavery: 'Should the slaves, so numerous in some of the southern States, be counted in apportioning the number of representatives to which the states were entitled? Or should these slaves be regarded as property rather than persons? The South ... wished to count its slaves when the question of representation in Congress arose but not when taxes were to be levied. A reasonable, if utterly illogical, solution was found in the decision to count five slaves as equal to three whites both in the apportionment of representatives and in the assessing of direct taxes' (Hicks, 1957, pp. 185ff.).

10 Another argument in favour of a stronger US government were the fears of the wealthier classes of the rising claims emanating from the inferior classes (see Beard, 1913, 1935).

11 See Peacock (1983), which emphasizes the 'on-the-job leisure factor', and Forte and di Pierro (1980).

12 On the utility functions of politicians, in addition to the path-breaking work of Downs (1957), see also Breton (1974, chapter 7), Breton and Scott (1978, chapter 8), and Peacock (1979, chapter 1).

13 Interest groups in the existing EEC setting have an official recognition and a convenient institutionalized place of action in the Economic and Social Committee with a special place reserved for agricultural interests. The influence of a corporate chamber in being able to reinforce sectional interest deserves more critical attention.

14 In a forthcoming paper (Forte, 1985a), I distinguish between two types of politicians, namely 'power and prestige maximizers' (political entrepreneurs) and 'safety seekers' (bureaucratic politicians). The first kind of politician will

pursue a strong Paretian strategy, subject to constraints, whereas the second kind of politician (and most bureaucrats) will pursue a maximin strategy, with a preference for the status quo whenever risks of losses are involved.

15 The discussion on measuring EEC burdens and benefits is highly complex, with respect to both the fiscal burdens and benefits and the losses and gains arising from EEC agricultural market regulations and border duties. See the recent report of the Institute of Fiscal Studies (1983).

16 I have discussed the methodological issues arising from the different interests of the different member countries in Forte (1984, 1985b).

17 This entitlement might be qualified by reference to the relative wealth of the respective countries.

18 The six nations clause is not required when the deliberation must be undertaken under proposal of the Commission: where the small nations, as we have seen, are over-represented. The table lists the percentage distributions of population, incomes and voting rights.

Countries	Population, 1982 (%)	Income, 1982[*] (%)	Council votes[**] (%)	Commission votes (%)
Germany	22.70	25.35	15.9	14.3
Italy	20.84	18.24	15.9	14.3
UK	20.74	18.35	15.9	14.3
France	19.90	22.02	15.9	14.3
Netherlands	5.20	5.34	7.9	7.1
Belgium	3.60	3.83	7.9	7.1
Greece	3.60	1.97	7.9	7.1
Denmark	1.90	2.94	4.8	7.1
Ireland	1.25	9.82	4.8	7.1
Luxembourg	0.13	0.14	3	7.1

[*] At purchasing power.   [**] Qualified majority.

19 Although a limit to them has been imposed following a new 'fiscal discipline' decision of the Council.

20 Wicksell's statement that 'freedom of movement, of occupation, religion, research and of the press, ... remain permanent features of the civilised world' appears a bit too optimistic. A binding EU constitution embodying these principles is clearly a logical outcome of his framework. For the statement that the exercise of a general regulatory power is *unavoidable* in order to have a well functioning free market, see Robbins (1937). For the statement that protectionist national regulations are also wrong from a socialistic interventionist point of view, see Wootton (1943).

11

International Agencies and the Peacock Critique

JOHN WILLIAMSON

11.1 INTRODUCTION

When I arrived as a young lecturer at the University of York, I took it for granted that governments, while sometimes stupid (especially when run by Conservatives), were essentially benevolent social institutions, at least so far as their subjects were concerned. I soon found this comforting Fabian assumption challenged by what I shall term the 'Peacock Critique', which held that governments are run by politicians and bureaucrats who may be maximizing a party or individual welfare function rather than any half-respectable specification of a social welfare function (see Peacock, 1979, ch. 1). With an embarrassingly long lag, I have come to accept the force of the Peacock Critique, and agree that it was a good idea to enquire into the likely motivation of the individuals responsible for implementing public policy before urging an extension to the role of governments.

As time has passed I have become ever more convinced of the force of the Peacock Critique. Today's *Washington Post* (of 1 August 1984) contains no less than four blatant examples of political auctioneering:

1 the decision of President Reagan, enthusiastically endorsed by Congress, to increases in social security pension benefits that were not required by the existing indexation provisions, thereby threatening the earlier heroic efforts of the Greenspan Commission to restore the solvency of the social security system;
2 a series of pork-barrel projects moving through Congress which provoked the comment by an appropriations committee staff member: 'There's probably more of this kind of thing this year when you compare it to non-election years, but for election years I don't sense it's any better or worse than usual';

3 approval by the Senate of a bill to continue selling electricity generated by the Hoover Dam for another 30 years at the rates set 50 years ago during the Depression, which are now 'one-fourth to one-fourteenth the national average';
4 administration action to tighten quota rules governing textile imports and increase the number of customs officials to fight 'textile bandits'.

The Reagan administration certainly seems to have done its best to create a case for mandatory curbs on the role of government, such as a balanced budget amendment, that it so ardently preaches.

When I write articles about the state of the world economy, I quite often end up by urging the international agencies to play a more energetic role. For example, I have at one time or another argued for the IMF to set its members current account targets; to develop its surveillance into the negotiation and policing of target zones for exchange rates; and to introduce a systematic element of anticyclical policy into its lending activities. (This list is not exhaustive.)

I suspect that the first time it occurred to me to wonder whether this propensity of mine might be vulnerable to the Peacock Critique was when I was musing on the confidence of another former colleague that his labours did indeed benefit humanity:

> If [the use of conditional liquidity is merely temporary] and if access to conditional liquidity is controlled by a presumptively wise international authority, there can scarcely be too much conditional liquidity in the world. By hypothesis, it can be used only by countries that are pursuing suitable policies, and such countries should have all the liquidity they need. (Fleming, 1961, p. 448)

The participants at this conference would seem to offer an ideal group before which to seek to justify the proposition that international agencies, unlike governments, are presumptively wise rather than presumptively self-serving. As a preliminary, it may be useful to lay out the standard view as to why we have created a set of international economic agencies. I shall then go on to discuss differences between the bureaucratic and political direction of national governments on the one hand and of international organizations on the other.

11.2 THE STANDARD PARADIGM

As a result of historical accident, the world is carved up into a collection of nation-states that have sufficiently cohesive internal organizations to be treated by international economists as agents analogous to the consumers and firms of standard economic theory. These countries seek to maximize their *national* self-interest, just as consumers and producers are assumed to maximize personal or corporate self-interest. Since many of the relationships between countries are not governed by competitive market forces, the question arises as to whether uncoordinated pursuit of national self-interest will lead to an efficient outcome. There is a burgeoning literature on the game-theoretic formulation of this problem (exemplified by the June 1984 conference of the London-based Centre for Economic Policy Research). The starting point is that uncoordinated national actions lead to a Nash equilibrium, which is in general dominated by cooperative equilibrium. Three of the classic examples are as follows.

Example A The world is in recession, but each country is afraid to expand unilaterally because this will generate either a current account deficit or inflation (or some of both). The problem is that a part of the benefit of demand expansion spills over abroad. A coordinated expansion would permit all to expand without generating a deficit or a depreciation to ignite inflation. The OECD needs to hitch up some locomotives.

Example B All countries have imposed a set of tariffs designed to maximize the national gains from trade. Multilateral free trade would be mutually advantageous, but no country has an incentive to dismantle its tariffs in the absence of reciprocal action. There is need for a GATT round.

Example C A country faces a payments crisis, as a result of some combination of external shocks and incompetent management. Its creditworthiness is exhausted; the imports that can be financed from prospective export revenues do not suffice to avoid prospective starvation and political disruption. For some mix of humanitarianism and strategic motivations, the 'rest of the [non-communist] world' wishes to provide enough help to ameliorate the hardships of the adjustment process. But naturally, each country would prefer the help to come from others: the benefits are a public good. There is need for conditional lending by the IMF.

The purpose of an international agency is therefore conceived to be that of providing expertise and institutional pressure for countries to take proper account of international spillover effects, and mechanisms whereby costs for the provision of international public goods can be shared, so that a cooperative equilibrium (Pareto optimum) can be achieved. The analogy to the economic role postulated for the state by Pigou or Baumol is evident. And the same questions as the Peacock Critique raised in that context deserve to be posed in the international context.

11.3 BUREAUCRATIC MOTIVATIONS

International organizations are bureaucracies. Bureaucrats like to receive good salaries. They like to have bigger bureaus. They are not traditionally noted for an entrepreneurial willingness to accept individual responsibility. They do not aim to work themselves out of a job (see, for example, Peacock, 1979, 1983).

In these respects, international agencies are probably fairly typical bureaucracies. International civil servants are certainly not underpaid: the pre-tax equivalent salary of a vice-president of the World Bank is about double the top salary in the US civil service (though not extravagant if compared instead to banks in the private sector). Some bureaus seem distinctly unproductive – but I know of no bureau chief who has drawn the implication that the size of his bureau should be pruned. And most international civil servants seem as risk-averse as other bureaucrats. Agencies that lose their function do not disappear: they find a new role and change their name (the OEEC), or expand what used to be peripheral activities and change their Articles (the IMF).

In the early years, many of the characteristic ills of bureaucracy may have been mitigated by the idealism of the individuals involved. This advantage has eroded over time, while a particular ill of the international bureaucracy – the nationality quota – has widened and strengthened its deadening grip. International agencies are also one degree further removed from democratic control (let alone from payment by results) than are national governments. Where budget decisions are taken by non-weighted voting while budgetary contributions are highly skewed, as in the United Nations, it is generally conceded that bureaucratic excesses are particularly flagrant.

In one respect, however, some international agencies exhibit a difference from some national bureaucracies which I (at least) consider to be much in their favour: they place a higher value on professional competence. Admittedly, I am here drawing on my personal experiences and comparing the IMF, which is the most economist-dominated of the international agencies (Coates, 1985), with HM Treasury, which is the apex of the British civil service and therefore a bastion of the 'gifted amateur'. I am uncertain how widely this contrast would generalize, but I shall suggest below that it is not accidental.

11.4 POLITICAL MOTIVATIONS: NATIONAL GOVERNMENTS

Textbook descriptions of the role of economists in the policy formulation process juxtapose a 'policy-maker', who knows/determines/represents public preferences with an economist, who understands how the world works. Between them, they generate an optimal set of policies, with no need for the economist to trouble his conscience with questions of moral philosophy. Economists need to worry only about improving their professional skills in comprehending better how the world works.

No economist will deny the importance of that task. Neither will the applied economist doubt the need to understand that the objective function he is seeking to maximize is a reflection of social rather than personal preferences (let alone of personal utility), and accordingly that it stems in some way from the political process. But the model is mischievous if it suggests that the economist can responsibly push the question of formulating social preferences off to others. The 'others' who stand above him in the governmental hierachy are ultimately politicians, whose utility functions are only too often very far indeed from any plausible specification of a social welfare function. The political business cycle has never been more in evidence, Almost no one believes that budget and current account deficits of the size forecast on present policies in the United States are long sustainable; and no one who does not believe that can accept the proximate aims emanating from the White House as a legitimate representation of public preferences.

The question of how economists should determine the objectives that they seek to promote when in public service is one that has received surprisingly little systematic attention. There is of course a formal literature in the theory of social choice, but it was surely not Arrow's Impossibility Theorem that prompted Martin Feldstein to incur the political odium that he did by speaking out for what economists recognized, virtually unanimously, to be reason and responsibility. It seems to me that economists in fact tend to share a surprisingly wide range of values. For example, we take it as axiomatic that the future costs of policies that bring current benefits should be discounted rather modestly, at a rate comparable to the discount rate of a typical consumer. This is not an instruction that we could rely on obtaining from the political masters from whom we supposedly take our orders as civil servants. Again, we value both efficiency and equity, and we despise the special interest groups that deny the importance of either (and especially those that are inimical to both). Once again, the political process does not always deliver instructions that are consistent with those values.

The philosophical basis of these widely shared values of economists is generally perceived to be distinctly shaky. Efficiency cannot be rigorously defined independently of distributional considerations, and the desirability of equity (let alone the desirable trade-off with efficiency when one reaches the frontier) cannot be derived from the hallowed Pareto criterion. My own inclination is to wonder about this less than I would have done formerly, and to wonder instead whether it might not be worthwhile to explore whether there is sufficient consensus to support some economists' version of the Hippocratic Oath.

Suppose, perhaps optimistically (for there are rewards to being a dissident, and there is little reason to suppose that the personal behaviour of economists is more altruistic than that of other groups in society), that there was sufficient consensus to establish a code that would specify in general but not vacuous terms the objectives that economists were obliged to promote by virtue of their acceptance in the profession. What impact would this have on the role of the economist in government?

At the very least, it would suggest that the advice an economist gives should go beyond

given that your proximate objective is X, the appropriate policy is Y

to add

have you realized that proximate objective Z might be conducive to greater social good [in the following sense...]?

More radically, it would tend to subvert the doctrine of ministerial responsibility – a doctrine already largely ignored by politicians who sensibly refuse to accept responsibility for what they do not control, but which is still the basis for muzzling the exercise and expression of professional expertise by those who serve them. Economists in government should have the right to be conscientious objectors if asked to serve as propogandists, merely rationalizing the decisions of their masters, as Harry Johnson used to charge them with doing. They should have the right – indeed, duty – to express publicly, say, before parliamentary select committees, their professional assessment of the sustainability of current policies, rather than being asked to defend existing policy independently of their convictions regarding its wisdom. (Thus my vision of the alternative role of the economist is one in which he becomes a more active participant in the political process, not a god who sets himself above it.)

To dream of such possibilities is to emphasize how divorced they are from present realities. One reason is that governments, especially single-party hierarchical governments in the Anglo-Saxon tradition, tend to be ideological. And ideology is not just a commitment to certain *values*, but a belief that general principles are sufficient to establish desirable policy actions, without any need to understand the specifics of the situation involved. I have sometimes thought that the most useful thing that economists do in government is to provide judgements on which constraints are binding in particular circumstances; but if your master (or mistress) believes as a matter of faith that inflation is always caused by an increase in the money supply (for example), he or she is not in a position to exploit such advice. Economists in such a situation are at best marginalized, at worst reduced to the role of propagandists.

11.5 POLITICAL FACTORS: INTERNATIONAL AGENCIES

In this respect international organizations are very different. They are not dominated by a single country, nor is there normally a dominant coalition of countries with ideological cohesion. Thus, neither power nor ideology can provide a basis for decision-making. Some other basis for deciding on a course of action has therefore to be found. At least among economic agencies, like the IMF, the World Bank and OECD, the alternative that has been found places major reliance on technical economic arguments.

This is not to claim that such decisions as these organizations succeed in reaching – for they do not always reach agreement at all – are necessarily those that would secure the best marks in a university examination. Who says something counts for more than the technical merit of the argument. Traditionally, however, arguments had to have some technical merit: no one was prepared to say 'I don't want this; I have a veto, so that's that.' One had to present a technical reason for using a veto if one was not to forfeit general respect, which – at least until recently – the players were loath to do. But technical reasons can be countered with new technical arguments and ingenious new technical proposals, until eventually a winning coalition can be assembled. The outcome may be a tortuous compromise dressed up in lofty phrases with some quite anomalous side-payments tacked on, but the process of reaching that agreement will almost certainly have involved some fairly esoteric economic arguments. Of course, where there is no compelling need to reach a decision, there may be no agreed outcome at all: precedents are extremely powerful, and the agency may simply continue to do what it was doing before.

International agencies in which economic arguments are so central to decision-making present economists with quite different opportunities to those available within national governments, or at least within the British government as I recall it (and matters have by all accounts deteriorated since then). Arguments are less easily dismissed just because they do not appeal to a superior in the hierachy (though I recall one such instance from my time in the IMF), or because they offend the dominant ideology. They are correspondingly more likely to influence the decision that is reached. (This is not to say that working in an international agency is necessarily more rewarding to those of us who measure our rewards by our input into public policy formation: the choice is, after all, basically between failing to influence arguments that lead to action, and having an impact on arguments whose outcome rarely influences the course of events.)

Admittedly, international organizations may themselves come to acquire reputations for adhering to a particular ideology. Thus, the IMF is often thought of as monetarist, the World Bank as an apostle of free markets, the OECD as Keynesian, GATT as free-trading. There is some basis of truth in these characterizations. The IMF did, early on, develop a simple monetary model of the balance of payments, and it has continued to use this as the basis for negotiating adjustment programmes with member countries, which are monitored primarily by the country's compliance with a target for domestic credit expansion. The World Bank does stress the need for incentives and efficiency, and preaches the virtues of market-oriented policies as a means to those ends. Keynesian models were in their heyday when the OECD first acquired its responsibilities for macroeconomic coordination, so it is not surprising that it employed such models extensively. GATT was set up as an instrument for liberalizing trade, and its staff continue to believe in the virtues of its *raison d'être*.

A general orientation need not, however, imply an ideological position as I previously defined that concept. The question that needs to be asked is not whether an organization has a well-defined purpose or a normal set of techniques for going about its business, but whether its actions are determined independently of the circumstances of the case. Economic theories are, in this view, not propositions of universal validity, but generalizations that are useful under certain circumstances; an important task of the economist is to clarify what that range of circumstances is for any particular theory. An approach is ideological only if all cases are forced into the same mould, even where this is inappropriate to the circumstances of the case.

In offering this interpretation of what is meant by an 'ideological approach' I am aware that I have made the concept subjective, since there is need for a judgement as to whether dissimilar treatment is appropriate. But this is as it should be: clearly, some people do believe the IMF (for example) to be ideological. My own judgement is that the Fund's general approach is appropriate to the typical problem with which it has to deal (Williamson, 1983), and also that it is possible to argue for modifications in that approach that are needed to deal with particular situations. In that sense I regard the IMF, and the other international agencies mentioned above, as reasonably free of ideology. Indeed, it would be surprising if this were not true, given the diverse ideological predispositions of the many governments that have a say in directing such agencies.

In addition to their lesser susceptibility to ideologues, there is a second reason for supposing that international agencies may be less susceptible to the Peacock Critique than national governments: they do not work to a single electoral cycle. When one country is willing to dismiss the unfortunate implications of conceding to special interest groups in the hope that the adverse general impact will be delayed until an election is safely over, other countries will be free of such pressure and may therefore support the agency in a stand against myopia. Even when an election is not imminent, international obligations may help a government to do what it would like to do because it believes it to be in the general long-run interest, but may hesitate to do because of sectional interests or short-run impacts. Tariff cuts and payments adjustment provide two obvious instances.

11.6 CONCLUDING REMARKS

It seems to me that there are some reasons for believing that international organizations are less vulnerable to what I have termed the 'Peacock Critique' than are national governments.[1] This is not primarily because of differing bureaucratic motivations, although I draw some hope from the greater role played in decision-making by economists, since professional pride is surely the most effective constraint on bureaucratic imperialism. The more important point is that their political direction is less prone to suffer from the tyranny of the ideologue.

With the exception of the Common Agricultural Policy, I find it hard to think of major initiatives of international organizations that could be regarded as seriously misguided. There has been no international equivalent of the Maudling or Barber boom, the monetary squeeze that pushed sterling over \$2.40 in 1980–1, Concorde or the repeated pre-Thatcher bailouts of British industry. Nor is it easy to recall minor idiocies comparable to those quoted above from the *Washington Post* of 1 August that have been perpetrated by international agencies. The weaknesses of the international organizations lie, rather, in what they leave undone because of the difficulties of reaching an agreement among such a disparate set of masters. Perhaps that provides the strongest justification of all for continuing to argue simultaneously that governments have too much power and that international agencies have too little.

NOTES

I am indebted to my colleagues I.M. Destler and Stephen Marris, as well as to participants at the Festschrift Conference, most particularly the discussant Chris Milner, for comments that have prompted extensive revisions. Naturally, responsibility remains mine alone.

1 Discussion at the conference questioned whether this optimistic assessment applies to all international agencies as opposed to the more technical ones on which I have focused.

12

Real Exchange Rates and Economic Development

HERBERT GIERSCH

12.1 THE SHORT AND THE LONGER VIEW

The public policy debate tends to be dominated by short-run considerations. This holds for Keynesian economists and for policy-makers in general. Both tend to have a time horizon not extending beyond a two- or three-year period. In focusing on the short run, they are likely to overlook the fundamentals below the surface. These fundamentals, I suggest, are more relevant than is usually assumed. They relate to the real sector and hence to markets that are slow to adjust. Adherents of the rational expectations school suffer from a similar bias. They stress the absorption and processing of new information and thus tend to see an economy with short-run equilibria. This makes them pay less attention to the operation of market forces, which are sluggish and tied to past plans and decisions, rational or not, many of which can be corrected only gradually in the course of time. But time lags and boomerang effects do matter. What is treated as an exogenous 'shock' in a rational expectations model is often, in a longer perspective, the more relevant part of economic life that has to be explained. Monetarists, it is true, have a longer time horizon when it comes to judging the Phillips curve and the effects of alternative monetary regimes; but their approach leads them to neglect institutional rigidities, including labour market problems. It is here that the supply-siders have a role to play, but only if they go beyond the tax issue to encompass the whole supply side in the spirit of classical economics.

It is the purpose of this paper to correct some of these shortcomings and to lengthen the time horizon in the public debate about exchange rates, notably about the dollar–DM rate. Long-term interest rates, most of all the real rate of interest and the profitability of investment, will be brought into focus. The hypothesis emerging from this paper is that the dollar is likely to remain strong for fundamental reasons, i.e. for reasons rooted in the real sectors of the US and European economies. Temporary declines for short-term reasons are not, of course, excluded. They should therefore not be viewed as disproving the central thesis: what matters in the longer run are the vitality of an economy and its place and role in world economic development.

The longer run is to be understood as comprising more than one decade and at least one turning point in what Schumpeter called a 'Kondratieff cycle'. This widening of the time horizon brings to mind the fact that the real exchange rate between the dollar and the Deutschmark, i.e. the exchange rate adjusted for relative inflation, is now (end of July 1984) close to what it was in the 1950s, when most people thought it to be in equilibrium. To be sure, the United States and the Europe of today are not the same as they were 30 years ago. But such historical comparisons may still serve as a useful background for forming a broad judgement about the present and the future.

In a shorter perspective, i.e. in comparison with the mid-1970s, the dollar appears to be grossly overvalued and US interest rates look exotic. Within a Keynesian framework of thought, both can be seen as the result of a large US budget deficit which the Federal Reserve is unwilling to finance (Marris, 1984; Blanchard and Dornbusch, 1984). Monetary and fiscal policy are seen to work against each other in the United States, and the overindebted countries have to carry the double burden of high interest rates and an expensive dollar. If only the US government could be induced to reduce its deficit sharply by raising some taxes or by reversing a previous income tax cut, both the dollar and real interest rates in the world would fall and find an acceptable equilibrium level (Bergsten, 1982). This is the view prevailing in the international economic policy discussion.

A dramatic picture presents itself when cyclical forces are brought to the foreground in this Keynesian framework. The strength of the US upswing that developed in 1983 despite high interest rates is then seen to be the result of deficit spending (Marris, 1984). Much of the investment appears to be of the induced type (described by the acceleration principle), just as are the capital imports that the United States needs in order to finance the current account deficit. These induced capital imports support the exchange rate of the dollar. Sooner or later, perhaps in 1985, the present business cycle will collapse. Then the world will experience both a sharp decline of US interest rates and a downfall of the dollar below its equilibrium level, causing disruptions and new imbalances in the world economy. So this story goes. But it may well be that in the United States the fundamental conditions for investment and growth, and hence for a strong dollar, have improved relative to the fundamentals in Europe so that the dollar can remain strong irrespective of cyclical forces.

Monetarists usually take a longer view than politicians and Keynesians. Their assertion that an exchange rate is the relative price of two monies appears trivial at first glance, but their insistence on the quantity theory of money and its implications for the monies' domestic purchasing power certainly extends the time horizon. Moreover, they stress the real component in nominal interest rates and would therefore, also join my train of thought towards (changes in) real exchange rates. The bridge to the fundamentals is the concept of confidence in the long-run stability of the currency's domestic purchasing power. How a shift of confidence from one currency to another leads to currency substitution, and thus changes the real exchange rate, shall be considered below.

In a monetarist perspective budget deficits are likely to destroy confidence. As Latin American experience – and earlier European experience – amply shows, budget deficits are often the result of fiscal irresponsibility; they can induce central banks to pursue an inflationary policy designed to finance the deficits and to reduce the real value of the outstanding public debt. But this is not what has happened so far in North America and present-day Western Europe. If markets were suspicious in this respect, the dollar would be weak rather than strong.

Financial analysts watching day-to-day developments relate the strong dollar to high US interest rates, which they as well as monetarists (Mascaro and Meltzer, 1983) partly attribute to the volatility of Federal Reserve (Fed) policy. But doubts come to mind immediately: would a less volatile Fed policy weaken the dollar? The answer will, of course, be 'no' on monetarist grounds. We come closer to the fundamentals when we raise the question how the US economy can afford to pay the risk premium for this volatility, given the fact that its real sector is prospering and obviously has fully adjusted to present interest rate levels. The answer is to be found in a correspondingly high profitability (or marginal efficiency) of investment, which can be due either to the cut in business taxes or to technological innovation or to the downward flexibility of real wages in the US labour market. In an interdependent system it is, of course, difficult to single out any one of these factors. But it is significant that they all belong to the real sector and explain why this sector has enough vitality to support a strong dollar.

12.2 PURCHASING POWER PARITY

Those who say that the dollar is overvalued have, of course, an implicit norm of what its exchange rate would be in 'normal' circumstances, or ought to be on efficiency grounds. Sometimes they implicitly or explicitly use a reference period or entertain the idea that the dollar will settle on a level in the middle between the high value it achieved in 1984 and its trough in 1978. All this boils down to the question of what fundamentals really determine the external value of a currency in the medium run.

The appropriate starting point is the purchasing power parity (PPP) doctrine which is based on the law of one price. This law holds for tradables between any two countries if trade is not restricted and if tariffs and taxes, transport and transactions costs are low enough to be ignored.

Deviations from this norm arise because the basket that is used to measure the purchasing power in the countries to be compared includes not only standardized commodities for which the law of one price may be taken to hold, but also goods and services that do not enter trade at all. We call them local goods or non-tradables. If the relation between the prices of tradable and the prices of non-tradables develops differently in the countries concerned, we will find that the exchange rate (which makes the price of tradables equal) will deviate from PPP. These are long-run deviations. We can observe them in international comparisons between more developed countries and less developed countries, and we think that they are also likely to play a role in a process of catching up or lagging behind. The major points and cases will be spelled out below.

Before doing so I propose to focus on a range of goods that are neither purely local goods (like the service of land in housing rents) nor standardized commodities to which the law of one price applies fairly well. These goods – call them 'manufactures' – are sold not in perfect markets but under conditions of monopolistic competition. They include such specific items as custom-tailored capital goods, consumer goods fulfilling country-specific tastes and new products that can earn a monopoly rent, but must create their own markets first. Although these manufactures – and a great number of quite specific services – are tradables, they are not strictly subject to the law of one price. Together with tradables and non-tradables, they form part of the PPP basket.

12.3 TEMPORARY DEVIATIONS FROM PPP

Changes in the price of these manufactures relative to the price of standardized commodities can lead to a deviation from PPP provided there is no compensating change in the relative price of non-tradables. Ignoring non-tradables for the moment, we can say that changes in the price of manufactures relative to the price of standardized commodities matter in our context if they affect the terms of trade. This is the case in the following examples.

A country removing restrictions on its foreign trade in manufactures must, at least temporarily, lower the price of its exports in order to squeeze itself as an aggressive seller into tight world markets; perhaps it also has to pay more for the import of intermediate goods. This deterioration of the terms of trade goes along with a devaluation of its currency in real terms. This benefits the export sector and the import substitution sector at the expense of the domestic sector: the latter shrinks relative to the international sector. Let me call this the case of an export drive. It applied to West Germany in the early 1950s.

The export drive is, of course, facilitated if the exchange rates are fixed to begin with and if they happen to be fixed in such a way that the country can run an export surplus and the central bank can accumulate the other country's currency. This was relevant for Europe and for much of the Western world during the period of the so-called 'dollar shortage'. While the process of dollar accumulation gradually achieved its purpose, the downward deviation from PPP ought to have been corrected gradually to avoid an overshooting. But such overshooting did take place. A dollar overhang developed which again led to a rather drastic reversal of the real exchange rate at the time when the Bretton Woods system broke down. An overshooting in the reverse direction – an excessive devaluation of the dollar as it happened in the 1970s – was perhaps necessary for shifting resources in Europe from the export sector to the domestic sector and in the United States from the domestic sector to the export sector. The United States had to become a relatively cheap country for Europeans, and Europe a relatively expensive country for tourists from America. 'Relative' here means compared with PPP, but even more so in comparison to the period when Europe responded to the so-called dollar shortage.

Another deviation from PPP equilibrium, which is also connected with the terms of trade, takes place when a country, instead of squeezing itself into export markets, finds its export mix of manufactured products faced with a high income elasticity of demand and uses this demand-pull for expanding its export volumes instead of raising prices. The international sector grows at the expense of the domestic sector. The terms of trade are worse than they could be. Sooner or later the country will, like West Germany at the end of the 1960s, discover that it has an oversized export sector. An adjustment process will gather momentum, either in the form of a domestic cost-push – higher wages and costs at the given exchange rate – or in the form of a currency revaluation at constant prices. This adjustment process amounts to an improvement in the country's terms of trade. All rents from superior design and quality, from reliability and punctuality, which were formerly used for promoting volumes will then be collected in the form of higher export prices. This improvement in the terms of trade goes along with an upward deviation from the previous real exchange rate, most likely also with an overshooting compared with long-run PPP.

Furthermore, changes in the terms of trade that involve a deviation from PPP, and thus have an effect on the real exchange rate, will have to be brought about to accommodate capital movements that are exogenous to the economic system. One case involves reparation payments under conditions of full employment. Their transfer in real terms requires a shift of resources from the domestic sector to the export sector and hence a real devaluation of the country's currency, so that the export sector and the import substitution sector find their terms of trade *vis-à-vis* the domestic sector improved.

A parallel case is that of a country that has lived on capital imports and has run into excessive debt. In order to regain confidence in its viability and to improve its standing in international capital markets, it must shift resources from the oversized domestic sector to the export (and import substitution) sector and thus improve its balance on current account. A real devaluation of the exchange rate, involving a worsening of its international terms of trade, is necessary in such a case to remedy an otherwise hopeless situation.

The last case refers to a country that insulates itself from cyclical fluctuations in international demand. In a worldwide recession, a firm can maintain its sales by undercutting its competitors' prices. A country full of such firms in its export and import substitution sectors, supported by downward flexibility of wages, could maintain a high level of employment by exhibiting such price flexibility. Its trade balance on current account will then improve, its terms of trade become worse. In comparison with PPP and the situation before the recession, the exchange rate will be considered undervalued. A good substitute for this is a devaluation. Although some observers will call this a beggar-thy-neighbour policy, the strategy is perfectly defensible if the recession has its origin abroad. No valid objection on cosmopolitical grounds can be raised against it. Clearly, if every country behaved in the same way, without delay the real quantity of money in the world (or the price of gold under a gold standard) would go up, and the Haberler–Pigou effect would come into play. In the case of such a simultaneous action temporary deviation from PPP would, of course, be observable. The preceding argument applies symmetrically to the case of a country insulating itself from a worldwide boom (Giersch, 1970).

12.4 SUSTAINED DEVIATIONS FROM PPP

So far we have used the notion of PPP in a fairly loose fashion by concentrating on manufactures and standardized commodities and leaving local goods and their prices out of the picture. It is now time to shift the emphasis. In the long run, there is no reason to believe that the prices of manufactures will behave differently from the prices of standardized commodities. Market imperfections and processes of the kind described above fade into the background, and the relative size of the domestic and the international sectors can be taken to be in equilibrium. This means that the rewards for capital and labour are the same across sectors within the country.

But this intersectoral equalization of factor rewards does not exclude intersectoral productivity differentials. Indeed, they become important for explaining permanent deviations from PPP. They matter in inter-country comparisions if – but only if – they are different in the countries to be compared. In order to bring this into sharp focus, we consider only local goods that are not traded at all and international goods (traded goods) for which the law of one price holds. The main proposition here is that the production of tradables is subject to the productivity whip of competition (or what Samuelson, 1984, calls a 'Darwinian–Toynbeean challenge process'), whereas local goods are produced behind the shelter of transport costs and hence with much slack (x-inefficiency) or with an inferior technology.

There is no reason to expect greatly different productivity differentials between countries that have attained similar levels of overall productivity and development. Nevertheless, there are always exceptions. Thus, we observe that some local goods in Europe and some services that are more strictly regulated on the old continent (e.g. air freight, road haulage, postal services) are distinctly more expensive in comparison with internationally traded goods than they are in the much larger markets of the New World. If the European Community (EC) would deregulate and form a really common market, Europe would be even cheaper for US visitors than it is now.

As a general rule, however, poorer countries should be cheaper in PPP terms than richer countries, just as poorer regions or cities in the same country tend to have a lower cost of living level than richer regions or cities, where the costs of local goods and services are boosted by the scarcity element in housing rents – unless these non-tradables are produced with a correspondingly high productivity. The rule of rich countries being expensive countries holds to the extent (1) that local goods have significant weight in the PPP basket, and (2) that in the course of the development process productivity in the international sector rises more than in the local sector. The second condition is essential. The proposition has been formulated by Balassa (1964), although somewhat differently, and can be traced back to Harrod (1933) and – with some modifications – even to Ricardo (1817).[1] As indicated, it can be supported by the presumption that competition is a productivity whip that operates more forcefully in the international sector than in the sector producing local goods.

As a corollary, countries in a catching-up process, i.e. countries becoming richer relative to their trading partners, will have an exchange rate that, although still undervalued in absolute PPP terms until they have fully succeeded in catching up, is becoming less and less undervalued. Compared with the past, the catching-up country will experience an upward revaluation in PPP terms. Some observers using the past as a norm may even (wrongly) interpret it as an overvaluation. The process bringing this about includes not only competition, which raises productivity in the international sector more than that in the local sector, but also the technology transfer from the more advanced countries. This presumably also affects the international sector more strongly, or earlier. Apart from the technology transfer, the catching-up country is likely to benefit from capital imports. This, again, will affect primarily its international sector, and not so much – or only with a time lag – its domestic sector. Capital imports, of course, mean a deficit in the external balance on current account, and those who (wrongly) judge the exchange rate with the norm of a current account equilibrium will see a strong (perhaps additional) reason to say that it is overvalued.

When the German Expert Council in 1964 passed its first judgement on the DM–dollar exchange rate, the dominant view of the public was that the (fixed) rate was still what it ought to be. This is why the Expert Council, considering the catching-up process and its effect on PPP, said that the Federal Republic of Germany, which had been a cheap country (in PPP terms) at the beginning of the catching-up process, should have ceased to be one; the exchange rate, therefore, was to be judged as undervalued, and a revaluation (or an upward float) was to be put on the policy agenda (SR, 1964/5). But none of us at the time thought that the revaluation required for these reasons would be more than 5–10 per cent. There is no reason to question this judgement in retrospect. As the real exchange rate of the dollar against the DM is now (July 1984) about 5 per cent higher than it was in 1964, the dollar on these (partial) grounds appears to be overvalued by 10–15 per cent. The undervaluation of the DM in the 1950s and the 1960s took care, of course, of the original 'dollar shortage' and contributed to the accumulation of the dollar overhang mentioned above. There is therefore no additional item to be added on this account if we make an historical comparison the basis of our judgement.

12.5 CURRENCY DISTURBANCES: THE DOWNFALL AND RENAISSANCE OF THE DOLLAR

Historical comparisons with the 1950s and 1960s are valid only to the extent that the decline and rise of the dollar in the 1970s can be considered an episode arising from exceptional circumstances. Without going into detail we may just note:

1 the financial implications of President Johnson's Great Society Programme;

2 the inflationary financing of the Vietnam war;
3 the price control experiment of the Nixon administration;
4 the overdue breakdown of the Bretton Woods system;
5 the 1973 oil shock;
6 Watergate;
7 the bad luck of the United States under the Carter administration; and
8 the rise of inflation (to almost 14 per cent) and of inflationary expectations until late 1979.

This period, however, also includes events in the real sector which can be taken to have led to a reversal of the trend. Worth mentioning are the deregulation of the trucking and airline industries; the creation of millions of new jobs in response to demographic changes; the emergence of new technology centres which had hardly any parallel in the rest of the world, perhaps not even in Japan; and the astonishing fact that real wages declined, partly under the impact of inflation, partly in response to demographic changes and increasing female participation rates. Immediately crucial for the dollar exchange rate was, of course, the monetary stance adopted in late 1979, which led to positive and high real rates of interest, which had been negative when the dollar was at its low.

A country like the United States, which previously performed a leadership role but lost ground in this respect to its competitors, will suffer a devaluation of its currency in real terms for the following reasons:

1 If technological leadership is being lost, the (transitory) monopoly rents from innovation or from superior quality will disappear: people will have to work harder to export more to pay for the same volume of imports.
2 Monetary leadership may be lost, in the sense that assets denominated in the country's currency, including cash, suffer a decline in foreign demand because foreigners (as well as domestic holders of such assets) lose confidence in the currency's long term stability in terms of domestic purchasing power. In order to describe this case I prefer to use the metaphor that 'portfolios emigrate' or that 'the currency area implodes'. Emigration in this sense implies immigration into another currency area, which tends to become larger (Giersch, 1977, para 6). The 'implosion' goes along with a devaluation of the real exchange rate in a process of currency substitution.

If a country such as the United States after 1979 resumes its leadership role in the field of technology, or as a trustworthy supplier of the Western world's international money, it will experience a sharp upward revaluation of its real exchange rate. Why then should we be so surprised about the renewed strength of the dollar?

12.6 GROWTH EQUILIBRIUM

What would real exchange rates look like in a smoothly growing world economy? A first answer is that they should not be judged by the yardstick of current account balance because there is a positive role to play for autonomous capital flows from richer to poorer countries. Wilhelm Röpke once said that people in the upper floors of the income pyramid tend to devote themselves to capital formation while the inhabitants of the lower floors take care of population growth. I prefer to use the metaphor of a Thünen cone (Giersch, 1949, 1979) for portraying the world economy, or any spatial system with rich centre and poor peripheries. The cone can grow in a smooth fashion, i.e. with a minimum of structural change, if the marginal efficiency of capital tends to rise everywhere at the same rate and if capital flows from the rich centre, where the marginal propensity to save is high, towards the periphery, where it is closer to zero. However smooth the growth process may be thought of, it must be sustained by the creation and application of new knowledge, presumably in the centre, in order to prevent a fall in the profit rate under the impact of Ricardian constraints (rising rents). But such innovative growth in the centre goes along with what we call 'locational innovations', This means that the optimum location for producing standardized commodities is moving from the centre towards the periphery.

To bring about this locational shift, the countries closer to the periphery must make themselves attractive by having their domestic resources 'undervalued' via the exchange rate. Undervaluation in this specific sense means 'in terms of costs for the production of standardized industrial commodities', for brevity's sake called 'Heckscher–Ohlin' goods. The counterpart to this are high and rising rents and wages for local labour in the centre; these push the locus of production of Heckscher–Ohlin goods out to the countries closer to the periphery. The structure of real exchange rates must reflect this structure of cost incentives. If the overvaluations and the undervaluations (in this sense) are not sufficiently pronounced, the process of locational shift (locational innovations) will be retarded. Retardation grants excessive time for process innovation to defend the old locations for Heckscher–Ohlin goods. A reversal of factor intensities is then likely to emerge, as we observe it in Thünen's stationary model in the case of wood, as a result of relatively high transport costs for this commodity. Defensive process innovations are of course, also promoted by protectionist policies. Undervaluations and overvaluations have to be more pronounced if, in addition to transport costs, such policy-induced resistances are to be overcome.

This spread argument for real exchange rates is a close cousin of the amendment to the PPP theorem discussed above in section 12.4. There the reason was the high price of local commodities in rich countries (say, housing rents) which are part of the PPP basket; here, however, the reason is the price of inputs for Heckscher–Ohlin goods and an international cost differential needed to induce and support this continuous process of locational innovations. There, it was a cross-section comparison that would make sense even if the world economy were in a stationary equilibrium; here, we have overvaluation and undervaluation as part and parcel of a moving equilibrium, as the incentive system necessary for bringing about the minimum adjustment needed for a process of trickling down. We may still say that the law of one price holds for standardized commodities (apart from transport costs) at any moment in time, but then we have to consider that the value of the stock of fixed capital used in producing these goods goes down in the advanced countries under the influence of an exchange rate that people may feel to be overvalued. At the same time, the low valuation of the exchange rates of the less advanced countries raises the marginal efficiency of capital for the (potential) production of Heckscher–Ohlin goods in these countries.

This model of a smoothly growing world economy offers itself as a reference system against which important disequilibrium cases can be judged. With regard to the United States and the dollar, we can summarize so far as follows:

1 As a rich country, the United States ought to run an export surplus to support the outflow of capital to poorer countries. Yet, given the fact that there are poorer countries which have overborrowed and must regain confidence on world capital markets by servicing – and perhaps temporarily repaying – their debt, a deficit in the US current account may help to prevent a debt crisis. Imagine what would happen if the United States now behaved in a similar way as it did in the interwar period, when Germany tried to pay off its reparation debt but failed because the final recipient – via the inter-allied war debt – did not cooperate by running a current account deficit.

2 A high valuation of the dollar may hurt numerous firms producing Heckscher-Ohlin goods and stimulate protectionist demands in the United States. Yet this is exactly the type of competitive pressure that is needed for the relocation of these industries to less advanced parts of the world economy.

12.7 GROWTH LEADERSHIP

Countries leading in world economic development must be engines of economic growth. Those who associate with the expansion of demand –

implying that demand is the limiting factor – focus on budget deficits. The 'Reagan deficit' is thus seen as a source of growth.

However, the same observers who support Keynesian remedies for unemployment and stagnation criticize this deficit for raising the level of interest rates in the world. Some of them would like Europe and Japan to have higher public deficits instead of the United States, implying (or not?) that the level of interest rates in the world would be different in that case. (Would it really be lower if the world economy substituted second-rate borrowers for the very best public borrower it presently has?)

Nevertheless the Reagan deficit deserves criticism, first, if it has to be considered as an act of dissaving for the world economy as a whole, or, second, if it implies a waste of capital compared with a situation in which total public expenditure in the United States were the same, but the counterpart of the deficit were (additional) productive investment – say, in infrastructure instead of public consumption or rearmament. As always, the resulting judgement depends upon the reference systems chosen and the way the alternatives are evaluated.

If the Reagan deficit is seen to be the result of the cut in income taxes and business taxes, one can well argue that this cut is equivalent to a productive investment, to the extent that it helped to improve the incentive system and to raise the motivation level in society, including the propensity to work, to invest and to innovate. It is true that our bookkeeping rules do not allow us to consider this as an investment, but in certain circumstances it may be a better form of investment than an outlay for hardware of the same magnitude. Whether this interpretation has some value, however, can be judged only in the long run, or perhaps in comparison with Europe, where taxes are higher and where motivation levels appear to be lower.

From a European perspective or a vantage point that permits a long-run view the United States can be seen to behave as an engine for world economic growth. Its real sector seems to have adjusted to the growth conditions of our time much better than the real sector in large parts of Europe. In order to support this view, we may note or recall the following interrelated points.

1 While Europe suffers from a level of real wages that is still too high (Giersch, 1978; Artus, 1985) and from a rigid wage structure which does not allow sufficiently for relative scarcities (excessive wages for unskilled workers and for workers in structurally weak regions; too small wage incentives – after taxes and deductions for social security – for attaining qualifications, for accumulating human capital and for moving to better paid jobs elsewhere), the United States has a balkanised and hence more flexible labour market and a union system that has become much weaker after the strike of the air controllers and the severe 1982 recession. Instead of shortening the working week and

reducing the retirement age, which is on the agenda in Europe, the United States has raised the retirement age and also the number of jobs that support going real wages.

2 In Europe, profits are still low compared with the interest that can be earned on financial assets (Dicke and Trapp, 1984). They fail to respond to the shortage of productive capital relative to the supply of labour – the combination of capital shortage and unemployment that emerged in the 1970s (Giersch, 1978). The US economy, on the other hand, has succeeded in raising profits to levels that match the high real rates of interest that exist and that are likely to prevail as long as the structural unemployment (or capital shortage unemployment) calls for giving capital formation the first priority in the growth process. This is mainly due to flexibility of the US labour market.

3 In large parts of Europe, including the north of West Germany, people still believe technology to have a labour-saving bias, as one may expect it to have if real wages are excessively high; therefore, they adopt an attitude that amounts to opposing technical progress (Europessimism). In the United States the population has never been really affected by such opinion trends and seems to have almost maintained, or even recently strengthened, its optimism towards the future course of economic development and technological advance.

4 In the United States public opinion seems to have recognized that government regulations and private barriers to entry weaken the economy's capacity to adjust to future developments. In Europe large sections of society still cling to policy conceptions and political ideas that are closer to state regulation, corporationism or the traditional guild society (Eurosclerosis). There may have been some shift to conservatism on both sides of the Atlantic, but conservatism in Europe essentially means conserving traditional structures rather than conserving the flexibility of society.

Taken together, these judgemental propositions (perhaps very subjective ones, short of further research which appears desperately needed in this field) suggest that the United States is already much better prepared for starting a new spurt in economic development – at least in comparison with Europe, perhaps less so in comparison with Japan. In this perspective, Europe is seen to be in the very early phase of an adjustment process that is likely to cover more than one of the short-term business cycles that we have become accustomed to observe. In my opinion (or my unspecified socioeconomic model), the transatlantic time lag in the real sector's adjustment to faster growth may well lie in the range of five to ten years. It could be shortened by a concerted movement towards freer trade among Western countries. Freer international trade would surely help to break up internal protection in Europe's domestic markets. In that case, the immense productivity source of international trade and of competition from abroad could be tapped. This would allow monetary policy to anticipate a somewhat faster growth of potential output. But the prospects for such a move within the next couple of years appear to be dim.

12.8 THE SHORT AND THE LONGER VIEW IN CONTRAST

The transatlantic time lag in the adjustment to high real rates of interest and to new technologies supports an explanation for the strength of the dollar and for the superior performance of the US economy which has its foundations in the real sector rather than in the monetary-fiscal policy mix. The following statements may help to bring the two alternative explanations into sharp contrast.

If the Reagan deficit is the villain of the piece, capital imports into the United States are of the induced type. They will fade away with the weakening of the present upswing, so that the dollar will decline to correct a current account deficit which corresponds with the budget deficit. If, however, it is the high marginal efficiency (profitability) of investment in the United States that is the dominant force in the scenario, the capital flows into that country are more of the autonomous type. They will then decline only slightly during the next recession, which itself will be weaker if autonomous investments in the United States remain fairly strong. To the extent that the profitability differential between the United States and Europe is decisive and does not substantially decline, the real exchange rate of the dollar will continue to have strong fundamental support.

The short-run explanation suggests that European countries ought to boost domestic demand by running higher fiscal deficits. They would weaken the induced flow of investible funds into the United States and thus contribute to bringing down the external value of the dollar. The longer-run explanation offered here suggests that Europe should imitate the United States in reducing real wages, in changing its attitude towards technical progress and in opening up its markets, so that European markets become more flexible and more attractive to potential entrepreneurs. It is only in such a process of revitalization that Europe will regain its former competitiveness in long-term capital markets. Only then will the fundamentals induce a weakening of the exchange rate of the dollar *vis-à-vis* European currencies – then, however, in combination with a faster growth of potential and actual output in Europe. In this longer-run perspective there is no reason to object to potentially higher budget deficits in Europe, if they arise not from higher public spending but from tax cuts, which raise the profitability of investment and, by reducing marginal taxes for wage-earners, raise the motivation level of the labour force and the whole population.

The dominance of the short-run explanation in the public discussion has drawbacks for a lasting therapy of Europe's economic problems. By making investors believe that the real value of the dollar will come down quickly, this explanation discourages US foreign direct investment in Europe. It also makes European firms pessimistic about the longer-run prospects for exporting to the US market. In the longer-run perspective, the high dollar will raise the profitability (marginal efficiency) of investment in Europe's export sector. This structure of exchange rates could well transmit part of the driving power for sustainable growth that the US economy develops to Europe and other countries, However, Europe is unlikely to take advantage of it if the high external value of the dollar is considered to be a short episode rather than a replay of the development that Europe experienced in the 1950s and 1960s.

The view that real interest rates will come down rather quickly makes investors believe that it is not worthwhile reversing the present bias in investment and even in applied research, which favours capital-intensive and labour-saving technologies in sharp contrast to a situation that displays a shortage of productive jobs in relation to an abundant supply of labour.

The idea that Europe – and West Germany in particular – needs just a little bit of fiscal expansion supports populist pressures. This may very well weaken the efforts to reduce the waste element in public expenditures in order to free resources for productive investment in the private sector, which would be the right response to Europe's capital shortage-cum-unemployment. Moreover, the concentration on vague macroeconomic concepts like deficit spending impairs the chances for tax cuts designed to promote capital formation and the creation of new firms on the old continent.

Emphasis on short-run measures to boost demand may do less harm in the United States, where real wages were brought down in the 1970s partly under the influence of unanticipated inflation. But in inflation-experienced Europe, with fairly centralized wage bargaining in many countries, the wage problem will have to be tackled directly. Central-ized unions always tend to maintain that unemployment is not their fault and must, therefore, be due to exogenous factors (like technical progress) or to a deficiency of overall demand. But although it is effective demand that matters, i.e. demand in relation to supply prices, the unions yield to strong membership pressure for raising real wages when demand improves so that 'job owners' fully benefit from any productivity advance, cyclical or trend-based. It is true that a learning process has started in Europe, here and there; but it may be swamped by a policy debate which ignores the microeconomic foundations and depicts the US policy as the source of the evil. The problem is not only the real wages paid out to the employees, but the numerous restrictive regulations and practices which raise the shadow wage for the employers, as they often make the hiring of new workers an almost irreversible decision. Irreversibility here and a belief in the reversal of the strengthening of the dollar add up to a situation that is not nearly as encouraging for Europe as the situation was under US growth leadership in the 1950s and 1960s.

12.9 CONCLUSIONS

If there is to be a brand name for distinguishing this longer-view interpretation of the present dollar–DM rate, it may be called a 'flagship hypothesis'. By raising the marginal efficiency of investment, the US economy is speeding up its trend rate of growth relative to the laggards in the convoy. The driving power is autonomous investment rather than induced investment of the accelerator type. The capital imports into the United States, which compensate for the crowding-out effect of the Reagan deficit, are therefore more trend-based than cyclical. They raise the external value of the dollar and thus weaken the competitive position of the less productive parts of US manufacturing, to the benefit of locations in countries with lower labour costs. Some of the laggards have to transfer debt services; others see the marginal efficiency of investment in their export sector improved, but have difficulty in making full use of this imparted and imported driving force. This speeding-up of the pacemaker and lagging of the followers is a plausible explanation for the transatlantic tensions in the field of economic policy.

At the end of a tiring series of reflections, an applied economist must try to arrive at a hard conclusion. To make it short, I would be more than mildly surprised if the real exchange rate of the dollar *vis-à-vis* the Deutschmark dropped by more than 10 or 15 per cent on average during any period of 12 months over the next three years.[2] This rests on the (realistic) condition that the United States remains on a monetary path which does not give rise to inflationary expectations (as it did in the second half of the 1970s). Moreover, the flagship hypothesis suggests that the range for the fluctuations of the dollar might even have a somewhat higher floor. In subsequent years Europe may well succeed in lowering this floor, just as the world may succeed in bringing down the real rate of interest by accelerating capital formation and economizing on the use of capital. But such success on the exchange rate front will largely depend upon how far the old continent regains its strength in curing Eurosclerosis.

NOTES

This paper was written in the summer of 1984 and addresses itself to explaining the foreign exchange situation at a time when the world was puzzled by a strong dollar and a strong US upswing. I am grateful for helpful comments on earlier drafts to many of my collaborators in the Kiel Institute of World Economics, notably R. Fürstenber, H. Schmieding and F. Wiess.

1 'Since gold rewards are proportional to efficiency in the output of tradable goods, highly efficient countries may find the gold cost of providing their ... services, in which proportional economies cannot be made, higher than in the less efficient countries .... The efficient contries will therefore tend to have a high cost of living' (Harrod, 1933, p. 68). And Ricardo notes: 'the prices of home commodities and those of great bulk, though of comparatively small value, are, independently of other causes, higher in those countries where manufactures flourish' (Ricardo, 1817, p. 23). For a discussion of Ricardo's contribution to the PPP theory see Officer (1982) and Samuelson (1984).

2 When this paper was drafted, towards the end of July 1984, the exchange rate was approximately DM 2.85 to the dollar.

Appendix
Alan T. Peacock:
Bibliography, 1949–84

BOOKS, MONOGRAPHS AND PAMPHLETS

The Economics of National Insurance. William Hodge and Co., London and Edinburgh, 1952.

National Income and Social Accounting (with Harold C. Edey). Hutchinson University Library, London, 1954. (Translated into Japanese and Portuguese).

The National Income of Tanganyika 1952–54 (with Douglas G.M. Dosser). Colonial Office Research Studies no. 26, Her Majesty's Stationery Office, London, 1958.

The Growth of Public Expenditure in the United Kingdom (with Jack Wiseman). Princeton University Press and Oxford University Press, 1961.

Analytical Concepts of Fiscal Policy with Special Reference to Developed Countries. Centro de Estudos de Estatistica Economica, Collectanea de Estudos no, 15, Lisbon, 1962.

Education for Democrats (with Jack Wiseman). Hobart Paper no. 25, Institute of Economic Affairs, London, 1965.

The Welfare Society. Unservile State Papers no. 2, 1961; rev. ed, 1966.

Educational Finance: Its Sources and Uses in the United Kingdom (with Howard Glennerster and Robert Lavers). Report no. 5 of Unit for Economic and Statistical Studies on Higher Education, Oliver and Boyd, Edinburgh and London, 1968.

Economic Aspects of Student Unrest (with A.J. Culyer). IEA Occasional Paper no. 26, Institute of Economic Affairs, London, 1968.

Fiscal Policy and the Employment Problem in Less Developed Countries (with G.K. Shaw). Development Centre of the Organization for Economic Co-operation and Development (OECD), 1971.

The Economic Theory of Fiscal Policy (with G.K. Shaw). Allen and Unwin, London, 1971; 2nd edn 1976. (Italian ed, 1972; Spanish ed, 1974).

The Political Economy of Public Spending, 1971 Mercantile Credit Lecture. University of Reading, 1972.

The Oil Crisis and the Professional Economist. Ellis Hunter Memorial Lecture, University of York, 1974.

Welfare Economics: A Liberal Restatement (with Charles Rowley). Martin Robertson, London, 1975. (Japanese ed, 1977).

The Composer in the Marketplace (with Ronald Weir). Faber Music Ltd, London, 1975.
The Credibility of Liberal Economics. Seventh Wincott Memorial Lecture, Institute of Economic Affairs, London, 1977.
The Economic Analysis of Government and Related Themes. Martin Robertson, Oxford, 1979.
The Public Sector Borrowing Requirement (with G.K. Shaw). Occasional Papers in Economics no. 1, University College at Buckingham, 1981.
Too Many Town Hall Staff? (with Martin Ricketts). Report for the Federation of Civil Engineering Contractors, London, 1982.
Inflation and the Performed Arts (with Eddie Shoesmith and Geoffrey Millner). Arts Council of Great Britain, London, 1983.

EDITED WORKS AND TRANSLATIONS

Translation from the German of *Grundlagen der theoretischen Volkswirtschaftslehre (Theory of the Market Economy)*, by Heinrich von Stackelberg. William Hodge, Edinburgh and London, 1952.
Income Redistribution and Social Policy (editor, and co-author of chapter 5 with P. Browning). Jonathan Cape, London, 1954.
Classics in the Theory of Public Finance (co-editor with R.A. Musgrave). International Economic Association/Macmillan, London, 1958.
Public Expenditure; Appraisal and Control (co-editor with D.J. Robertson and author of chapter 1). Scottish Economic Society/Oliver and Boyd, Edinburgh and London, 1963.
Government Finance and Economic Development (co-editor, and co-author of chapter 14 with Gerald Hauser). Organization for Economic Co-operation and Development (OECD), Paris 1965.
Public Finance as an Instrument of Economic Development (Editor, and author of chapter 1). Papers prepared for a study course, Technical Co-operation Programme of the OECD. Organization for Economic Co-operation and Development (OECD), Paris, 1965.
Quantititive Analysis in Public Finance (editor, and author chapter 1 and co-author of chapter 8 with Elliot Morss). Praeger Publishers, New York, 1969.
Structural Economic Policies in West Germany and the United Kingdom (editor, and author of various chapters). Anglo-German Foundation, London, 1980.
The Political Economy of Taxation (co-editor, and co-author of chapter 1 with Francesco Forte). Basil Blackwell, Oxford, 1981.
The Regulation Game: How British and West German Firms Bargain with Government (editor and contributor). Basil Blackwell, Oxford, 1984.

CONTRIBUTIONS TO OFFICIAL REPORTS AND ENQUIRIES

Reform of Income Tax and Social Security Payments. Report of the Committee set up by the Liberal Party Organization (member). London, 1950.
Report of the Commission of Enquiry into the Natural Resources and Population Trends of the Colony of Fiji (Commission member). Legislative Council of Fiji Council Paper no. 1 Suva, Fiji, 1960.

A Survey of Education within the Framework of Social and Economic Development in Afghanistan (member of Mission and contributor). UNESCO, 1962.

Report of the Committee on the Generation and Disribution of Electricity in Scotland. (Committee member). Cmnd 1859, Her Majesty's Stationery Office, 1962.

Report of the Committee on the Impact of Rates (Allen Committee) (Committee member). Her Majesty's Stationery Office, 1965.

Royal Commission on Health of the Government of Newfoundland and Labrador, Vol 3, Appendix: 'The Economic and Financial Implications of an Expansion of Medical Services in Newfoundland'. October 1966.

Report of the Presidential Fiscal Reform Commission of the Government of Colombia (Musgrave Commission) (Commission member). Bogota, Colombia, 1969.

The Economics of Public Expenditure and its Consequences for Parliamentary Control (with Jack Wiseman). First Report from the Select Committee on Procedure, Cmnd 410, Her Majesty's Stationery Office, 1969.

Public Policy and the Scrutiny of Taxation (with Jack Wiseman). Second Special report for the Select Committee on Procedure, Session 1969–70. Her Majesty's Stationery Office, 1970.

Report of the Arts Council Enquiry into Orchestral Resources in Britain (Peacock Report) (Chairman of the Enquiry). Arts Council of Great Britain, 1970.

How Entry into the Common Market May Affect Britain's Invisible Earnings (main contributor). Report Submitted to the Committee on Invisible Exports by the Economists Advisory Group, July 1971.

Royal Commission on the Constitution 1969–73. (Commission member). Report presented to Parliament by Command of Her Majesty, October 1973 (co-signatory (with Lord Crowther-Hunt) of the Memorandum of Dissent).

ARTICLES

'The Finance of the Welfare State' (unsigned), *The Round Table*, June 1949.

'The National Insurance Funds', *Economica*, 16(3) 1949.

'The Finance of British National Insurance', *Public Finance*, 5(3), 1950.

'Keynesianische Nationalokonomie und Anti-Inflations-Politik', *Zeitschrift fur die Gesamte Staatswissenschaft*, 106(4), 1950.

'Recent German Contributions to Economics', *Economica*, 17(2), 1950.

'National Insurance and Economic Policy', *The Banker*, December 1950.

'Alternative Presentations of the Social Accounts', *Accounting Research*, January 1951.

'A Note on the Theory of Income Redistribution' (with D. Berry). *Economica*, 18(1), 1951.

'Sur la theorie des depenses publiques', *Economie Appliquée*, 1951.

'The Problem of Economic Power: Review Artcle of Walter Eucken's Unser Zeitalter der Misserfolge', *Weltwirtschaftliches Archiv*, 68(1), 1952.

'Theory of Population and Modern Economic Analysis. I', *Population Studies* 6(2), 1952.

'Social Security and Inflation: A Study of an Adjustable Pensions Scheme', *Review of Economic Studies*, 20(3), 1952/3.

'Wage Claims and the Pace of Inflation (1945–51)' (with W.J.L. Ryan), *Economic Journal*, 63(2), 1953.
'Malthus in the Twentieth Century', in *Introduction to Malthus* (ed. David Glass). Watts and Co., London, 1953.
'The Hyperbarbarous Technology', *Westminster Bank Review*, November 1953.
'Public Finance and the Welfare State', *The Banker*, 1953.
'Politique fiscale et budget national en Grand-Bretagne', *Revue de Science et de Legislation Financieres*, 1953.
'Theorie moderne de l'incidence de l'impot et securite sociale', *Revue de Science et de Legislation Financieres*, 1954.
'Theory of Population and Modern Economic Analysis. II', *Population Studies*, March 1954.
'The Economics of Pension Funds' (with F.W. Paish), *Lloyds Bank Review*, October 1954.
'The Economics of Dependence 1952–82' (with F.W. Paish), *Economica*, 21(4) 1954.
'Economic Theory and the Concept of an Optimum Population', in *The Numbers of Animals and Man* (ed. J.B. Cragg and N.W. Pirie). Oliver and Boyd, Edinburgh and London, 1955.
'Neuere Entwicklungen in der Theorie der "Fiscal Policy"', *Finanzarchiv* 16, 1955.
'The Future of Government Expenditure', *District Bank Review*, June 1955.
'Das Finanz-und Steuersystem Grossbritanniens', *Handbuch der Finanzwissenschaft*, 2nd ed (ed. Wilhelm Gerloff and Fritz Neumark). J.C.B. Mohr (Paul Siebeck), Tübingen, 1956.
'The Finance of State Education in the United Kingdom' (with J. Wiseman), *Year Book of Education, 1965*. Evans Brothers, London, 1956.
'Tax Policy and the Budget, 1956', *British Tax Review*, June 1956.
'A Note on the Balanced Budget Multiplier', *Economic Journal* 66(2), 1956.
'Sozialpolitik in Liberaler Sicht', *Schweizer Monatshefte*, March 1957.
'Production Functions and Population Theory' (review article), *Population Studies*, March 1957.
'The Economic Writings of Frances Horner', *Scottish Journal of Political Economy* 5(2), 1957.
'The Economics of National Superannuation', *Three Banks Review*, September 1957.
'Some Observations on the Reports of the Royal Commission on the Taxation of Profits and Income', *National Tax Journal*, 10(3), 1957.
'The Savings–Investment Problem in Contemporary Britain', *International Congress for the Study of Savings Problems*. Imprimerie Nationale, Paris, 1957.
'From Political Economy to Economic Science', Inaugural Lecture as Professor of Economic Science, University of Edinburgh, *University of Edinburgh Gazette*, 1957.
'Welfare in the Liberal State' (unsigned), chapter V of *The Unservile State Essays in Liberty and Welfare* (ed. George Watson). George Allen and Unwin, London, 1957.
'Input–Output Analysis in an Underdeveloped Country: A Case Study' (with Douglas Dosser), *Review of Economic Studies*, 25(1), 1957/8.
'Fiscal Policy and the Composition of Government Purchases' (with I.G. Stewart), *Public Finance*, 13(2), 1958.

'Monetary Policy and Central Bank Organization', *Scottish Bankers Magazine*, May 1958.

'The Government as an Employer' (with Thomas L. Johnston), *Westminster Bank Review*, August 1958.

'L'Economiste dans la litterature', *Revue de Science Financiere*, 1958.

'Les Depenses gouvernmentales et la structure du marche', *Revue de Science Financiere*, 1959.

'The Public Sector and the Theory of Economic Growth', *Scottish Journal of Political Economy*, 7(1), 1959.

'The Rehabilitation of Classical Debt Theory', *Economica* 26(2), 1959.

'Regional Input–output Analysis and Government Spending' (with Douglas Dosser), *Scottish Journal of Political Economy*, 7(3), 1959.

'Eine Analyse der Britischen Entwicklung aum Wohlwahrtstaar', *IFO-Studien*, 5(122), 1959.

'Politique Economique et Calcul du Revenue National Specialement dans les Pays Sous-Developees', *Revue de Science Financiere*, 1959.

'The Government as a Buyer', *The Purchasing Journal*, January 1960.

'The New Attack on Localized Unemployment', *Lloyds Bank Review*, January 1960.

'Built-in Flexibility and Economic Growth', in *Stabile Preise in wachsender Wirtschaft* (ed. Gottfried Bombach). J.C.B. Mohr (Paul Siebeck), Tübingen, 1960.

'Economic Problems of a Multi-racial Society – The Fiji Case', *Scottish Journal of Political Economy*, 8(1), 1961.

'The Past and Future of Public Spending' (with Jack Wiseman), *Lloyds Bank Review*, April 1961.

'The International Distribution of Income 1949 and 1957' (with S. Andic), *Journal of the Royal Statistical Society*, series A (General), 124(2), 1961.

'Stabilization and Planning in African Countries', (with Douglas Dosser), *Public Finance*, 18(3), 1962.

'The Control and Appraisal of Public Investment in the United Kingdom', *Finanzarchiv*, 22(1), September 1962.

'Economic Advice to Government in the United Kingdom', in *Probleme der normativen Okonomik und der wirtschaftpolitischen Beratung* (ed. Erwin v. Berkerath and Herbert Giersch). Dunker and Humblot, Berlin, 1963.

'Economic Analysis and Government Expenditure Control', *Scottish Journal of Political Economy*, 10(1), 1963.

'Economic Growth and the Demand for Qualified Manpower', *District Bank Review*, June 1963.

'Economics of a Net Wealth Tax for Britain', *British Tax Review*, November–December 1963.

'The International Distribution of Income with "Maximum Aid"' (with Douglas Dosser), *Review of Economics and Statistics*, November 1964.

'Problems of Government Budgetary Reform', *Lloyds Bank Review*, January 1964.

'The Political Economy of Social Welfare', *Three Banks Review*, December 1964.

'Monetary and Fiscal Policy in Relation to African Development', in *Economic Development for Africa South of the Sahara* (ed. E.A.G. Robinson), Proceedings of a Conference held by the International Economic Association. Macmillan, London, 1964.

'Towards a Theory of Inter-Regional Fiscal Policy', *Public Finance*, 20(1-2) (Essays in honour of Fritz Neumark), 1965.

'The Social Accounting of Education' (with Robert Lavers), *Journal of the Royal Statistical Society* series A, 129(3), 1966.

'Economic Growth and the Principles of Educational Finance in Developing Countries' (with Jack Wiseman), chapter 6 of *Financing of Education for Economic Growth*. OECD, Paris, 1966.

'The Economics of Taxing Advertising', *Accountancy*, March 1966.

'Fiscal Surveys and Economic Development' (with Suehan Andic), *Kyklos*, 19(4), 1966.

'A Conceptual Scheme for the Analysis of Data on Educational Finance', in *Methods and Statistical Needs for Educational Planning*. OECD, Paris 1967.

'Consumption Taxes and Compensation Finance' (with John Williamson), *Economic Journal*, 77(1), 1967.

'The New Doctor's Dilemma' (with J.R. Shannon), *Lloyds Bank Review*, January 1968.

'Public Patronage and Music: An Economist's View', *Three Banks Review*, March 1968.

'Measuring the Efficiency of Government Expenditure' (with Jack Wiseman), chapter 3 of *Public Sector Economics* (ed. A.R. Prest) Manchester University Press, 1968.

'Stability, Growth and Budgetary Planning', chapter II of *The Budget Today*, College of Europe. St Catherine's Press, Bruges, 1968.

'The Welfare State and the Redistribution of Income' (with J.R. Shannon), *Westminster Bank Review*, August 1968.

'Welfare Economics and Public Subsidies to the Arts', *Manchester School of Economic and Social Studies*, 37(4) 1969.

'Public Expenditure as a Source of Finance for Medical care in Britain' (with Jack Wiseman), Appendix B of *Health Services Financing*. British Medical Association, London, 1970.

'Public Expenditure Research at the University of York', *Openbare Uitgaven*, June 1971.

'Justifying the Subsidy', *Opera*, 1971.

'Fiscal Measures to Improve Employment in Developing Countries: A Technical Note' (with G. K. Shaw), *Public Finance*, 26(3), 1971.

'Invisible Earnings' (with R.A. Cooper), chapter 8 of *The Economics of Europe: What the Common Market Means for Britain* (ed. John Pinder). Charles Knight, London, 1971.

'Fiscal Measures to Improve Employment in Developing Countries: A Reply' (with G. K. Shaw), *Public Finance*, 27(1), 1972.

'The Public Finance of Inter-Allied Defence Provision', *Essays in Honour of Antonio de Vito De Marco*. Cacucci Editore, Bari, 1972.

'The Multiplier and the Valuation of Government Expenditures', *Finanzarchiv*, 30(3), 1972.

'Pareto-Optimality and the Political Economy of Liberalism' (with Charles K. Rowley), *Journal of Political Economy*, 80(3), 1972.

'Welfare Economics and the Public Regulation of Natural Monopoly' (with Charles K. Rowley), *Journal of Public Economics*, 1(2), 1972.

'Fiscal Means and Political Ends', *Essays in Honour of Lionel Robbins* (ed. Maurice Peston and Bernard Corry). Weidenfeld and Nicolson, London, 1972.

'New Methods of Appraising Government Expenditure: An Economic Analysis', *Public Finance*, 27(2), 1972.

'Welfare Economics and the Public Regulation of Natural Monopoly: A Reply' (with Charles K. Rowley), *Journal of Public Economics*, 2(1), 1973.

'An Economic Analysis of the British Tax Credit Proposals' (with Alan Maynard), *Institute for Fiscal Studies*, March 1973.

'Cost–Benefit Analysis and the Political Control of Public Investment', *Cost Benefit and Cost Effectiveness* (ed. J. N. Wolfe). George Allen and Unwin, London, 1973.

'The Economic Value of Musical Composition', *Beitrage zu einer Theorie der Sozialpolitik* (ed. Bernhard Kulp and Wolfgang Stuzel). Dunker and Humblot, Berlin, 1973.

'Cultural Accounting' (with Christine Godfrey), *Social Trends*, no. 4, HMSO, London, 1973.

'Fiscal Measures to Create Employment: The Indonesian Case' (with G. K. Shaw), *Bulletin for International Fiscal Documentation*, 27(4), 1973.

'The Economics of Museums and Galleries' (with Christine Godfrey), *Lloyds Bank Review*, January 1974.

'The Treatment of Government Expenditure in Studies of Income Distribution', *Public Finance and Stabilization Policy: Essays in Honour of Richard Musgrave* (ed. Warren L. Smith and John L. Culbertson). North-Holland, Amsterdam, 1974.

'Economic Policy and the Finance of Intermediate Level Governments', *Royal Commission on the Constitution 1969–1973*, vol. II, Memorandum of Dissent, Cmnd 5460-1. HMSO, London, 1974.

'The Problems of The Performing Arts and Economic Analysis', chapter 7 of *Understanding Economics* (ed. Bing Chen). Little, Brown and Co., Boston, 1974.

'The Economic Analysis of Negative Income Taxation' (with Alan Maynard), in *Economic Policies and Social Goals* (ed. A. J. Culyer), York Studies in Economics. Martin Robertson, London, 1974.

'International Linkage Models and the Public Sector' (with Martin Ricketts), *Public Finance* 30(3), 1975.

'The Treatment of the Principles of Public Finance', in *The Wealth of Nations. Essays on Adam Smith* (ed. Andrew S. Skinner and Thomas Wilson). Clarendon Press, Oxford, 1976.

'The "Output" of the London Orchestras 1966–75', *The Musical Times*, August 1976.

'The Political Economy of the "Dispersive Revolution"', *Scottish Journal of Political Economy*, 23(3), 1976.

'The Political Economy of Devolution. The British Case', in *The Political Economy of Fiscal Federalism* (ed. Wallace E. Oates). Procedures of the Berlin Conference of ISPE, January 1976. Heath, Lexington, Massachusetts.

'Giving Economic Advice in Difficult Times', *Three Banks Review*, March 1977.

'Stabilization and Distribution Policy', in *Grenzen der Umverteilung* (ed. Martin Pfaff). Duncker and Humblot, Berlin, 1978.

'Combined Defence and International Economic Co-operation', (with Keith Hartley), *The World Economy* 1(3), 1978.

'Do We Need to Reform Direct Taxes?', *Lloyds Bank Review*, July 1978.

'Trade Unions and Economic Policy', in *Trade Unions: Public Goods or Public Bads?* Institute of Economic Affairs Readings no. 17. Institute of Economic Affairs, London, 1978.

'The Economics of Bureaucracy: An Inside View', in *The Economics of Politics*, Institute of Economic Affairs Readings no. 18. Institute of Economic Affairs, London, 1978.

'The growth of the Public Sector and Inflation' (with Martin Ricketts), in *The Political Economy of Inflation* (ed. Fred Hirsch and John H. Goldthorpe). Martin Robertson, London, 1978.

'Is Fiscal Policy Dead?' (with G. K. Shaw), *Banca Nazionale Del Lavoro Quarterly Review*, June 1978.

'Preserving the Past: An International Economic Dilemma', in *Nur Oekonomie is keine Oekonomie* (Festschrift for B.M. Biucchi) (Ed. Pio Caroni *et al.*). Verlag Paul Haupt, Bern, 1978.

'Approaches to the Analysis of Government Expenditure Growth' (with Jack Wiseman), *Public Finance Quarterly*, 7(1) 1979.

'On the Anatomy of Collective Failure', *Public Finance*, 32(1), 1980.

'Studying Economic Policy', Foreword to *Current Issues in Economic Policy* (ed. R. M. Grant and G. K. Shaw). Philip Allan, Oxford, 1980.

'The British Economy and Its Problems', in *Britain: Progress or Decline?* (ed. Richard Rose). Macmillan, London, 1980.

'Inter-governmental Fiscal Relations in a Unitary State: The Example of the United Kingdom' (with Martin Ricketts), in *Handbuch der Finanzwissenschaft* (ed. Fritz Neumark and Norbert Andel), 3rd edn. J. C. B. Mohr (Paul Siebeck), Tübingen, 1981.

'Fiscal Theory and the Market for Tax Reform', in *The Reform of Tax Systems* (ed. F. Forte and K. Roskamp). Wayne State University Press, Detroit, 1981.

'Government Expenditure and the Radical Left', *Journal of Economic Affairs*, 1(3), 1981.

'Model Building and Fiscal Policy: Then and Now', *Finanzarchiv*, 39(1), 1981.

'Fiscal Policy in a Monetarist's World', *Report of the Proceedings of the Thirty-Third Tax Conference of the Canadian Tax Foundation*. Toronto, 1982.

'Controlle microeconomici e macroeconomici della spesa pubblica', *Einaudi notizie*, Fondazione Luigi Einaudi, Milan, 1982.

'The LSE and Post-war Economic Policy', *Atlantic Economic Journal*, 10(1), 1982.

'Calculating the Revenue Loss from Evasion' (with G. K. Shaw), *Journal of Economic Affairs* 2(4), 1982.

'Is Tax Revenue Loss Overstated?' (with G. K. Shaw), *Journal of Economic Affairs*, 2(3), 1982.

'Tax Evasion and Tax Revenue Loss' (with G. K. Shaw), *Public Finance*, 37(2), 1982.

'The Disaffection of the Taxpayer', Presidential Address to the Atlantic Economic Society, Miami Beach, October 1982, *Atlantic Economic Journal*, 11(1), 1983.

'The Politics of Culture and the Ignorance of Political Scientists: A Reply to F. F. Ridley', *Journal of Cultural Economics*, June 1983.

'Reducing Government Expenditure: A British View', in *Reassessing the Role of Government in the Mixed Economy* (ed. Herbert Giersch). J. C. B. Mohr (Paul Siebeck), Tübingen, 1983.

'Welfare Economics, Public Finance and Selective Aid Policies', in *Reflections on a Troubled World Economy: Essays in Honour of Herbert Giersch* (ed. Fritz Machlup, Gerhard Fels and Hubertus Muller-Groeling). Trade Policy Research Centre/Macmillan, London, 1983.

'Mittelfristige Finanzpolitik in einer monetaristischen Welt – Das Beispiel Grossbritannien', *Zeitschrift fur Wirtschaftspolitik*, 32(1), 1983.

'Public *X*-Inefficiency: Informational and Institutional Constraints', in *Anatomy of Government Deficiencies* (ed. Horst Hanusch). Seringer-Verlag, Berlin, 1983.

'Education Voucher Schemes – Strong or Weak?' *Journal of Economic Affairs*, 3(2), 1983.

'The Political Economy of Strukturpolitik', *Zeitschrift fur die gesamte Staatswissenschaft*, 140(2), 1984.

'Preface' and 'Tax Sharing: The West German Example' (with Lesley Wakefield), in *Fiscal Decentralisation* (ed. Thomas Wilson). Anglo German Foundation, London, 1984.

'Economics, Inflation and the Performing Arts', in *Inflation and the Performing Arts* (ed. Hilda Baumol and William J. Baumol). New York University Press, 1984.

'Privatisation in Perspective', *Three Banks Review*, December 1984.

'Disability Policy in the United Kingdom' (with M. J. M. McCrostie) in *Public Policy Towards Disabled Workers*. (ed. R. Haveman et al), Cornell University Press, Ithaca and London, 1984.

References

ALCHIAN, A. AND DEMSETZ, H. (1972) 'Production, Information Costs and Economic Organisation'. *American Economic Review*, vol. 62.

ARTUS, J. (1985) *An Empirical Evaluation of the Disequilibrium Real Wage Hypothesis* (forthcoming).

ASHWORTH, J. (1982) 'The Supply of Labour', in J. Creedy and B. Thomas (eds) *The Economics of Labour*. Butterworths, Sevenoaks

ATKINSON, A. B. AND STIGLITZ, J. E. (1980) *Lectures on Public Economics*. McGraw-Hill, Maidenhead, Berkshire.

ATTIYEH, R. E., BACH, G. L. AND LUMSDEN, K. G. (1969) 'The Efficiency of Programmed Learning in Teaching Economics: The Results of a Nationwide Experience'. *American Economic Review*, vol. 59.

ATTIYEH, R. AND LUMSDEN, K. G. (1971) 'University Students' Initial Understanding of Economics: The Contribution of the A-level Economics Course and of Other Factors.' *Economica*, vol. 38.

BALASSA, B. (1964) 'The Purchasing Power Parity Doctrine: A Reappraisal'. *Journal of Political Economy*, vol. 72.

BALDWIN, S. (1981) *The Financial Consequences of Disablement in Children: Final Report*. Social Policy Research Unit, Working Paper DHSS 76, University of York.

BARRO, R. J. AND GORDON, D. B. (1983) 'Rules, Discretion and Reputation in a Model of Monetary Policy'. *Journal of Monetary Economics*, vol. 12.

BARRY, NORMAN (1983) *Unanimity, Agreement and Liberalism*. University of Buckingham Discussion Papers in Economics no 22.

BAUMOL, W. J. (1958) 'On the Theory of Oligopoly'. *Economica*, vol. 25.

BAUMOL, W. J. AND BOWEN, W. G. (1965) 'On the Performing Arts: The Anatomy of their Economic Problems'. *American Economic Review*, vol. 55.

BAUMOL, W. J. AND BRADFORD, D. F. (1970) 'Optimal Departures from Marginal Cost Pricing'. *American Economic Review*, vol. 60.

BAUMOL, W. J. *et al.* (1962) 'The Role of Cost in the Minimum pricing of Railroad Services'. *Journal of Business*, vol. 35; reprinted in Munby (1968).

BEARD, CHARLES A. (1913, 1935) *An Economic Interpretation of the Constitution of the United States*. Macmillan Press, New York.

BECKER, G. S. (1983) 'A Theory of Competition Among Pressure Groups for Political Influence'. *Quarterly Journal of Economics*, vol. 98.

BECKERMAN, W. AND CLARK, S. (1982) *Poverty and Social Security in Britain*. Oxford University Press.

BENTHAM, JEREMY (1978) *Principles of Civil Code* (first published in 1803), in C.B. Macpherson, *Property*. (University of Toronto Press.)

BERGSTEN, C. FRED (1982) 'The International Implication of Reagonomics', *Kieler Vorträge*, vol. 96.

BLANCHARD, O. AND DORNBUSCH, R. (1984) 'US Deficits, the Dollar and Europe'. *Banca Nazionale del Lavoro Quarterly Review*, no. 148.

BLAUG, M. (1980) *Methodology of Economics*. Cambridge University Press.

BORCHERDING, T. E., BUSH, W. C. AND SPANN, R. M. (1977) 'The Effects on Public Spending of the Divisibility of Public Outputs in Consumption, Bureaucratic Power and the Size of the Tax Sharing Group'. In T.E. Borcherding (ed.), *Budgets and Bureaucrats: The Sources of Government Growth*. Duke University Press, Durham, North Carolina.

BRADFORD, DAVID (1969) 'Balance on Unbalanced Growth'. *Zeitschrift fur National-ökonomice*, December.

BRAINARD, W. (1967) 'Uncertainty and the Effectiveness of Policy'. *American Economic Review*, vol 57.

BRAY, M. M. (1982) 'Learning, Estimation and the Stability of Rational Expectations'. *Journal of Economic Theory*, vol. 29.

BRETON, ALBERT (1974) *The Economic Theory of Representative Government*. Macmillan Press, London.

BRETON, ALBERT AND SCOTT, ANTONY (1978) *The Economic Consitution of Federal States*. University of Toronto Press.

BRETON, A. AND WINTROBE, R. (1975) 'The Equilibrium Size of a Budget-maximizing Bureau'. *Journal of Political Economy*, vol. 83.

BRETON, A. AND WINTROBE, R. (1982) *The Logic of Bureaucratic Conduct*. Cambridge University Press, New York.

BRITTAN, S. (1973) *Is there an Economic Consensus? An Attitude Survey*. Macmillan Press, London.

BUCHANAN, J. (1965) 'An Economic Theory of Clubs'. *Economica*, vol. 32.

BUCHANAN, J. (1970) *Costs and Choice*. Markham, Chicago.

BUCHANAN, J. (1976) 'Public Goods and Natural Liberty'. In T. Wilson and A.S. Skinner (eds), *The Market and the State*. Clarendon Press, Oxford.

BUCHANAN, J. AND THIRLBY, G. F. (eds) (1973) *LSE Essays on Cost*. Weidenfeld and Nicolson, London.

BUCHANAN, J. AND TULLOCK, G. (1962) *The Calculus of Consent: Logical Foundations of Constitutional Democracy*. University of Michigan Press, Ann Arbor, Michigan.

BUITER, W. AND MILLER, M. (1984) 'The Macroeconomic Consequences of a Change of Regime'. *Brookings Papers on Economic Activity*.

BUTTON, K. J. AND FLEMING, M. C. (1982) 'The Predictive Power of A-level Attainment: A Case Study'. *Educational Research*, vol. 24.

CAIRNES, A. (1976) 'The Market and the State'. In T. Wilson and A.S. Skinner (eds), *The Market and the State*. Clarendon Press, Oxford.

CARTER, C. (1984) *The Purposes of Government Expenditure*. Policy Studies Institute, London.

CAVACO-SILVA, ANIBAL A. (1977) *Economic Effects of Public Debt*. Martin Robertson, Oxford.

CAVACO-SILVA, ANIBAL A. (1982) 'Public Debt: Allocative Effects'. *Economica* vol. 49.

CLARK, JOHN BATES (1914) *The Distribution of Wealth*. Macmillan Press, New York.

CLARK, R. L. AND SPENGLER, J. J. (1980) *The Economics of Individual and Population Ageing*. Cambridge University Press.
COATES, A. W. (1985) *The Role of Economists in International Agencies.* (forthcoming)
COHEN, M. D. (1974) 'The Importance of Member Preferences in Committee Assignment: An Assessment against Optimal Standards and a Single Process Model'. Unpublished paper.
Congressional Quarterly (Weekly Report), 21 April 1984.
CROPSEY, J. (1975) 'Adam Smith and Political Philosophy'. In A. S. Skinner and T. Wilson (eds), *Essays on Adam Smith*. Clarendon Press, Oxford.
CURRIE, D. A. (1982) 'Macoeconomic Policy Design and Control Theory: A Failed Partnership'. Unpublished paper.
DE ALESSI, L. (1969) 'Implications of Property Rights for Government Investment Choices'. *American Economic Review*, vol. 59.
DEMSETZ, H. (1967) 'Toward a Theory of Property Rights'. *American Economic Review*, vol. 57.
DEMSETZ, H. (1968) 'Why Regulate Utilities? *Journal of Law and Economics*, vol. 11.
DHSS (DEPARTMENT OF HEALTH AND SOCIAL SECURITY) (1983) *Elderly People in the Community: Their Service Needs*. HMSO, London.
DICKE, H. AND TRAPP, Z. (1984) 'Zinsen, Gewinne und Nettoinvestitionen zu den Bestimmungsfaktoren der Sachvermögensbildung westerdeutscher Unternehmen'. *Kiel Discussion Paper*, no. 99.
DILMOT, A. W., KAY, J. A. AND MORRIS, C. N. (1984) *The Reform of Social Security*. Oxford University Press.
DORNBUSCH, R. (1980) *Open Economy Macroeconomics*. Basic Books, New York.
DOWNS, A. (1957) *An Economic Theory of Democracy*. Harper and Row, New York.
DOWNS, A. (1967) *Inside Bureaucracy*. Little, Brown, Boston.
DREZE, J. H. (1966) 'Some Post-war Contributions of French Economists to Theory and Policy'. *American Economic Review*, vol. 56.
ECKSTEIN, O. (1981) *Core Inflation*. Prentice-Hall, Englewood Cliffs, New Jersey.
EDGEWORTH, F. Y. (1925a) 'The Pure Theory of Taxation' (First published in *Economic Journal*, 1897). In Edgeworth (1925b).
EDGEWORTH, F. Y. (1925b) 'Papers Relating to Political Economy', vol. 11. Macmillan Press, London.
EKELUND, R. B. AND HERBERT, R. F. (1983) *A History of Economic Theory and Method* (2nd edn). McGraw-Hill, Maidenhead,Berkshire.
EQUAL OPPORTUNITIES COMMISSION (1908) *The Experience of Caring for Elderly and Handicapped Dependants: Survey Report*. EOC, Manchester.
ERMISCH, J. (1983) *The Political Economy of Demographic Change*. Policy Studies Institute/Heinemann, London.
EUROPEAN COMMISSION (1977) *Report of the Study Group on the Role of Public Finance in European Integration* (McDougall Report). European Commission, Brussels.
FAITH R. L., LEAVENS, D. R. AND TOLLINSON, R. D. (1982) 'Antitrust Pork Barrel'. *Journal of Law and Economics*, vol. 25.
FAMA, E. F. (1980) 'Agency Problems and the Theory of the Firm'. *Journal of Political Economy*, vol. 88.

FARRELL, M. J. (1958) 'In defence of Public Utility Price Theory'. *Oxford Economic Papers*, vol. 10.

FELS, R. (1970) 'Multiple Choice Questions in Elementary Economics' In K. G. Lumsden (ed.), *Recent Research in Economics Education*. Prentice-Hall, Hemel Hempstead, Hertfordshire.

FINCH, J. AND GROVES, D. (1983) *A Labour of Love: Women Work and Caring*. Routledge and Kegan Paul, London.

FLEMING, J. MARCUS (1961) 'International Liquidity: Ends and Means'. *IMF Staff Papers*, vol. 8.

FORTE, FRANCESCO (1984) *Oltre guesta Europa*. Rusconi, Milan.

FORTE, FRANCESCO (1985a) 'Democracy as a Public Good'. *Economia delle Scelte Pubbliche*, (forthcoming).

FORTE, FRANCESCO (1985b) 'Il Bilancio nell'economia pubblica Giaffre'. Rusconi, Milan.

FORTE, FRANCESCO AND DI PIERRO, ALBERTO (1980) 'A Pure Model of Public Bureaucracy'. *Public Finance*, vol. 35.

FRIEDMAN, M. (1953) 'The Effects of Full Employment Policy on Economic Stability: A Formal Analysis'. In his *Essays on Positive Economics*. University of Chicago Press.

FRIEDMAN, M. (1957) *A Theory of the Consumption Function*. Princeton University Press.

DE GRAAF, J. (1957) *Theoretical Welfare Economics*. Cambridge University Press, London.

GIERSCH, H. (1949) 'Economic Union Between Nations and the Location of Industries'. *Review of Economic Studies*, vol. 17.

GIERSCH, H. (1970) 'Entrepreneurial Risk Under Flexible Exchange Rates'. In *Approaches to Greater Flexibility of Exchange Rates: The Burgenstock Papers*. Princeton University Press.

GIERSCH, H. (1977) 'IMF Surveillance Over Exchange Rates', In R. Mundell and J. J. Polak (eds), *The New International Monetary System*. New York.

GIERSCH, H. (1978) Preface. In H. Giersch (ed.), *Capital Shortage and Unemployment in the World Economy*. J. C. B. Mohr, Tübingen.

GIERSCH, H. (1979) 'Aspects of Growth, Structural Change and Employment: A Schumpeterian Perspective'. *Weltwirchschaftliches Archiv*, vol. 115.

GOVERNMENT ACTUARY'S DEPARTMENT (1984) *Population Projections 1981–2021*. Office of Population and Census Statistics, London.

GRIER, K. B. (1984) 'Congressional Preferences and Federal Reserve Policy: A Principal–Agent Approach'. Unpublished paper.

HARBERGER, A. (1971) 'Three Basic Postulates for Applied Welfare Economics'. *Journal of Economic Literature*, vol. 9.

HARBERGER, A. (1978) 'On the Use of Distributional Weights in Social Cost Benefit Analysis'. *Journal of Political Economy*, vol. 86.

HARBURY, C. D. AND SZRETER, R. (1968) 'The Influence upon University Performance of the Study of Economics at School'. *Journal of the Royal Statistical Society*, vol. 131.

HARROD, R. F. (1933) *International Economics*. Cambridge University Press, London.

HARSANY, JOHN C. (1953) 'Cardinal Utility in Welfare Economics and the Theory of Risk Taking' *Journal of Political Economy*, vol. 61.

HARSANY, JOHN C. (1976) *Essays in Ethics, Social Behaviour and Scientific Explanation*, Reidel, Dordrecht.

HEIM, A. (1968) *AH5 Group Test of High Grade Intelligence*. National Bureau of Economic Research, Cambridge, Massachusetts.

HELLER, WALTER W. (1951) 'Compulsory Lending: The World War II Experience'. *National Tax Journal*, vol. 4.

HENWOOD, M. AND WICKS, M. (1984) *The Forgotten Army: Family Care and Elderly People*. Family Policy Studies Centre, London.

HMSO (1984) *The next Ten Years: Public Expenditure and Taxation into the 1990s*, Cmnd 9189. HMSO, London.

HICKS, D. (1957) *The Federal Union: A History of the United States to 1877*. Riverside Press, Cambridge, Massachusetts.

HIRSCHMAN, A. O. (1981) *Essays in Trespassing Economics to Politics and Beyond*. Cambridge University Press.

HIRST, M. (1985) 'Moving On: Transfer from Child to Adult Services for Young People with Disabilities'. Social Policy Research Unit, University of York.

HOCHMAN, M. M. AND ROGERS, J. R. (1964) 'Pareto-optimal Redistribution'. *American Economic Review*, vol. 54.

HOLZMAN, FRANKLYN D. (1957) 'An Estimate of the Tax Element in Soviet Bond'. *American Economic Review*, vol. 47.

HOTELLING, H. (1938) 'The General Welfare in Relation to the Problems of Taxation and of Railway and Utility Rates'. *Econometrica*, vol. 6; reprinted in K.J. Arrow and T. Scitovsky (eds), *Readings in Welfare Economics*. Irwin Press, Homewood, Illinois, 1969.

INSTITUTE OF FISCAL STUDIES (1983) 'Report on the Pilot Study'. *Economia Europea*, vol. 4.

JEWSON, M. G. AND MECKLING, W. M. (1976) 'Theory of the Firm–Managerial Behaviour, Agency Costs and Ownership Structure'. *Journal of Financial Economics*.

JOHNSTON, J. (1960) *Statistical Cost Analysis*. McGraw-Hill, New York.

KAHN, A. E. (1974) 'Economic Theory as a Guideline for Government Intervention and Control: A Comment'. *Journal of Economic Issues*, vol. 8.

KEYNES, J. M. (1936) *The General Theory of Employment, Interest and Money*. Macmillan Press, London.

KYDLAND, E. G. AND PRESCOTT, E. C. (1977) 'Rules Rather than Discretion: The Inconsistency of Optimal Plans'. *Journal of Political Economy*, vol. 85.

LERNER, A. P. (1944) *Economics of Control*. Macmillan Press, London.

LEVIN, E., SINCLAIR, I. AND GORBACH, P. (1983) *The Supporters of Confused Elderly People at Home*. National Institute for Social Work Research Unit, London.

LITTLE, I. M. D. (1957) *Critique of Welfare Economics*. Oxford University Press.

LOCKE, JOHN (1960) *Two Treatises of Government*, ed. P. Laslett. Mentor Books, New York.

LUMSDEN, K. G., ATTIYEH, R. AND SCOTT, A. (1980) *Economics Education in the UK*. Heinemann, London.

LUMSDEN, K. G. AND RITCHIE, C. J. (1975) 'The Open University: A Survey and Economic Analysis'. *Instructional Science*.

LUMSDEN, K. G. AND SCOTT, A. (1982) 'An Output Comparison of Open University and Conventional University Students'. *Higher Education*, vol. 2.

LUMSDEN, K. G. AND SCOTT, A. (1983) 'The Efficacy of Innovative Teaching Techniques in Economics: The UK Experience'. *American Economic Review*, vol. 73.

LUMSDEN, K. G. AND SCOTT, A. (1984) 'How to Maximise Golden Opinions'. *Applied Economics*, vol. 16.

MARRIS, S. (1984) 'The Dollar Problem Statement on H. J. Res. 585, before the US House of Representatives Committee on Banking and Urban Affairs, Subcommittee on Domestic Monetary Policy'. Washington, D.C.

MASCARO, A. AND MELTZER, A. H. (1983) 'Long and Short Term Interest Rates in a Risky World'. *Journal of Monetary Economics*, vol. 12.

MAYNARD, A. K. AND SMITH, J. C. C. (1983) *The Elderly: Who Cares? Who Pays?* Nuffield/York Portfolio no. 1. Nuffield Provincial Hospitals Trust, London.

MELODY, W. H. (1974) 'The Marginal Utility of Marginal Analysis in Public Policy'. *Journal of Economic Issues*, vol. 8.

METCALFE, D. (1984) 'On the Measurement of Employment and Unemployment'. *National Institute Economic Review*, no. 109.

MIGUÉ, J. L. AND BÉLANGER, G. (1974) 'Toward a General Theory of Managerial Discretion'. *Public Choice*, vol. 17.

MILL, JOHN STUART (1921) *Principles of Political Economy* (first published in 1849). Longman, London.

MILL, JOHN STUART (1972) 'Utilitarianism' (first published in 1861). In M. B. Acton (ed.), *Utilitarianism, On Liberty and Considerations of Representative Government*. Dent and Sons, London.

MILLER, G. J. (1977) 'Bureaucratic Compliance as a Game on the Unit Square'. *Public Choice*, vol. 23.

MILLWARD, R. (1971) *Public Expenditure Economics: An Introductory Application of Welfare Economics*. McGraw-Hill, Maidenhead, Berkshire.

MINFORD, A. P. L. (1984) 'State Expenditure: A Study in Waste'. *Economic Affairs*, vol. 4.

MISHAN, E. (1971) *Cost–Benefit Analysis*. Allen and Unwin, London.

MIZUTA, M. (1975) 'Moral Philosophy and Civil Society'. In A. S. Skinner and T. Wilson (eds), *Essay on Adam Smith*. Clarendon Press, Oxford.

MODIGLIANI, F AND BRUMBERG, R. (1954) 'Utility Analysis and the Consumption Function: An Interpretation of Cross Section Data'. In K. Kurihara (ed.), *Post-Keynesian Economics*. Rutgers University Press, Rutgers, New Jersey.

MUNBY, D. (ed.) (1968) *Penguin Modern Economics Readings: Transport*. Penguin Books, Harmondsworth, Middlesex.

MUSGRAVE, R. A. (1959) *The Theory of Public Finance*. McGraw-Hill, New York.

MUSGRAVE, R. A. (1970) 'Pareto-optimal Redistribution: A Comment'. *American Economic Review*, vol. 60.

MUSGRAVE, R. A. (1974) 'Maxi-Min, Uncertainty and the Leisure Trade-off'. *Quarterly Journal of Economics*, vol. 88.

MUSGRAVE, R. A. (1976) 'Adam Smith on Public Finance and Distribution'. In T. Wilson and A. S. Skinner (eds), *The Market and the State*. Clarendon Press Oxford.

MUSGRAVE, R. A. (1983) 'Private Labor and Common Land'. In G. Break (ed.), *State and Local Finance*. University of Wisconsin Press, Madison, Wisconsin.

MUSGRAVE, R. A. AND PEACOCK, A. T. (eds) (1967) *Classics in the Theory of Public Finance*. International Economic Association/St Martin's Press, New York.

NAGEL, T. (1975) 'Libertarianism Without Foundations'. *Yale Law Journal*, vol. 85.

NELSON, J. R. (ed) (1968) *Marginal Cost Pricing in Practice*. Prentice-Hall, Englewood Cliffs, New Jersey.

NISKANEN, W. A. (1971) *Bureaucracy and Representative Government*. Aldine-Athortan, Chicago and New York.

NISKANEN, W. A. (1975) 'Bureaucrats and Politicians'. *Journal of Law and Economics*, vol. 18.

NISSEL, M. AND BONNERJEA, K. (1982) *Family Care of the Handicapped Elderly: Who Pays?* Policy Studies Institute, London.

NOVE, A. (1973) *Efficiency Criteria for Nationalised Industries*. Allen and Unwin, London.

NOZIK, R. (1974) *Anarchy, State and Utopia* Basic Books, New York.

OATES, WALLACE E. (1972) *Fiscal Federalism*. Harcourt Brace, New York.

OFFICER, L. H. (1982) *Purchasing Power Parity and Exchange Rates*. London.

OLSSON, MANCUR (1965) *The Logic of Collective Action, Public Goods and the Theory of Groups*. Harvard University Press, Cambridge, Massachusetts.

OORT, C. (1958) *Decreasing Costs as a Problem in Welfare Economics*. Drukkerij Holland, Amsterdam.

ORZECHOWSKI, W. (1977) 'Economic Models of Bureaucracy: Survey, Extensions and Evidence'. In T. E. Borcherding (ed.), *Budgets and Bureaucrats: The Sources of Government Growth*. Duke University Press, Durham, North Carolina.

PAISH, F. W. (1966) *Studies in an Inflationary Economy*. Macmillan Press, London.

PAISH, F. W. (1970) *How the Economy Works and Other Essays*. Macmillan Press, London.

PAISH, F. W. AND PEACOCK, A. T. (1954) 'Economics of Dependence (1952–82)'. *Economica*, vol. 21.

PARKER, G., BALDWIN, S. AND GLENDENNING, C. (1984) *Informal Care and Carers: A Research Review and Recommendation for Future Research*. Social Policy Research Unit Working Paper, DHSS 183, University of York.

PARKINSON, C. N. (1970) *Parkinson's Law and Other Studies in Administration*. Ballantine Books, New York.

PEACOCK, A. T. (1961) *The Welfare Society*. Unservile State Paper no. 2.

PEACOCK, A. T. (1963) 'Economic Analysis and Government Expenditure Control'. *Scottish Journal of Political Economy*, vol. 10.

PEACOCK, A. T. (1975) 'The Treatment of the Principles of Public Finance in the Wealth of Nations'. In A. S. Skinner and T. Wilson (eds), *Essays on Adam Smith*. Clarendon Press, Oxford.

PEACOCK, A. T. (1979) *The Economic Analysis of Government*. Martin Robertson, Oxford.

PEACOCK, A. T. (1983) 'Public X-Inefficiency: Informational and Institutional Constraints'. In H. Hanusch (ed.), *Anatomy of Government Deficiencies*. Springer Verlag, Heidelberg.

PEACOCK, A. T. AND SHAW, G. K. (1971) *The Economic Theory of Fiscal Policy*. Allen and Unwin, London.

PESTON, M. H. (1980) *Whatever Happened to Macroeconomics?* Manchester University Press.

PESTON, M. H. (1982) *Theory of Macroeconomic Policy* (2nd edn). Philip Allan, Oxford.

PESTON, M. H. (1984) 'The Elementary Macroeconomic Consequences of Public and Private Sector Money Wages'. *Queen Mary College Discussion Paper*, no. 116.

PIGOU, A. C. (1928) *Study of Public Finance*. Macmillan Press, London.

PIGOU, A. C. (1943) 'The Classical Stationary State'. *Economic Journal*, vol. 53.

PIGOU, A. C. (1944) *Lapses from Full Employment*. Macmillan Press, London.

PREST, A. R. (1969) 'Compulsory Lending Schemes'. *IMF Staff Papers*, vol. 16.

RAWLS, JOHN (1971) *A Theory of Justice*. Harvard University Press, Cambridge, Massachusetts.

RICARDO, D. (1817) *Principles of Political Economy and Taxation* (ed. E. C. K. Granner). London 1927.

ROBBINS, L. (1937) *Economic Planning and International Order*. Macmillan Press, London.

ROBBINS, L. (1938) 'Interpersonal Comparisons of Utility'. *Economic Journal*, vol. 48.

ROBBINS, L. (1955) 'The Teaching of Economics in Schools and Universities'. *Economic Journal*, vol. 65.

ROHDE, D. AND SHEPSLE, K. A. (1973) 'Democratic Committee Assignments in the House of Representatives: Strategic Aspects of a Social Choice Process'. *American Political Science Review*.

ROWLEY, C. K. AND PEACOCK, A. T. (1975) *Welfare Economics: A Liberal Restatement*. Martin Robertson, Oxford.

RUGGLES, N. (1947) 'The Welfare Basis of the Marginal Cost Pricing Principle'. *Review of Economic Studies*, vol. 17.

RUGGLES, N. (1949) 'Recent Developments in the Theory of Marginal Cost Pricing' *Review of Economic Studies*, vol. 19: reprinted in Turvey (1968a).

SACHVERSTANDIGENRAT ZUR BEGUTACHTUNG DER GESAMTWIRTSCHAFT-LICHEN ENTWICKLUNG, JAHRESGUTACHTEN (1964) Deutscher Budestag, Drucksache IV/2890, Par 33-42.

SAMUELSON, P. A. (1948) *Foundations of Economic Analysis*. Harvard University Press, Cambridge, Massachusetts.

SAMUELSON, P. A. (1984) 'Second Thoughts on Analytical Income Comparisons'. *Economic Journal*, vol. 94.

SADLER, T. AND TSCHIRHART, J. T. (1980) 'The Economic Theory of Clubs: An Evaluative Survey'. *Journal of Economic Literature*, vol. 18.

SCANLON, T. M. (1982) 'Contractualism and Utilitarianism'. In Amarthya Sen and Bernard Williams (eds), *Utilitarianism and Beyond*. Cambridge University Press.

SEN, AMARTHYA (1970) *Collective Choice and Social Welfare*. Oliver and Boyd, London.

SEN, AMARTHYA AND WILLIAMS, BERNARD (EDS) (1982) *Utilitarianism and Beyond*. Cambridge University Press.

SHEPSLE, K. A. (1975) 'A Model of the Congressional Committee Assignment Process: Constrained Maximization in the Institutional Setting'. *Public Choice*, vol. 21.

SHOUP, CARL S. (1944) 'Forced Loans'. In *Curbing Inflation Through Taxation*. Tax Institute, New York.

SHOUP, CARL S. (1969) *Public Finance*. Weidenfeld and Nicolson, London.

SIDGWICK, HENRY, (1883) *The Principles of Political Economy*. Macmillan Press, London.

SIEGFRIED, J. J. (1979) 'Male/Female Differences in Economics Education: A Survey'. *Journal of Economic Education*, vol. 10.

SILBERTSON, A. (1972) 'Economies of Scale in Theory and Practice'. *Economic Journal*, vol. 83.

SMITH, A. (1964) *The Wealth of Nations*. (first published in 1776). Glasgow.

SMITH, A. (1969) *The Theory of Moral Sentiments*, ed. E. G. Weston. Liberty Classics, Indianapolis.

SMITH, C. A. (1955) 'Survey of Empirical Evidence on Economies of Scale in NBER'. In *Business Concentration and Price Policy*. Princeton University Press.

STIGLER, G. J. (1975a) *The Citizen and the State: Essays on Regulation*. University of Chicago Press.

STIGLER, G. J. (1975b) *Smith's Travels on the Ship of State*. In A. S. Skinner and T. Wilson (eds), *Essays on Adam Smith*. Clarendon Press, Oxford.

TOBIN, J. (1980) *Asset Accumulation and Economic Activity*. Basil Blackwell, Oxford.

TOWNSDEN, R. B. (1983) 'Forecasting the Forecasts of Others'. *Journal of Political Economy*. vol. 91.

TULLOCK, G. (1965) *The Politics of Bureaucracy*. Public Affairs Press, Washington D.C.

TURVEY, R. (1964) 'Marginal Cost Pricing in Practice'. *Economica*, vol. 31.

TURVEY, R. (ED.) (1968a) *Penguin Readings in Modern Economics: Public Enterprise*. Penguin Books, Harmondsworth, Middlesex.

TURVEY, R. (1968b) *Optimal Pricing and Investment in Electricity Investment*. Allen and Unwin, London.

TURVEY, R. (1969a) 'Marginal Cost'. *Economic Journal*, vol. 79.

TURVEY, R. (1969b) 'The Second Best Case for Marginal Cost Pricing'. In J. Margolis and H. Guitton (eds), *Public Economics*. Macmillan Press, London.

TURVEY, R. AND ANDERSON, D. (1975) *Electricity Economics*. Johns Hopkins University Press, Baltimore.

US GOVERNMENT PRINTING OFFICE (1984) 'Federal Civilian Workforce Statistics'. In monthly release, Workforce Analysis and Statistics Division, Office of Personal Management, April.

VAN GRAAF, I. (1957) *Theoretical Welfare Economics*. Cambridge University Press.

VAN GRAAF, I. (1962) 'On Making Recommendations in a Democracy'. *Economic Journal*, vol. 72.

VAUGHN, K. I. (1980) 'Does it Matter that Costs are Subjective?' *Southern Economic Journal*, vol. 46.

VICKREY, WILLIAM (1965) 'Marginal Utility by Reactions to Risk'. *Econometrica*, vol. 13.

VICKREY, W. (1955) 'Some Implications of Marginal Cost Pricing for Public Utilities'. *American Economic Review*, vol. 45.

VINER, J. (1927) 'Adam Smith and Laissez-faire'. *Journal of Political Economy*, vol. 35; reprinted in Viner (1958).

VINER, J. (1958) *The Long View and the Short View*. The Free Press, Glencoe, Illinois.

WALKER, D. (1955) 'The Direct–Indirect Tax Problem; Fifteen Years of Controversy'. *Public Finance*, vol. 10.

WALL, N. (1982) 'University Economics and School Economics: The Classics and Bridges'. *Economics*, vol. 18.

WALTERS, A. A. (1963) 'Production and Cost Functions: An Econometric Study'. *Econometrica*, vol. 31.

WALTERS, A. A. (1968) *The Economics of Road User Charges*. Johns Hopkins University Press, Baltimore.

WEBER, M. (1947) *The Theory of Social and Economic Organisation*. W. Hodge, Edinburgh.

WEINGAST, B. A. (1984) 'The Congressional–Bureaucratic System: A Principal–Agent Perspective'. *Public Choice*, vol. 30.

WEINGAST, B. A. AND MORGAN, M. J. (1983) 'Bureaucratic Discretion or Congressional Control? Regulatory Policy Making by the Federal Trade Commission'. *Journal of Political Economy*, vol. 91.

WICKSELL, KNUT (1958) 'A New Principle of Just Taxation', trans. J. M. Buchanan. *Finanz Teoretische Untersuchungen* (first published in Wicksell, 1896). In R. A. Musgrave and A. T. Peacock (eds), *Classics in the Theory of Public Finance*. Macmillan Press, London.

WICKSELL, KNUT (1896) *Finanztheoretische Untersuchungen*. Fischer, Jena.

WILLIAMS, A. (1972) 'Cost–Benefit Analysis: Bastard Science and/or Insidious Poison in the Body Politic'. *Journal of Public Economics*, vol. 1.

WILLIAMSON, J. H. (1966) 'Profit, Growth and Sales Maximisation', *Economica*, vol. 33.

WILLIAMSON, J. (1983) *IMF Conditionality*. Institute for International Economics, Washington.

WILLIAMSON, O. E. (1964) *The Economics of Discretionary Behaviour: Managerial Objectives in a Theory of the Firm*. Prentice-Hall, Englewood Cliffs, New Jersey.

WILSON, T. (1976) 'Sympathy and Interest'. In T. Wilson and A. S. Skinner (eds), *The Market and the State*. Clarendon Press, Oxford.

WINCH, D. (1969) *Economics and Policy*. Hodder and Stoughton, London.

WISEMAN, J. (1957) 'The Theory of Public Utility Price: An Empty Box'. *Oxford Economic Papers*, vol. 9; reprinted in Buchanan and Thirlby (1973).

WISEMAN, J. (1959) 'The Theory of Public Utility Prices: A Further Note'. *Oxford Economic Papers*, vol. 11.

WOOTTON, B. (1943) 'Socialism and Federalism'. In P. Rannsome (ed.), *Studies in Federal Planning*. Macmillan Press, London.

WUST, HERBERT F. (1981) *Federalismus Grundlage für Effiziency in der Staatwirtschaft Vadenhoeck Ruprecht*. Göttingen.

YOUNG, WARREN L. (1973) 'Compulsory Loans and Consumption – Savings Behaviour, Some Micro- and Macro-economic Aspects'. *Public Finance* vol. 31.

Index